Happy Birthday 17/6/13,

G000061909

Britain's
Best
Pubs

AA Lifestyle Guides

Advertising Sales:
advertisementsales@theAA.com

Editorial:
lifestyleguides@theAA.com

Typeset by AA Lifestyle Guides

Printed and bound by Graficas, Estella, Spain

Editorial contributors: Philip Bryant

Cover credits:
Front Cover:The Anchor Inn
Back Cover: (t) The Nags Head;
(c) The Westleton Crown;
(b) The Fish House

A CIP catalogue record for this book is available from the British Library

ISBN: 978-0-7495-6789-7

Published by AA Publishing, which is a trading name of AA Media Limited, whose registered office is:
Fanum House,
Basing View,
Basingstoke,
Hampshire RG21 4EA
Registered number 06112600

theAA.com/shop

A04570

Britain's Best
Pubs

Contents

Welcome	**4**
Using the Guide	**5**

AA Ratings and Awards	**8**
Useful Information	**11**

England	**14**
Berkshire	**16**
Buckinghamshire	**21**
Cambridgeshire	**30**
Cheshire	**35**
Cornwall	**41**
Cumbria	**50**
Devon	**60**
Dorset	**81**
Durham, County	**86**
Essex	**88**
Gloucestershire	**93**
Greater Manchester	**108**
Hampshire	**110**
Herefordshire	**124**
Hertfordshire	**128**
Kent	**132**
Lancashire	**139**
Leicestershire	**147**
London	**149**
Norfolk	**153**
Northamptonshire	**159**

Northumberland	**164**
Nottinghamshire	**168**
Oxfordshire	**170**
Shropshire	**184**
Somerset	**186**
Staffordshire	**195**
Suffolk	**199**
Surrey	**206**
East Sussex	**209**
West Sussex	**217**
Warwickshire	**228**
West Midlands	**232**
Wight, Isle of	**234**
Wiltshire	**238**
Worcestershire	**250**
North Yorkshire	**252**
South Yorkshire	**266**
West Yorkshire	**268**
Scotland	**270**
Wales	**280**

Maps	
Location Maps	**299**
County Map	**312**

Indexes	
Location index	**315**
Pub index	**326**

Welcome

Britain's Best Pubs is for anyone who enjoys eating and drinking well in formal or informal surroundings. Where stars have been awarded, you can relax in the knowledge that accommodation has been inspected and rated by the AA.

Britain's Best

In this fully updated and revised guide to Britain's Best Pubs you'll find a selection of pubs and hostelries from cosy inns on old coach routes to smart gastro-pubs in towns and cities. Though very different in conception and setting, they all share a commitment to providing refreshment and serving good food based on fresh (and local where possible) produce cooked to order. Hospitality is warm and welcoming, and real ales and well-known brands are offered alongside decent wines. The index and map sections at the back of this guide will help you to find a wide range of towns and villages to visit in search of an authentic pub experience. To help you make the most of your visit we've included recommended places to see in the area of your choice.

A Place to Stay

Room prices for single and double occupation are shown where the accommodation has been inspected and rated by the AA under our Hotel and Guest Accommodation Schemes. Many places will also offer variable rates and special offer breaks so it's worth asking when you book.

Accommodation varies from pubs with two or three rooms, to much grander inns and hotels with all the extras (although most of the places included in this guide have fewer than 20 rooms). Whatever their size or style, all the places selected for inclusion in Britain's Best Pubs have the same best qualities in common: good food, beer served in relaxed and inviting surroundings and great value for money.

Using the Guide

Britain's Best Pubs has been designed to enable you to find both establishments and locations quickly and efficiently. Each entry provides clear information about the opening hours, food, facilities, and nearby recommended places to visit.

See page 3 to browse the main gazetteer section by county. If you want to find a pub in a specific location use the Location Index (page 315). Alternatively, use the Pub Index (page 326) to find an establishment by name.

Finding your way

The main section of the guide is divided into three main parts covering England, Scotland and Wales. The counties within each of these sections are ordered alphabetically as are the town or village locations (shown in capital letters as part of the address) within each county. Finally, the establishments are listed alphabetically under each location name. Towns names featured in the guide are shown in the map section at the back of the guide.

The Old Inn

★ ★ ★ ◉ ♨ INN
Address: Ash Lane, WHITCHURCH, Salisbury, SA38 2PP
Tel: 01963 300123
Email: oldinn@pubgroup.co.uk
Website: www.pubgroup.co.uk/oldrectory
Map ref: 3 TQ32
Directions: Next to church at S end of Whitchurch
Open: 11.30–3 5.30–11 (Sun 12-3) ♨ L 11–2
D 7–9 ⏹ L 12–2 D 6–9 Rooms: 8 en suite S £35–40 D £75–100 Facilities: Gardens Parking
Notes: ⊕ Free House ♦ ⟿ ♟ 7

Tucked away down a leafy lane, The Old Inn is the perfect place for a relaxing drink and a good meal. This old inn has been beautifully restored and extended, with its character carefully preserved. The perfect place for walkers hiking the nearby Ridgeway, the garden offers a shady retreat for lunch and in colder weather log fires and leather sofas provide a warm and welcome resting place. There are two bars, where meals can also be enjoyed, as well as a comfortable and spacious oak-beamed restaurant providing a more formal environment. The menu makes good use of local organic produce with well-cooked dishes that will satisfy the heartiest appetite. The en suite bedrooms are simply furnished and decorated with many thoughtful extras.

Recommended in the area

Salisbury Cathedral; New Forest National Park; Stonehenge and Salisbury Plain

❶ Stars and Symbols

A star rating denotes where an entry has been inspected under one of two separate schemes; either the AA Guest Accommodation Scheme or the AA Hotel Scheme.

Pubs rated under the Guest Accommodation Scheme have been given a descriptive category designator: B&B, Guest House, Farmhouse, Inn, Restaurant with Rooms or Guest Accommodation.

Pubs in the Hotel Scheme also have their own descriptive designator: Hotel, Town House Hotel, Country House Hotel, Small Hotel.
See pages 8–10 for more information on the AA ratings and awards scheme.

continued

5

Egg cups 🥚 and Pies 🥧

These symbols denote where the breakfast or dinner are really special, and have an emphasis on freshly prepared ingredients.

Rosette awards ⊛

This is the AA's food award (see page 9 for further details).

❷ Contact Details

The pub address includes a locator or place name in capitals (e.g. NORWICH). Within each county, entries are ordered alphabetically first by this place name and then by the name of the establishment.

Telephone and fax numbers, and e-mail and website addresses are given where available and are believed correct at the time of going to press but changes may occur. The latest establishment details can be found at theAA.com.

❸ Map Reference

Each establishment in this guide is given a map reference for a location which can be found in the atlas section at the back of the guide. It is composed of the map page number (1–13) and two-figure map reference based on the National Grid.

For example: **Map 05 SU48**

05 refers to the page number of the map section at the back of the guide

SU is the National Grid lettered square (representing 100,000sq metres) in which the location will be found

4 is the figure reading across the top and bottom of the map page

8 is the figure reading down each side of the map page

❹ Directions

Where possible, directions have been given from the nearest motorway or A road.

❺ Open

Indicates the opening hours of the establishment and, if appropriate, any dates when it may be closed for business.

🍽 Bar Meals

Indicates the times and days when the proprietors have told us that bar food can be ordered.

🍽 Restaurant

Indicates the times and days when proprietors have told us that food can be ordered from the restaurant. Please be aware that last orders could vary by up to 30 minutes.

❻ Room Information

Room information is only shown where accommodation has been inspected by the AA. The number of letting bedrooms with a bath or shower en suite are indicated. Bedrooms that have a private bathroom adjacent may be included as en suite. Further details on private bathroom and en suite provision may also be included in the description text (see ❾).

Always phone in advance to ensure that the establishment has the room facilities that you require.

Prices: Charges shown are per night except where specified. **S** denotes bed and breakfast per person (single). **D** denotes bed and breakfast for two people sharing a room (double).

In some cases prices are also given for family rooms, also on a per night basis. Prices are indications only, so check what is included before booking.

❼ Facilities
This section lists a selection of facilities offered by the pub such as garden details or children's play area. If you have young children it may be worth checking what facilities are available.

Additional facilities, such Wi-fi, or notes about other services (e.g. if credit card details are not accepted) may be listed here.

Parking is listed if available. Other types of parking (on road or Park and Ride) may also be possible; check the descriptions for further information. Phone the establishment in advance of your arrival if unsure.

❽ Notes
This section provides specific details relating to:

Pub Status:
⊕ This symbol is followed by text that indicates the name of the brewery to which the pub is tied or the company which owns it, or where the pub is a free house and independently owned and run.

♟ Indicates the number of wines available by the glass.

Children:
⬩♦ This indicates that the pub is child friendly and might provide a children's menu or portions, a play room area or a family room.

Dogs:
🐕 All establishments should accept assist/guide dogs. (Under the Discrimination Disability Act 1995 access should be allowed for guide dogs and assistance dogs). Some places that do accept dogs may restrict the size and breed, where dogs are allowed on the premises, and the rooms into which they can be taken. Please check the policy when booking.

Key to symbols

★	Black stars (see page 8)
☆	Yellow Stars (see page 8)
★	Red Stars (see page 8)
%	Hotel Merit Score
◉	AA Rosette (see page 9)
☖	Breakfast Award in Guest Accommodation scheme
�	Dinner Award in Guest Accommodation scheme
3 TQ28	Map reference
S	Single room
D	Double room
⬩♦	Children allowed
🐕	Dogs allowed in area indicated
Wi-fi	Wireless network connection
⬛	Bar meals
⬩◎⬩	Restaurant meals
L	Lunch
D	Dinner
⊕	Pub status (Chain or Free House)
♟ 30	Number of wines available by the glass

Smoking policy:
Smoking in public areas is now banned in England, Scotland and Wales.

Many pubs provide an outdoor covered area or outbuilding for smokers. The proprietor can designate one or more bedrooms with ventilation systems where the occupants can smoke, but communal areas must be smoke-free.

❾ Description
The description of the pub includes amongst other information, a background to the establishment, the beers and drink available, the type of eating options and, where relevant, information about the accommodation.

❿ Recommended in the area
This indicates local places of interest, and potential day trips and activities.

AA Ratings and Awards

Star ratings shown in Britain's Best Pub guide indicate where the accommodation available has been inspected by the AA under either its Guest Accommodation or Hotel Schemes.

Guest Accommodation and Hotel Schemes

The AA inspects and rates establishments under two different accommodation schemes. Guest houses, B&Bs, farmhouses, inns and Restaurants with Rooms are rated under the Guest Accommodation Scheme and hotels are rated under the Hotel Scheme. Establishments recognised by the AA pay an annual fee according to the rating and the number of bedrooms. This rating is not transferable if an establishment changes hands.

Common Standards

A few years ago, the accommodation inspection organisations (The AA, VisitBritain, VisitScotland and VisitWales) undertook extensive consultation with consumers and the hospitality industry which resulted in new quality standards for rating establishments. Guests can now be confident that a star-rated B&B or a hotel anywhere in the UK and Ireland will offer consistent quality and facilities.

The system of ratings also uses descriptive designators to classify the establishment – see pages 9 and 10 for a fuller explanation.

★ Stars

AA Stars classify accommodation at five levels of quality, from one at the simplest, to five at the highest level of quality in the scheme.

★ Yellow stars indicate that the accommodation in the Guest Accommodation Scheme is in the top ten per cent of its star rating. Yellow stars only apply to 3, 4 and 5 star establishments.

★ Red stars highlight the best hotels in each star rating category within the AA Hotel Scheme.

Check theAA.com for up-to-date information and current ratings.

The Inspection Process

Establishments applying for AA recognition are visited by a qualified AA accommodation inspector as a mystery guest. Inspectors stay overnight to make a thorough test of the accommodation, food and hospitality. After paying the bill the following morning, they identify themselves and ask to be shown around the premises. The

inspector completes a full report, resulting in a recommendation for the appropriate star rating. After this first visit, the establishment will receive an annual visit to check that standards are maintained. If it changes hands, the new owners must re-apply for a rating.

Guests can expect to find the following minimum standards at all levels:
- Pleasant and helpful welcome and service, and sound standards of housekeeping and maintenance
- Comfortable accommodation equipped to modern standards
- Bedding and towels changed for each new guest, and at least weekly if the room is taken for a long stay
- Adequate storage, heating, lighting and comfortable seating
- A sufficient hot water supply at reasonable times
- A full cooked breakfast. (If this is not provided, the fact must be advertised and a substantial continental breakfast must be offered.)

Designators (Guest Accommodation)
All AA rated guest accommodation is given one of six descriptive designators to help potential guests understand the different types of accommodation available in Britain. The following are included in this guide.

INN: Traditional inns often have a cosy bar, convivial atmosphere, good beer and pub food. Those listed in the guide will provide breakfast in a suitable room, and should also serve light meals during licensing hours. The character of the properties vary according to whether they are country inns or town establishments. Check arrival times as these may be restricted to opening hours.

B&B: Accommodation is provided in a private house run by the owner and with no more than six guests. There may be restricted access to the establishment particularly in the late morning and the afternoon.

AA Rosette Awards

Out of the many thousands of restaurants in the UK, the AA identifies some 1,900 as the best. The following is an outline of what to expect from restaurants with AA Rosette Awards. For a more detailed explanation of Rosette criteria please see theAA.com

@ Excellent local restaurants serving food prepared with care, understanding and skill, using good quality ingredients.

@@ The best local restaurants, which aim for and achieve higher standards, better consistency and where a greater precision is apparent in the cooking. There will be obvious attention to the selection of quality ingredients.

@@@ Outstanding restaurants that demand recognition well beyond their local area.

@@@@ Amongst the very best restaurants in the British Isles, where the cooking demands national recognition.

@@@@@ The finest restaurants in the British Isles, where the cooking stands comparison with the best in the world.

GUEST HOUSE: Provides for more than six paying guests and usually offers more services than a B&B, for example dinner, which may be served by staff as well as the owner. London prices tend to be higher than outside the capital, and normally only bed and breakfast is provided, although some establishments do provide a full meal service. Check on the service and facilities offered before booked as details may change during the currency of this guide.

continued

9

FARMHOUSE: A farmhouse usually provides good value B&B or guesthouse accommodation and excellent home cooking on a working farm or smallholding. Sometimes the land has been sold and only the house remains, but many are working farms and some farmers are happy to allow visitors to look around, or even to help feed the animals. However, you should always exercise care and never leave children unsupervised.

The farmhouses are listed under towns or villages, but do ask for directions when booking.

RESTAURANT WITH ROOMS: These restaurants offer overnight accommodation with the restaurant being the main business and open to non-residents. The restaurant usually offers a high standard of food service, and often has been awarded an AA Rosette.

GUEST ACCOMMODATION: Establishments that meet the minimum entry requirements are eligible for this designator.

Designators (Hotels)

All AA rated hotels are given a descriptive designator to identify the different types of hotel available. Included in this guide:

HOTEL: The majority of establishments in this guide come under the category of Hotel.

TOWN HOUSE HOTEL: A small, individual city or town centre property, which provides a high degree or personal service and privacy

COUNTRY HOUSE HOTEL: These may vary in size and are located in a rural area.

SMALL HOTEL: Has less than 20 bedrooms and is managed by its owner.

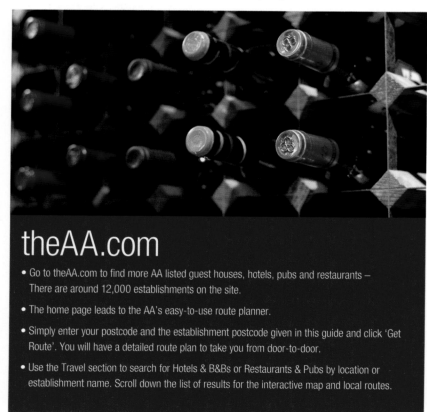

theAA.com

- Go to theAA.com to find more AA listed guest houses, hotels, pubs and restaurants – There are around 12,000 establishments on the site.

- The home page leads to the AA's easy-to-use route planner.

- Simply enter your postcode and the establishment postcode given in this guide and click 'Get Route'. You will have a detailed route plan to take you from door-to-door.

- Use the Travel section to search for Hotels & B&Bs or Restaurants & Pubs by location or establishment name. Scroll down the list of results for the interactive map and local routes.

Useful Information

If you're unsure about any of the facilities offered, always check with the establishment before you visit or book accommodation. Up-to-date information on all pubs in this guide can be found at the travel section of theAA.com

Fire Precautions and Safety
Many of the establishments listed in the guide are subject to the requirements of the Fire Precautions Act of 1971. All establishments should display details of how to summon assistance in the event of an emergency at night.

🐕 Dogs
Some establishments that accept dogs may restrict the size and breed of dogs permitted. Under the Discrimination Disability Act 1995 access should be allowed for guide dogs and assistance dogs.

👨‍👦 Children
Child-friendly pubs have a children allowed symbol at the end of the entry under Notes. When booking a meal you would be advised to check that children are welcome.

Smoking Regulations
Please see page 7.

Facilities for Disabled Guests
The final stage (Part III) of the Disability Discrimination Act (access to Goods and Services) came into force in October 2004. This means that service providers may have to consider making permanent physical adjustments to their premises. For further information, see the government website www.disability.gov.uk. The establishments in this guide should all be aware of their responsibilities under the Act. We recommend that you always telephone in advance to ensure that the establishment you have chosen has appropriate facilities.

Complaints

Readers who have any cause to complain about accommodation, food and drink or service are urged to do so on the spot. This should provide an opportunity for the proprietor to correct matters. If a personal approach fails in connection with accommodation, readers can write to the editor of the guide at Lifestyle Guides, Fanum House, Basingstoke, Hants RG21 4EA.

The AA may at its sole discretion investigate any complaints received from guide users for the purpose of making any necessary amendments to the guide. The AA will not in any circumstances act as a representative or negotiator or undertake to obtain compensation or enter into any correspondence or deal with the matter in any other way whatsoever. The AA will not guarantee to take any specific action.

Bank and Public Holidays 2011

New Year's Day Holiday	3rd January
New Year's Holiday (Scotland)	4th January
Good Friday	22nd April
Easter Monday	25th April
Royal Wedding	29th April
Early May Bank Holiday	2nd May
Spring Bank Holiday	30th May
August Holiday (Scotland)	2nd August
Summer Bank Holiday	29th August
St Andrew's Day (Scotland)	30th November
Christmas Day Holiday	26th December
Boxing Day Holiday	27th December

Thousands of places to stay throughout the UK & Ireland

i View information on thousands of AA recognised establishments and other accommodation

☑ Access to online booking facilities for selected establishments

Extensive range and choice of accommodation

Get the most out of your trip with AA Travel

Exclusive discounts for AA Members and eligible customers at participating hotels

Terms and conditions apply

ENGLAND

Little Langdale, Lake District National Park, Cumbria

14th-century Donnington Castle gatehouse

The Chequers Brasserie

Address: Dean Lane, COOKHAM DEAN, SL6 9BQ
Tel: 01628 481232
Fax: 01628 481237
Email: info@chequersbrasserie.co.uk
Website: www.chequersbrasserie.co.uk
Map ref: 3 SU88
Directions: From A4094 in Cookham High St towards Marlow, over rail line. 1m on right
Open: all day all week 11-11 ⏚ ⏺ **L** Mon-Sat 12-2.30, Sun 12-9.30 **D** Mon-Thu 6.30-9.30, Fri-Sat 6.30-10, Sun 12-9.30 **Facilities:** Parking Garden Wi-fi **Notes:** ⊕ FREE HOUSE ⏚ ⏚ 14

The Chequers is a popular gastro-pub in this pretty Thames Valley village, where *Wind in the Willows* author Kenneth Grahame spent his childhood, and where artist Stanley Spencer was born and spent most of his working life. Both would have been familiar with the encompassing wooded hills and Victorian and Edwardian villas surrounding the village green. Open the pub door to the small intimate bar area and you are greeted by oak beams, maybe an open fire, comfortable seating and real ales from Marlow's Rebellion and Adnams breweries, and Cotswold Brewing's speciality lagers. Dining takes place in either the main older part of the building, the Conservatory, a private dining room or outside on the small lawned area. A good-value lunch blackboard lists dishes such as free-range Cumberland spiced sausages with Cheddar-mashed potato and onion gravy. The main and specials menus change regularly to feature warm salad of smoked chicken, chorizo and black pudding topped with soft-poached duck egg; seared calves' liver and smoked bacon with sage-mashed potato, caramelised baby onions and red wine sauce; and dressed Cornish crab with Marie Rose sauce, and lemon and dill mayonnaise. The all-day Sunday roast has been claimed to be the best in Berkshire.

Recommended in the area

Cliveden; Burnham Beeches; Bekonscot Model Village

The Queen's Arms Country Inn

★★★★ INN
Address: EAST GARSTON, RG17 7ET
Tel: 01488 648757
Fax: 01488 648642
Email: info@queensarmshotel.co.uk
Map ref: 3 SU37
Directions: M4 junct 14, 4m onto A338 to Great
Shefford, then East Garston **Open:** all week
Rooms: 8 en suite (1 GF) **S** £80-£130 **D** £80-£130
Facilities: Parking Garden **Notes:** ♨ ⌁

Hunting enthusiast and head chef Matt Green-Armytage has partnered with Lucy Townsend to
show customers of this Lambourn Valley inn what good taste means – in every respect. The food,
for example, is made from the freshest seasonal produce available, with regularly changing menus
offering Maldon oysters with sweet and sour red wine onions; braised pig's cheeks with white pudding
mash and scrumpy sauce: steamed Cornish sea bass with fennel and tomato dressing; and game and
poultry from local shoots and farms. The terrace and large garden are popular in the warmer months.
Horses almost outnumber people in this area, so why not spend a day riding.
Recommended in the area
Uffington White Horse; Ashdown House (NT); Ridgeway National Trail

The Crown & Garter

★★★★ ◌ INN
Address: Inkpen Common, HUNGERFORD, RG17 9QR
Tel: 01488 668325
Email: gill.hern@btopenworld.com
Website: www.crownandgarter.com
Map ref: 3 SU36 **Directions:** From A4 to Kintbury
& Inkpen. At village store left into Inkpen Rd, Inkpen
Common 2m **Open:** all week 12-3 5.30-11 (Sun
12-5 7-10.30) **Closed:** Mon & Tue lunch ⌑ ⍟ **L**
Wed-Sat 12-2, Sun 12-2.30 **D** Mon-Sat 6.30-9.30
Rooms: 9 en suite (9 GF) **S** £69.50 **D** £99 **Facilities:** Parking Garden Wi-fi **Notes:** ⊕ FREE HOUSE ☕ 9

A family-owned, personally run 17th-century inn in a really pretty part of Berkshire, its ancient charm
can best be seen in the bar area, where there's a huge inglenook fireplace and beams. You can eat
in the bar, the restaurant, or in the enclosed beer garden, choosing from a variety of dishes all freshly
prepared on the premises from local produce. There are daily fish and seafood specials available. Eight
separate, spacious en suite bedrooms are situated around a pretty cottage garden.
Recommended in the area
Newbury Racecourse; Combe Gibbet; Highclere Castle

The Swan Inn

★★★★ 🛏 🍴 INN

Address: Craven Road, Lower Green, Inkpen,
HUNGERFORD, RG17 9DX
Tel: 01488 668326 **Fax:** 01488 668306
Email: enquiries@theswaninn-organics.co.uk
Website: www.theswaninn-organics.co.uk
Map ref: 3 SU36 **Directions:** S down Hungerford
High St (A338), under rail bridge, left to Hungerford
Common. Right signed Inkpen (3m) **Open:** 12-2.30
7-10 (Sat noon-11pm Sun noon-4) **Closed:** 25-26

Dec 🏖 **L** all wk 12-2 **D** all wk 7-9.30 🍽 **L** Wed-Sun 12-2.30 **D** Wed-Sat 7-9.30 **Rooms:** 10 en suite
S £70-£85 D £85-£105 **Facilities:** Parking Garden Wi-fi **Notes:** ⊕ FREE HOUSE 🛉

Retaining much of its character, this 17th-century inn is owned by local organic beef farmers (there's a
farm shop too) and menus feature their own and local organic produce. Vegetarian, fish and children's
menus are available. The beamed inn is set below Walbury Iron Age hill fort, and enjoys spectacular
views. Four real ales from Butts Brewery are offered, plus an organic wine list.

Recommended in the area

Kennet and Avon Canal; Newbury Racecourse; Avebury Stone Circle

Kennet and Avon Canal, Newbury

Bird In Hand Country Inn

Address: Bath Road, KNOWL HILL,
Twyford, RG10 9UP
Tel: 01628 826622 & 822781
Fax: 01628 826748
Email: sthebirdinhand@aol.com
Website: www.birdinhand.co.uk
Map ref: 3 SU87
Directions: On A4, 5m W of Maidenhead,
7m E of Reading Open: all day all week
🏃 🍴 food served all day Rooms: 15 (6 GF)
S £40-£75 D £60-£120 Facilities: Parking Garden Wi-fi
Notes: 🍺 FREE HOUSE ♦♠ ⚑ ♞ ♥ 20

Dating back to the 14th century, this charming country inn has been owned by the same family for three generations. Legend has it that George III granted it a royal charter in the 18th century for the hospitality he was shown, and a royal welcome is still the order of the day. A local award-winner, today the inn serves a host of well kept real ales and a large selection of wines by the glass in the oak-panelled bar, which in winter boasts a huge open fire. In summer months, a pretty beer garden and fountain patio provide the backdrop for the brick-built barbecue and spit roast. Inside, an extensive menu is available from both the bar and the attractive restaurant, which overlooks the courtyard and fountain. Diners can choose from a range of traditional dishes, such as hearty steak and kidney pudding with Guinness, pork belly in Calvados or whole roast stuffed quail with apricot and thyme, through to European-based options such as tapas, mezze and paella. There are also a number of daily specials and a cold buffet is available at lunchtime. The inn's en suite bedrooms have all been refurbished and include many modern facilities such as Wi-fi and direct-dial telephones.
Recommended in the area
Legoland; Odds Park Farm; Wellington Country Park

BUCKINGHAMSHIRE

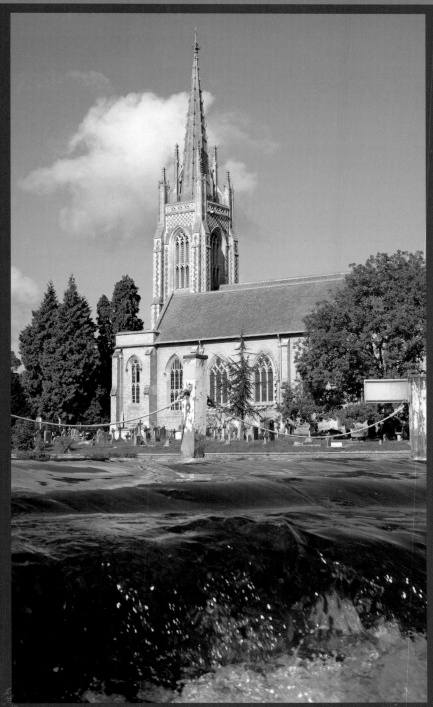

All Saints church at Marlow by the River Thames

The Crooked Billet

Address: 2 Westbrook End, Newton Longville,
nr BLETCHLEY, MK17 0DF
Tel: 01908 373936
Email: john@thebillet.co.uk
Website: www.thebillet.co.uk
Map ref: 3 SP83 **Directions:** M1 junct 13, follow
signs to Buckingham. 6m, signed at Bottledump rdbt
to Newton Longville **Open:** noon-2.30 5-11 (Sun
noon-4) **Closed:** Mon L 🍺 🍽 L Tue-Sat 12-2, Sun
12-4 **D** Mon-Sat 7-9.30 **Facilities:** Parking Garden **Notes:** 🍺 GREENE KING 👫 🍷 200

While it retains much traditional charm, with original oak beams, open log fires and a large garden,
the top attraction is the food and wine offered by husband-and-wife team John and Emma Gilchrist.
Emma's weekly-changing menus are based on the finest ingredients, local where possible, and the
suppliers - right down to the 'people of Newton Longville for growing our vegetables and herbs' - are
all acknowledged in print. On offer is a range of sandwiches, wraps, burgers and goodies on toast,
and a seven-course 'whole table only' tasting menu. Falling somewhere between these two extremes
are main menu starters of garlic roasted hand-dived scallops with butternut squash purée, crisp sage
and lardons; house-cured sliced duck breast, pecorino shavings, white honey truffle, purple fig and
thyme. Then might come mild monkfish and king prawn curry, lemon and coriander rice with onion
fritter; or overnight roasted crispy pork belly braised Puy lentils, tarragon and baby onions. Desserts
include Muscat poached pear, tonka bean ice cream and a bar of 'Fruit & Nut'; or apple, blackberry and
almond tart, rosehip flavoured custard with blackberry ice cream. The cheese board has won heaps of
awards, as has John Gilchrist for compiling 'best wine' lists, including his 300-bin selection here.
Recommended in the area
Woburn Abbey; Bletchley Park; Leighton Buzzard Railway

The Royal Oak

Address: Frieth Road, BOVINGDON GREEN, Marlow, SL7 2JF
Tel: 01628 488611
Fax: 01628 478680
Email: info@royaloakmarlow.co.uk
Website: www.royaloakmarlow.co.uk
Map ref: 3 SU88
Directions: From Marlow, take A4155. In 300yds right signed Bovingdon Green. In 0.75m pub on left
Open: all day all week 11-11 (Sun 12-10.30) **Closed:** 26 Dec
🍺 🍴 L Mon-Fri 12-2.30, Sat 12-3, Sun 12-4 D Sun-Thu 6.30-9.30, Fri-Sat 6.30-10 **Facilities:** Parking Garden Wi-fi
Notes: ⊕ SALISBURY PUBS LTD 🏠 🐾 🍷 20

Drive up the hill out of Marlow and you'll soon come across this old whitewashed pub. Sprawling gardens, fragrant kitchen herbs and a sunny terrace suggest that it is well looked after. Red kites, which were re-introduced to the Chilterns in 1989, now frequently soar majestically overhead. The interior is both spacious and cosy, with a snug with wood-burning stove, a rose-red dining room and rich dark floorboards. Plush fabrics and heritage colours create a warm background for the early evening regulars gathered around a cryptic crossword, or playing a tense game of cards. The imaginative British food is a big draw, not least because it derives from fresh, seasonal and, as far as possible, local produce. Fish, of course, has to travel, but a belief in good food ethics means choosing new and interesting varieties from sustainable sources. Other menu suggestions might include veal and rosemary sausage casserole with Boston baked beans; and crispy pork belly with pig's cheeks on sticky red cabbage and cider gravy. Real ales from Rebellion Brewery in Marlow Bottom keep beer miles to a minimum.

Recommended in the area

Cliveden (NT); Burnham Beeches; Hughenden Manor

The Red Lion

Address: CHENIES, Chorleywood, Rickmansworth, WD3 6ED
Tel: 01923 282722 **Fax:** 01923 283797
Email: theredlionchenies@hotmail.co.uk
Website: www.theredlionchenies.co.uk
Map ref: 3 TQ09
Directions: Between Rickmansworth & Amersham on A404, follow signs for Chenies & Latimer
Open: all week Mon-Sat 11-2.30 5.30-11 (Sun 12-3 6.30-10.30) **Closed:** 25 Dec **L** Mon-Sat 12-2, Sun 12-2.15 **D** Mon-Sat 7-10, Sun 7-9.30 **Facilities:** Parking Garden **Notes:** FREE HOUSE 10

Michael Norris has been at this popular hostelry for over twenty years, and under his expert direction the pub has achieved considerable renown. He is keen to stress that this is a pub that does food, not a restaurant that does beer, but that's not to say that the quality and range of food on offer is in any way an afterthought. Michael has put together a menu that has something for everyone, with a wide range of snacks, starters and main meals. Among the listings you'll find the ever-popular jacket potatoes; pasta carbonara; and a tasty beef, mustard and cheese pie, plus a number of more exotic dishes that might include Moroccan chicken breast with couscous; pork fillet with prunes; oxtail with root vegetables; and fresh tuna loin with roasted Mediterranean vegetables. But even with all this choice, it would be a shame not to try the famous Chenies lamb pie. Needless to say, the real ales on offer are kept in perfect condition and there are some good wines to choose from too. The Red Lion is not far outside the M25 at junction 18 and is well worth making a detour to enjoy its pleasant, country-pub atmosphere – the way that pubs used to be before piped music and fruit machines were invented – and the garden makes for enjoyable alfresco summer lunches.

Recommended in the area

Legoland; Bekonscot Model Village; Odds Farm Park Rare Breeds Centre

The Swan Inn

Address: Village Road, DENHAM, UB9 5BH
Tel: 01895 832085
Fax: 01895 835516
Email: info@swaninndenham.co.uk
Website: www.swaninndenham.co.uk
Map ref: 3 TQ08
Directions: From A40 take A412. In 200yds follow Denham Village sign on right. Through village, over bridge, last pub on left
Open: all day all week 11-11 (Sun 12-10.30)
Closed: 26 Dec **L** Mon-Fri 12-2.30, Sat 12-3, Sun 12-4 **D** Sun-Thu 6.30-9.30, Fri-Sat 6.30-10 **Facilities:** Parking Garden Wi-fi **Notes:** SALISBURY PUBS LTD 20

The Swan is probably everyone's idea of the traditional country inn – Georgian, double-fronted and covered in wisteria. The surprise, though, is that the secluded village of Denham is really no distance at all from the bright lights of both London and its premier airport at Heathrow. The interior is cosily welcoming, with a large log fire and pictures picked up at local auctions, while outside is a sunny terrace, and gardens large enough to lose the children in (only temporarily, of course). Though The Swan is still very much a pub, the quality of the food is a great attraction, with fresh, seasonal produce underpinning a menu that reinvigorates some old favourites and makes the most of market availability with daily specials. For a starter or light meal look to the 'small plates' section, where you'll find Marlow Rebellion (a local beer) steamed mussels with garlic herbs and onion rye bread; and pan-fried balsamic chicken livers on 'eggy bread' brioche with crispy pancetta. Among the main meals there is plenty of variety, from slow-cooked Chiltern lamb shoulder on smoked potato mash to Indian-spiced mackerel.

Recommended in the area

Burnham Beeches; Cliveden (NT); Dorney Court

The Nags Head

★★★★ ⊛ INN

Address: London Road, GREAT MISSENDEN, HP16 0DG
Tel: 01494 862200
Fax: 01494 862685
Email: goodfood@nagsheadbucks.com
Website: www.nagsheadbucks.com
Map ref: 3 SP80
Directions: 1m from Great Missenden on London Rd. From A413 (Amersham to Aylesbury) turn left signed Chiltern Hospital. After 500mtrs pub on corner of Nags Head Ln & London Rd
Open: all day all week ▣ ⓣ◎❙ L Mon-Sat 12-2.30, Sun 12-3.30 D all wk 6.30-9.30 **Rooms:** 5 en suite D £90-£120 **Facilities:** Parking Garden Wi-fi **Notes:** ⊕ FREE HOUSE ⚬⚬ ⌁ ♟ 19

Situated in the valley of the River Missbourne in the glorious Chilterns, the inn is ideally situated within walking distance of the picturesque village of Great Missenden, yet near major road and rail networks. The inn has been tastefully refurbished to a high standard, retaining the many original 15th-century features including low oak beams and a large inglenook fireplace, plus a large garden. The building comprises an award-winning gastro-pub and restaurant together with beautifully furnished double and twin bedrooms. The Nags Head has played host to a variety of TV series and has been visited by many famous names, including prime ministers and the children's author Roald Dahl; a replica of the inn recently featured in the film animation of his book *Fantastic Mr Fox*. The English and French fusion dishes on the extensive menu, and daily specials board, use the highest quality, locally sourced produce whenever possible; expect home-smoked fish, saddle of lamb from a nearby farm, and locally made cheeses. To accompany, there's a carefully selected, global wine list, as well as beers and local ales on tap.

Recommended in the area

Roald Dahl Museum; Bekonscot Model Village; Whipsnade Zoo

The Hand and Flowers

◉◉◉

Address: 126 West Street, MARLOW, SL7 2BP
Tel: 01628 482277 **Fax:** 01628 401913
Email: theoffice@thehandandflowers.co.uk
Website: www.thehandandflowers.co.uk
Map ref: 3 SU88
Directions: M4 junct 9, A404 N into Marlow, A4155 towards Henley-on-Thames. Pub on outskirts on right
Open: 12-2.30 6.30-9.30 (Sun 12-3.30)
Closed: 24-26 Dec, 1 Jan D, Sun eve ▙ L Mon-Sat 12-2.30 D Mon-Sat 6.30-9.30 ⦿ L all wk 12-2.30 D all wk 6.30-9.30
Facilities: Parking Garden Wi-fi **Notes:** ⊕ GREENE KING ⬩⬩ ⚑ 11

Six years ago, Tom and Beth Kerridge reopened this 18th-century, whitewashed pub just outside Marlow, and there seems to be no stopping its progress. The interior is an easygoing combination of flagstone floors, beams, exposed stone walls, neutral colours, leather banquettes and cloth-free tables. Tom is the chef, and he's frequently in the spotlight for his regularly changing, seasonal menus of simple yet elegant modern British and rustic French food. Among dishes which have helped him earn three AA Rosettes are starters of crayfish Scotch egg or truffled pork terrine with toasted sour dough, and main course favourites of slow cooked duck breast with Savoy cabbage, duck fat chips and gravy, Weymouth plaice with sweetcorn purée, girolles, brown shrimps and Chablis shallots, or cutlet of lamb with lamb breast and caramel poached chicory. Round off with tonka bean pannacotta with mango and Pedro Ximenez jelly, or passionfruit and white chocolate trifle. The famous set lunch typically offers cream of celeriac soup, followed by cassoulet and blackberry fool with bramble jelly, while on Sundays there are roasts. Two of the four stylish cottage suites have private terraces with hot tubs.

Recommended in the area

Cliveden (NT); Burnham Beeches; Hughenden Manor

The Old Queens Head

Address: Hammersley Lane, PENN, HP10 8EY
Tel: 01494 813371
Fax: 01494 816145
Email: info@oldqueensheadpenn.co.uk
Website: www.oldqueensheadpenn.co.uk
Map ref: 3 SU99
Directions: B474 (Penn road) through Beaconsfield
New Town towards Penn, approx 3m left into School
Rd, left in 500yds into Hammersley Ln. Pub on corner
opp church

Open: all day all week 11-11 (Sun 12-10.30) **Closed:** 26 Dec ⓑ ⓘ **L** Mon-Fri 12-2.30,
Sat 12-3, Sun 12-4 **D** Sun-Thu 6.30-9.30, Fri-Sat 6.30-10 **Facilities:** Parking Garden Wi-fi
Notes: ⓦ SALISBURY PUBS LTD ⦿ ⑂ ⓟ 20

The Old Queens Head exudes bags of character and atmosphere. The Dining Room, originally a barn,
dating from 1666, but with several later additions, now provides lots of cosy corners. Many hours
have been well spent at local auctions finding sympathetic old furniture and pictures, while warm
heritage colours blend with glowing dark floorboards, flagstones, rugs and classic fabrics. Although
first and foremost a pub, it is just as ready to serve a light bite at lunchtime, or a fabulous dinner,
special occasion or not. There's even free Wi-fi for those who have to work while eating. Experienced
staff provide good service and plenty of good old-fashioned hospitality. The food balances Classic
with Modern British, resulting in a menu with plenty of choice, such as Chiltern Hills venison and wild
mushroom suet pudding on purple sprouting broccoli with girolle and game jus; and grilled plaice on
lemon and thyme risotto with prawn beignet. A sunny terrace overlooks the large garden and the village
church of St Margaret's. There are great walks nearby in the ancient beech woodlands.

Recommended in the area

Bekonscot Model Village; West Wycombe; Legoland

Chequers Inn

★★★ 75% ❀ HOTEL

Address: Kiln Lane, WOOBURN COMMON,
Beaconsfield, HP10 0JQ
Tel: 01628 529575 **Fax:** 01628 850124
Email: info@chequers-inn.com
Website: www.thechequersatwooburncommon.co.uk
Map ref: 3 SU98 **Directions:** M40 junct 2, A40
through Beaconsfield Old Town to High Wycombe. 2m
from town left into Broad Ln. Inn 2.5m **Open:** noon-
mdnt 🍺 **L** Mon-Fri 12-2.30, Sat 12-10, Sun 12-9.30
D Mon-Thu 6-9.30, Fri 6-10, Sat 12-10, Sun 12-9.30 ⊗ **L** 12-2.30 **D** 7-9.30 **Rooms:** 17 (8 GF)
S £85-£99.50 **D** £90-£107.50 **Facilities:** Parking Garden Wi-fi **Notes:** ⊕ FREE HOUSE ⋕ ♟ 14

Steeped in history, this family-run 17th-century coaching inn is tucked away in The Chilterns. With oak
beams, quiet corners and flagstone floors it's a charming blend of old and new. Dine in the attractive
restaurant, country bar or contemporary lounge. Fresh, seasonal produce is used in dishes such as
beef fillet with wild mushrooms and béarnaise sauce. There are 17 beautifully appointed bedrooms.
Recommended in the area
Cliveden (NT); Burnham Beeches; Bekonscot Model Village

West Wycombe House

CAMBRIDGESHIRE

Mathematical Bridge over the River Cam

The Crown

Address: Bridge Road, BROUGHTON,
Huntingdon, PE28 3AY
Tel: 01487 824428
Email: info@thecrowninnrestaurant.co.uk
Website: www.thecrowninnrestaurant.co.uk
Map ref: 3 TL27
Directions: Just off A141 between Huntingdon
& Warboys, by church in village centre
Open: all wk Mon-Fri 11.30-3 6.30-11 (Sat 11.30-
11, Sun 11.30-10.30) 🍽 L 12-2.30 D 7-10
Facilities: Parking Garden **Notes:** ⊕ FREE HOUSE ♦♦ 🚶 ♥ 10

Horse chestnut trees surround the picturesque grounds of this family-run, 18th-century Grade II-listed village pub situated in the hamlet of Broughton. In previous times it was a saddlery, stables and a piggery, but you wouldn't know any of this from the attractive bar and restaurant styled in traditional country pub with contemporary touches, providing a warm, comfortable and homely environment. On sunny days head outside to eat on the patio and enjoy the garden. Simple and hearty perfectly sums up the food ethos here, the kitchen using nothing but the finest, fresh local ingredients. This is complemented by a hand picked wine list and a well stocked bar complete with regularly changing guest ales. Since fresh, seasonal food is the best for flavour and quality, dishes are created and the menu changes as required so advantage can be taken of the best available produce. At lunchtime expect Cumberland sausage with mustard mash, Broughton burger, and roasted vegetable and mozzarella lasagne. The main menu might suggest pan-fried peppered duck breast, chargrilled rib-eye steak, or seared sea bass fillet. High levels of personal service makes The Crown the perfect venue for a business meeting dinner, intimate meal or a family get-together.

Recommended in the area

Huntingdon Racecourse; The Raptor Foundation; St Ives

The Anchor Inn

★★★★ ◎ RESTAURANT WITH ROOMS
Address: Sutton Gault, ELY, CB6 2BD
Tel: 01353 778537 **Fax:** 01353 776180
Email: anchorinn@popmail.bta.com
Website: www.anchorsuttongault.co.uk
Map ref: 4 TL58 **Directions:** From A14, B1050
to Earith, take B1381 to Sutton. Sutton Gault on left
Open: all week 12-2.30 7-10.30 (Sat 12-3 6.30-11
Sun 12-4 6.30-10) **Closed:** 25-26 Dec eve
◎ L Mon-Sat 12-2, Sun 12-2.30 D Mon-Fri 7-9,
Sat 6.30-9.30, Sun 6.30-8.30 **Facilities:** Parking Garden **Notes:** ⊞ FREE HOUSE ♦♦ ♟ 12

Built in 1650 to provide shelter for workers digging the New Bedford River to help drain the Fens, The
Anchor Inn has evolved to combine modern comforts with timeless charm and character. Scrubbed pine
tables on uneven tiled floors, antique prints, period furniture and winter log fires all enhance the cosy,
intimate atmosphere of this family-run free house. The pub has won wide recognition for its stylish
accommodation and British cuisine with European influences, using the best of local ingredients.
Recommended in the area
Ely Cathedral; Oliver Cromwell's House; Ely Museum

Grafham Water

The Cock Pub and Restaurant

Address: 47 High Street, HEMINGFORD GREY,
Huntingdon, PE28 9BJ
Tel: 01480 463609
Email: cock@cambscuisine.com
Website: www.cambscuisine.com
Map ref: 3 TL27
Directions: 2m S of Huntingdon and 1m E of A14
Open: all week 11.30-3 6-11 †©! L all wk 12-2.30
D all wk 6.15-9.30 **Facilities:** Parking Garden
Notes: ⊕ FREE HOUSE ⫯† ⫯† ⚑ 14

Down-to-earth, but passionately run, this pub stands in the heart
of a pretty village on the Great Ouse, the fourth longest river
in the UK. The traditional bar is separate from the bustling, country-style restaurant, and since food
is not served in the pub area it is ideal for those who just want a pint of one of the four real ales from
breweries all within an hour's drive, or village-brewed Cromwell cider. Service in the restaurant
is professional and friendly, with food guided by the seasons, fresh and fully prepared on site.
Lunchtime might offer beef, cinnamon and chilli stew with butter bean mash, or great sausages made
by the chefs onsite. In the evening try a starter of spinach gnocchi, wild mushrooms, pinenuts and
ricotta; or roasted fig, walnut and Stilton salad with green peppercorn dressing: then roast duck breast,
potato bake, sprouting broccoli, beetroot and blackberries; or, from the daily changing fish board,
monkfish with prosciutto, potato rösti, green vegetables, chorizo and red wine sauce. Speaking of wine,
many are from the Languedoc, reflecting frequent research visits by the owners and staff. There is
a delightful garden for summer dining. The August bank holiday weekend beer festival and barbecue
is a cracking event.

Recommended in the area

Imperial War Museum Duxford; Grafham Water; Houghton Mill

The Bell Inn Hotel

★★★ 81% ⌬ HOTEL

Address: Great North Road, STILTON,
Peterborough, PE7 3RA
Tel: 01733 241066 **Fax:** 01733 245173
Email: reception@thebellstilton.co.uk
Website: www.thebellstilton.co.uk
Map ref: 3 TL18
Directions: From A1(M) junct 16 follow signs for
Stilton. Hotel on main road in village centre
Open: all week noon-2.30 6-11 (Sat 12-3 6-12, Sun

noon-11) **Closed:** 25 Dec ⌬ **L** Mon-Sat 12-2.30, Sun all day **D** all wk 6-9.30 ⌬ **L** Sun 12-2 **D** Mon-
Sat 7-9.30 **Rooms:** 22 en suite (3 GF) **S** £67-£110 **D** £92-£130 **Facilities:** Parking Garden **Notes:** ⌬
FREE HOUSE ⌬ ⌬ 8

Historically an important stop on the Great North Road between London and York, this beautiful old
stone-built inn is one of the country's best surviving examples of a mid 17th-century coaching house.
The village is the birthplace of Stilton cheese and if you expect to find this delicacy well represented
here, you will - try Stilton pâté with walnuts and griotinne cherries, for instance. The softly lit bistro,
where contemporary art complements the low ceilings and exposed beams, offers fillet of sea bass
on crayfish and pea risotto, for example, while in the first-floor, beamed restaurant, sip your aperitif in
one of the leather armchairs while choosing from the traditionally and internationally influenced menu.
Typical would be seared scallops, pancetta, broad beans and hollandaise sauce, and rack of English
lamb, galette potato and garlic purée. Legend has it that from one of the restaurant windows Dick
Turpin jumped on to his horse Black Bess and escaped whoever was pursuing him. Today, however,
you can eat in the attractive courtyard in peace and tranquillity with friendly staff in attendance.
Recommended in the area
Nene Valley Railway; Burghley House; Rutland Water

CHESHIRE

The City Walls and King Charles' Tower, Chester

The Bhurtpore Inn

Address: Wrenbury Road, ASTON,
Nantwich, CW5 8DQ
Tel: 01270 780917
Email: simonbhurtpore@yahoo.co.uk
Website: www.bhurtpore.co.uk
Map ref: 6 SJ64
Directions: Just off A530 between Nantwich
& Whitchurch. Turn towards Wrenbury at x-rds
in village
Open: all week 12-2.30 6.30-11.30 (Fri-Sat 12-12,
Sun 12-11) **Closed:** 25-26 Dec, 1 Jan 🍺 🍴 **L** Mon-Fri 12-2 **D** Mon-Fri 6.30-9.30 (Sat 12-9.30,
Sun 12-9) **Facilities:** Parking Garden **Notes:** ⊕ FREE HOUSE ⊪ 🐕 🍷 11

The George family has a bit of a thing about this traditional village pub. In 1849 James George leased it from the local Combermere estate, from which descendant Philip George bought it in 1895, only to sell it six years later to a Crewe brewery. Ninety years later, in 1991, Simon and Nicky George were looking to buy their first pub and came across the boarded-up, stripped-out Bhurtpore. It ticked just about every box. Although it has been a pub since at least 1778, it was the 1826 Siege of Bhurtpore in India, where Lord Combermere had distinguished himself, that inspired its current name. With eleven real ales always available, a large selection of bottled beers and seven continental beers on tap, it is truly a free house. The award-winning food is fresh, home made and reasonably priced, both in the bar and the restaurant. Starters include spicy lamb samosas, and pork and black pudding patties with coarse grain mustard. Finish with spiced raisin and ginger pudding with toffee sauce. Behind the pub is a lawn with countryside views. At the centre of the local community, the pub is home to an enthusiastic cricket team, a group of cyclists known as the Wobbly Wheels and folk musicians.

Recommended in the area

Hack Green Secret Bunker; Cholmondeley Castle; Historic Nantwich; Stapeley Water Gardens

The Pheasant Inn

★★★★★ 🛏 INN

Address: BURWARDSLEY, Nr Tattenhall, CH3 9PF
Tel: 01829 770434 **Fax:** 01829 771097
Email: info@thepheasantinn.co.uk
Website: www.thepheasantinn.co.uk
Map ref: 6 SJ55 **Directions:** A41 (Chester to
Whitchurch), after 4m left to Burwardsley. Follow
'Cheshire Workshops' signs **Open:** all day all week
🍴 ⬤ **L** all wk (no food Mon 3-6) **D** all wk (no food
Mon 3-6) **Rooms:** 12 en suite (5 GF) **Facilities:**
Parking Garden Wi-fi **Notes:** ⊞ FREE HOUSE ⬤ 🐾

In a peaceful corner of Cheshire, yet this 300-year-old sandstone former farmhouse is just 15 minutes' drive from Chester. An alehouse from the mid-17th century, since the early 19th century only five families have been licensees. As well as the wooden-floored, heavy-beamed bar, you can take your drinks out into the stone-flagged conservatory, courtyard or terrace. The menu offers light bites and deli-boards; a gastropub-style selection; and British and European fare. Stay over in one of the country-style bedrooms.

Recommended in the area

Beeston Castle; Cheshire Candle Workshops; Oulton Park

Albion Inn

Address: Park Street, CHESTER, CH1 1RN
Tel: 01244 340345
Email: christina.mercer@tesco.net
Website: www.albioninnchester.co.uk
Map ref: 5 SJ46
Directions: In city centre adjacent to Citywalls &
Newgate **Open:** all week 12-3, Tue-Fri 5-11, Sat
6-11, Sun 7-10.30, Mon 5.30-11 **Closed:** 25-26
Dec, 1-2 Jan 🍴 ⬤ **L** all wk 12-2 **D** Mon-Sat 5-8
Notes: ⊞ PUNCH TAVERNS 🐾 ♿

Many a young lad would have spent his last night in Civvy Street in what is now Chester's last Victorian corner pub, before heading for the Western Front in the First World War. Mike and Christina Mercer's traditional three-room interior - Vault, Snug and Lounge – evokes those times with Great War pictures, posters and advertisements. Regionally sourced 'trench rations' include boiled gammon and pease pudding; McConickies corned beef hash; filled Staffordshire oatcakes; fish pie; and a selection of club and doorstep sandwiches. Four cask ales are on tap, alongside malts and New World wines.

Recommended in the area

Roman Wall, Chester; Ness Gardens; Cholmondeley Castle

The Cholmondeley Arms

★★★ INN

Address: CHOLMONDELEY, Malpas, SY14 8HN
Tel: 01829 720300 Fax: 01829 720123
Email: info@cholmondeleyarms.co.uk
Website: www.cholmondeleyarms.co.uk
Map ref: 6 SJ55
Directions: On A49, between Whitchurch &
Tarporley Open: all day all week Closed: 25 Dec
L Mon-Fri 12-2.30, Sat-Sun 12-9.30 D Mon-Fri
6-10, Sat-Sun 12-9.30 Rooms: 6 en suite (3 GF)
S £55 D £70-£90 Facilities: Parking Garden Wi-fi Notes: ⊕ FREE HOUSE ♦♦ ➤ ♀ 10

Set in the Cheshire countryside adjacent to Cholmondeley Castle, the Cholmondeley Arms is a friendly and relaxing gastro-pub. Whether you visit to sample the award-winning food or the CAMRA accredited real ales, it is sure to be an enjoyable experience. Relax by the open log fire after a walk in the surrounding hills, a trip to Cholmondeley Castle, a round of golf or a busy day at work. You can make use of our Wi-fi whether you are on business or a leisurely break at this quintessentially English pub.
Recommended in the area
Cholmondeley Castle Gardens; The Croccy Trail; Beeston Castle; The Sandstone Trail

The Dog Inn

★★★★ INN

Address: Well Bank Lane, Over Peover,
KNUTSFORD, WA16 8UP
Tel: 01625 861421 Fax: 01625 864800
Email: thedoginnpeover@btconnect.com
Website: www.doginn-overpeover.co.uk
Map ref: 7 SJ77
Directions: S from Knutsford take A50. Turn into
Stocks Ln at The Whipping Stocks pub. 2m
Open: all week 11.30-3 4.30-11 (Sat-Sun all day)
L all wk 12-2.30 D all wk 6-9 Rooms: 6 en suite S £60 D £80 Facilities: Parking Garden Wi-fi
Notes: ⊕ FREE HOUSE ♦♦ ➤ ♀ 10

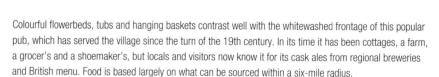

Colourful flowerbeds, tubs and hanging baskets contrast well with the whitewashed frontage of this popular pub, which has served the village since the turn of the 19th century. In its time it has been cottages, a farm, a grocer's and a shoemaker's, but locals and visitors now know it for its cask ales from regional breweries and British menu. Food is based largely on what can be sourced within a six-mile radius.
Recommended in the area
Tatton Park (NT); Jodrell Bank Observatory; Capesthorne Hall

The Davenport Arms

Address: Congleton Road, MARTON, SK11 9HF
Tel: 01260 224269 **Fax:** 01260 224565
Email: enquiries@thedavenportarms.co.uk
Website: www.thedavenportarms.co.uk
Map ref: 6 SJ86
Directions: 3m from Congleton off A34
Open: noon-3 6-mdnt (Fri-Sun noon-mdnt) **Closed:**
Mon L (ex BH) ▨ L Tue-Sat 12-2.30, Sun 12-3 **D**
Tue-Thu 6-9, Sun 6-8.30 ▨ L Tue-Fri 12-2.30, Sat
12-9, Sun 12-8 **D** Tue-Fri 6-9, Sat 12-9, Sun 12-8
Facilities: Parking Garden Wi-fi **Notes:** ⊞ FREE HOUSE ♦♦ ♀ 9

The Davenports were royal foresters who once wielded considerable power in this neck of the woods. In the traditional bar of this true country pub, with its exposed brickwork, cushioned settles, leather sofas and wood burning stove, you will find well kept real ales usually sourced from local micro-breweries. Traditional and more contemporary dishes, all freshly made on the premises from seasonal local produce, are served in the bar or separate restaurant. There is a play area in the secluded garden.
Recommended in the area
Quarry Bank Mill (NT); Capesthorne Hall (NT); Oulton Park

The Goshawk

Address: Station Road, MOULDSWORTH, CH3 8AJ
Tel: 01928 740900
Fax: 01928 740965
Website: www.thegoshawkpub.co.uk
Map ref: 6 SJ57
Directions: A51 from Chester onto A54. Left onto
B5393 towards Frodsham. Enter Mouldsworth, pub
on left opposite rail station
Open: all week noon-11 (Sun noon-10.30)
Closed: 25 Dec & 1 Jan ▨ ▨ food served all day
Facilities: Parking Garden **Notes:** ⊞ WOODWARD & FALCONER PUBS ♦♦ ♀ 14

On the edge of the Delamere Forest, The Goshawk is just 15 minutes' drive from Chester. The imaginative menu ranges from pub classics to more sophisticated fare. Everything is freshly prepared and you can eat in the bar, lounge or restaurant areas. A wide choice of wines from around the world is offered as well as real ales such as Piffle beer, Weetwood ales and the changing casks of the week. There is a good play area for children, and the decking outside overlooks a fine crown bowling green.
Recommended in the area
Go Ape at Delamere Forest; Mouldsworth Motor Museum; Sail Sports Windsurfing Centre

The Swettenham Arms

Address: Swettenham Lane, SWETTENHAM,
Congleton, CW12 2LF
Tel/fax: 01477 571284
Email: info@swettenhamarms.co.uk
Website: www.swettenhamarms.co.uk
Map ref: 7 SJ86 **Directions:** M6 junct 18 to
Holmes Chapel, then A535 towards Jodrell Bank.
3m right (Forty Acre Lane) to Swettenham
Open: all week noon-3.30 6-11 (Sat-Sun noon-11)

🍺 🍽 L Mon-Fri 12-2.30, Sat-Sun 12-9.30 D Mon-Fri 6.30-9.30, Sat-Sun 12-9.30 **Facilities:** Parking Garden Wi-fi **Notes:** 🛢 FREE HOUSE 👫 🐕 🍷 12

Abundant hanging baskets, a nature reserve and an adjoining lavender and sunflower meadow guarantee an enduring memory of this fine 16th-century former nunnery, now unspoilt country inn. It has a warm and inviting atmosphere, along with speciality wines, ales and ciders, and a kitchen that relies on excellent Cheshire produce. Start with rabbit and baby leek terrine, then follow with rack of lamb with basil mousse and ratatouille, or seared sea bass and langoustine risotto.
Recommended in the area
Quinta Arboretum; Dane Valley walks; Little Moreton Hall

The Bear's Paw

★★★★★ 🛏 INN
Address: School Lane, WARMINGHAM,
Crewe, CW11 3QN
Tel: 01270 526317
Email: info@thebearspaw.co.uk
Website: www.thebearspaw.co.uk
Map ref: 7 SJ76 **Directions:** M6 junct 18, A54,
A533 towards Sandbach. Follow signs for village
Open: all day all week noon-11 🍺 🍽 Mon-Thu

12-9.30, Fri-Sat 12-10, Sun 12-8 **Rooms:** 14 en suite S £79-£120 D £99-£140 **Facilities:** Parking Garden Wi-fi **Notes:** 🛢 FREE HOUSE 👫 🐕 🍷 10

This charming yet stylish 19th-century gastro-pub reaches the heart of the community through the employment of good old-fashioned inn-keeping principles. It's warm and friendly; it serves six real ales from local micro-breweries in its large, reclaimed oak-floored bar; and it provides wholesome food made from the best of locally sourced seasonal produce. A daily-changing menu might list steak and Weetwood ale pie; trio of oxtail; or pan-fried grey mullet. There are luxurious boutique-style bedrooms available.
Recommended in the area
Hack Green Secret Nuclear Bunker; Palms Tropical Oasis; Trent & Mersey Canal

CORNWALL

St Ives harbour

The Halzephron Inn

Address: GUNWALLOE, Helston, TR12 7QB
Tel: 01326 240406
Fax: 01326 241442
Email: halzephroninn@tiscali.co.uk
Website: www.halzephron-inn.co.uk
Map ref: 1 SW62
Directions: 3m S of Helston on A3083,
right to Gunwalloe, through village. Inn on left
Open: all week Closed: 25 Dec
♿ ⏺ L all wk 12-2 D all wk 7-9
Facilities: Parking Garden
Notes: ⊕ FREE HOUSE ♙ ♟ 8

The name of this ancient inn derives from 'Als Yfferin', old Cornish for 'cliffs of hell', and this is an appropriate description of its situation on this hazardous but breathtaking stretch of coastline. Once a haunt of smugglers, the pub is located close to the fishing village of Gunwalloe and stands just 300 yards from the famous South Cornwall footpath. The only pub on the stretch between Mullion and Porthleven, today it offers visitors a warm welcome, a wide selection of ales and whiskies, and meals prepared from fresh local produce. These may be served outside, with views of the surrounding fields to the back or the ocean to the front, or inside, in a number of dining areas, from cosy nooks to a separate dining area or a family room (there's a thoughtful junior menu). Lunch and dinner bring a choice of fresh Cornish fare, accompanied by home-made granary or white rolls, plus daily-changing specials that might include roast monkfish tail wrapped in bacon on a seafood risotto, or seafood chowder. To follow there may be bread and butter pudding or hot chocolate fudge cake with Cornish cream. There's also a good wine list, with a choice of half-bottles.

Recommended in the area

Trevarno Gardens; Goonhilly Satellite Earth Station; RNAS Culdrose

The Crown Inn

★ ★ ★ INN
Address: LANLIVERY, Bodmin, PL30 5BT
Tel: 01208 872707
Email: thecrown@wagtailinns.com
Website: www.wagtailinns.com
Map ref: 1 SX05
Directions: Signed from A390. Follow brown sign about 1.5m W of Lostwithiel
Open: all day all week 🍽 food served all day
Rooms: 9 en suite (7 GF)
Facilities: Parking Garden Wi-fi **Notes:** ⊕ FREE HOUSE 🍴 🐾

This charming pub was built in the 12th century for the men constructing St Brevita's church next door. Such great age means everything about it oozes history – its thick stone walls, granite and slate floors, glass-covered well, low beams, open fireplaces and distinctive bread oven. The bar serves beers from Sharps of Rock and Skinners of Truro, and ten wines by the glass from a reasonably priced wine list. With Fowey harbour not far away, the menu will undoubtedly offer fresh crab, scallops, mackerel and more, while other local produce includes meats from a butcher in Par, fruit and vegetables from a local grocer and dairy products from Lostwithiel. At lunchtime, try chef's smoked mackerel pâté, or a proper Cornish pasty. Dinner might begin with an appetiser of marinated olives and ciabatta bread, followed by a starter of locally smoked duck, Cornish charcuterie, or pan-seared scallops. Main courses include Greek-style salad; steaks with chips, onion rings and rocket and Parmesan salad; whole baked sea bass stuffed with lemon and fennel; and Laura's cheesy ratatouille. Some of the comfortable en suite rooms include children's beds, and in some dogs are welcome. The pretty front garden is lovely in warm weather.

Recommended in the area

Restormel Castle; Lanhydrock House (NT); China Clay Country Park

The Bush Inn

Address: MORWENSTOW, Bude, EX23 9SR
Tel: 01288 331242
Website: www.bushinn-morwenstow.co.uk
Map ref: 1 SS21
Directions: Exit A39, 3m N of Kilkhampton,
2nd right into village of Shop. 1.5m to Crosstown.
Inn on village green
Open: all day all week 11am-12.30am
🍴 ⚜ L all wk D all wk
Facilities: Parking Garden Notes: ⚭ ⚹ ☂ 9

Said to be one of Britain's oldest pubs, The Bush Inn was originally built as a chapel in AD 950 for pilgrims en route to Spain. It became a pub some 700 years later and has provided sustenance for visitors for hundreds of years. Smugglers and wreckers were among them, drawn by the inn's dramatic and isolated clifftop location on the north Cornish coast; nowadays the views over the Tidna Valley and the Atlantic Ocean are just as stunning as they must have been then. The unspoilt interior features stone-flagged floors, old stone fireplaces, a Celtic piscina carved from serpentine set into a wall behind the cosy bar, and a 'leper's squint' – a tiny window through which the needy could grab scraps of food. Today the meals are very different, with the emphasis on fresh local produce, including beef from the inn's own farm. Local shoots provide the game, and seafood comes from home waters. In winter, warming dishes include red wine and blue cheese risotto and venison stew, all served with Cornish real ales and a variety of fine wines. In summer, diners can enjoy a plate of mussels or beer-battered pollock and chips in the garden, which contains sturdy wooden play equipment. There are three bed and breakfast rooms and self-catering accommodation is also available.

Recommended in the area

Clovelly; Morwenstow Church and Hawker's Hut (NT); Boscastle

The Pandora Inn

Address: Restronguet Creek, MYLOR BRIDGE,
Falmouth, TR11 5ST
Tel: 01326 372678 **Fax:** 01326 378958
Email: info@pandorainn.com
Website: www.pandorainn.com
Map ref: 1 SW83
Directions: From Truro/Falmouth follow A39, left
at Carclew, follow signs to pub **Open:** all day all
week 10.30am-11pm **Closed:** 25 Dec 📖 🍴 food
served all day Sun-Thu 10.30-9, Fri-Sat 10.30-9.30
Facilities: Parking Garden Wi-fi **Notes:** 🌐 ST AUSTELL BREWERY 🍴 🐕 🍷 15

One of the best known inns in Cornwall, The Pandora is set by the water in the beautiful surroundings
of Restronguet Creek. Parts of the thatched, cream-painted building date back to the 13th century,
and its flagstone floors and low beamed ceilings suggest that little can have changed since. The
atmosphere is splendidly traditional, with lots of snug corners, three log fires and a collection of
maritime memorabilia. The inn is named after the good ship Pandora, sent to Tahiti to capture the
Bounty mutineers. Unfortunately it was wrecked and the captain court-marshalled so, forced into early
retirement, he bought the inn. A full range of drinks is served, including fine wines and beers from
St Austell Brewery, HSD and Tribute. The award-winning kitchen team offers the same menu in the
bars or upstairs in The Upper Deck restaurant. When the sun shines, the tables and chairs set out on
the new pontoon provide an experience akin to walking and eating on water. Food is taken seriously
here, and the lunchtime and evening menus are supplemented by daily specials displayed on boards.
Ingredients are sourced from Cornish farmers and fishermen, and local seafood - some caught from the
pub's own pontoon - is a speciality of the house.

Recommended in the area

Trelissick Gardens (NT); National Maritime Museum; Pendennis Castle

Driftwood Spars

★★★★ ⇔ GUEST ACCOMMODATION

Address: Trevaunance Cove, ST AGNES, TR5 0RT
Tel: 01872 552428 **Fax:** 01872 553701
Email: info@driftwoodspars.co.uk
Website: www.driftwoodspars.co.uk
Map ref: 1 SW75
Directions: A30 onto B3285, through St Agnes, down hill, left at Peterville Inn, onto road for Trevaunance Cove **Open:** all day all week 11-11 (Fri-Sat 11-1am, 25 Dec 11am-2pm) ⬛ **L** all wk 12-

2.30 **D** all wk 6.30-9.30 (winter 6.30-9) ⭐ **L** Sun 12-2.30 **D** all wk 7-9, (winter Thu-Sat 7-9) **Rooms:** 15 (5 GF) **S** £45-£66 **D** £86-£102 **Facilities:** Parking Garden Wi-fi **Notes:** ⊕ FREE HOUSE ⬩⬩ ⌁ ⚑ 10

Just a short distance from the beach, this family-run, award-winning old pub has a dining room with sea view, three cosy bars, two beer gardens and a micro-brewery. Locally sourced produce is at the heart of the pub's food ethos, including fish landed daily at Newlyn. Among the specials are wild rabbit fricassée, and whole roast Cornish sole. The bedrooms, some overlooking the Atlantic, are pretty special too.

Recommended in the area

The Eden Project; Tate St Ives; South West Coastal Path

The Victory Inn

Address: Victory Hill, ST MAWES, TR2 5DQ
Tel: 01326 270324
Fax: 01326 270238
Email: contact@victory-inn.co.uk
Website: www.victory-inn.co.uk
Map ref: 1 SW83
Directions: Take A3078 to St Mawes. Pub up Victory Steps adjacent to harbour
Open: all day all week 11am-mdnt ⬛ **L** all wk 12-3

D all wk 6-9.30 ⭐ **L** all wk 12-3 **D** all wk 6-9.15
Facilities: Garden Wi-fi **Notes:** ⊕ PUNCH TAVERNS ⬩⬩ ⌁

This friendly fishermen's local, with spectacular harbour views, is named after Nelson's flagship, HMS Victory, and is now an award-winning dining pub, offering the freshest of local seafood. The blackboard specials change according to the day's catch, with dishes such as fresh crab salad; lobster thermidor; cod and chips; crab and mushroom omelette; and trio of fish with squid ink risotto. There's also pub grub and lunchtime snacks. In addition to local real ales, there's a decent selection of wines.

Recommended in the area

The Eden Project; Falmouth Maritime Museum; St Mawes Castle

The Cornish Arms

Address: Churchtown, ST MERRYN,
Padstow, PL28 8ND
Tel: 01841 532700 **Fax:** 01841 521496
Email: cornisharms@rickstein.com
Website: www.rickstein.com
Map ref: 1 SW87
Directions: From Padstow follow signs for St Merryn
then Churchtown **Open:** all wk 11am-11pm (25 Dec
open 2hrs only, winter 3-5pm) (Summer & school
hol open all day) ▲ L all wk 12-3 D all wk 6-9
Facilities: Parking Garden Wi-fi **Notes:** ⊕ FREE HOUSE ♦♦ ♠ ♀ 11

In 2010 Rick Stein became the pub's new tenant, adding to his Padstow-based empire. Luke Taylor, who has worked with Stein for a decade, is responsible for the well-received, simple British menu featuring crab salad; grilled Cornish hake; whole roasted sea bass; or Tywardreath pork and garlic sausages. St Austell brewery supplies great ales, while from Sharp's come Chalky's Bark and Bite, named in memory of Stein's late, show-stealing Jack Russell. Speaking of which, dogs on leads are welcome.

Recommended in the area

Tate St Ives; Bodmin Moor; Shire Horse and Carriage Museum

The Eden Project

The Mill House Inn

Address: TREBARWITH, Tintagel, PL34 0HD
Tel: 01840 770200
Fax: 01840 770647
Email: management@themillhouseinn.co.uk
Website: www.themillhouseinn.co.uk
Map ref: 1 SX08
Directions: From Tintagel take B3263 S, right after
Trewarmett to Trebarwith Strand. Pub 0.5m on right
Open: 11-11 (Fri-Sat 11am-mdnt, Sun noon-10.30)
Closed: 25 Dec ᕒ **L** Mon-Sat 12-2.30, Sun 12-3

D all wk 6.30-8.30 ⃝ **D** all wk 7-9 **Facilities:** Parking Garden Wi-fi **Notes:** ⊕ FREE HOUSE ⁙ ⁙

The Mill House dates back to 1760, and was a working mill until the 1930s. It is situated on the north
Cornish coast in a beautiful woodland setting, just half a mile from the surfing beach at Trebarwith
Strand, and a short distance from King Arthur's legendary castle. The Mill offers first class food and
accommodation (eight elegant rooms, all with en suite facilities) in a charming stone building. The
slate-floored bar with its wooden tables, chapel chairs and wood burning stove has a family friendly
feel. You may also choose to eat on the partly-covered tiered terraces (with heaters) at the front. A
new restaurant opened in July 2008 and is designed to blend in with the existing features of the Mill.
Traditional bar lunches such as snakebite-battered local haddock or a Cornish smoked fish platter are
followed by selections on the evening restaurant menu such as duo of Tintagel duck served with swede
and carrot purée or grilled local halibut with spinach and prawn ragout. Sharps and Tintagel Brewery
local ales together with an imaginative wine list complement the regularly changing menus, which
make use of the best locally sourced ingredients. The Mill House is licensed for wedding ceremonies
and is a perfect location for receptions, parties and conferences.

Recommended in the area

Trebarwith Surfing Beach; Tintagel Castle; Delabole Wind Farm

The Springer Spaniel

Address: TREBURLEY, Nr Launceston, PL15 9NS
Tel: 01579 370424
Email: enquiries@thespringerspaniel.org.uk
Website: www.thespringerspaniel.org.uk
Map ref: 1 SX37
Directions: On A388 halfway between
Launceston & Callington
Open: all week noon-2.30 6-10.30 ▤ ⭢◉⭠ L all wk
12-1.45 **D** all wk 6.15-8.45 **Facilities:** Parking
Garden **Notes:** ⊕ FREE HOUSE ⭡ ⭢

A friendly, traditional pub in the heart of the Cornish countryside offering delicious food, delectable ales, fine wines and great service. The old walls of The Springer Spaniel conceal a cosy bar with high-backed wooden settles, farmhouse-style chairs and a wood-burning stove to keep the chill out on colder days. There is a cosy candlelit restaurant, and for better weather a landscaped garden with outdoor seating. The menu features imaginative, contemporary dishes as well as traditional favourites and specialises in local, seasonal food including organic meat from the owners' farm.

Recommended in the area

Cotehele (National Trust); Mining Heritage Centre; Sterts Theatre, Upton Cross

Cotehele House

CUMBRIA

Lanercost Cricket Club

Drunken Duck Inn

★★★★★ ◉◉ ⧯ INN

Address: Barngates, AMBLESIDE, LA22 0NG
Tel: 015394 36347
Fax: 015394 36781
Email: info@drunkenduckinn.co.uk
Website: www.drunkenduckinn.co.uk
Map ref: 5 NY30
Directions: From Kendal on A591 to Ambleside, then follow Hawkshead sign. In 2.5m inn sign on right, 1m up hill **Open:** all week **Closed:** 25 Dec
🍴 L all wk 12-4 ⊚ D all wk 6-9.30
Rooms: 17 en suite (5 GF) S £71.25-£142.50 D fr £95
Facilities: Parking Garden Wi-fi **Notes:** ⊕ FREE HOUSE ⊪ ⧉ 17

This 17th-century inn is surrounded by 60 private acres of beautiful countryside. In spring, you can barely move for flowers, and all year round there are striking views of fells and lakes. Under the same family ownership since 1977, the Drunken Duck has been refurbished with a stylish mix of modern luxury and old world charm. Expect plenty of sofas to lounge in, a pretty residents' garden, and glamorous bedrooms. The bar, with its antique settles and log fires, serves beers from the inn's own Barngate Brewery. These have been named after much loved dogs: Cracker, Tag Lag and Chester's Strong and Ugly. The award-winning candlelit restaurant offers intelligent, modern British cuisine, with the same menu offered at lunch and dinner, supplemented by specials. Start with crab and shrimp tortellini with prawn bisque and rocket, followed by braised belly pork and black pudding with boulangère wilted lettuce, Calvados apples and sauce. Leave room for rhubarb and duck egg custard tart with clotted cream, or you could try the gourmet cheese list.

Recommended in the area

Lake District Visitor Centre; Armitt Museum; Windermere Steamboat Centre

The Boot Inn

Address: BOOT, Eskdale Valley, CA19 1TG
Tel: 019467 23224
Email: enquiries@bootinn.co.uk
Website: www.bootinn.co.uk
Map ref: 5 NY10 **Directions:** From A595 follow signs for Eskdale then Boot **Open:** all week
Closed: 25 Dec ᴸ ⚬ L all wk 12-3 **D** all wk 6-8.30 ⚬ **D** all wk 6-8.30 Feb-Nov (Mid Nov-mid Dec & mid Jan-Feb D only, Xmas exceptions) **Facilities:** Parking Garden Wi-fi **Notes:** ⊕ ROBINSONS ⋔ ⋔

Whether you are in the bar with its crackling log fire, in the light and airy conservatory, or in the dining room, which dates back to 1578, you can expect a warm welcome from Caroline, Sean and the friendly staff at The Boot Inn. Enjoy a drink in the bar or the snug and plan a day in some of the best scenery and walking areas in England. Hungry walkers will enjoy the home-made hearty dishes – Cumbrian Tatie Pot, Boot pie and Bewley's Cumberland sausage with mash. There is a garden with boules pitch, and traditional games, pool table and plasma screen TV available in the bar.

Recommended in the area

Muncaster Castle; La'al Ratty Steam Train; Whitehaven Rum Story; Eskdale, Lake District National Park

Terrace gardens at Muncaster Castle

The Sun Coniston

Address: CONISTON, LA21 8HQ
Tel: 015394 41248
Fax: 015394 41219
Email: thesun@hotelconiston.com
Website: www.thesunconiston.com
Map ref: 5 SD39
Directions: From M6 junct 36, A591, beyond
Kendal & Windermere, then A598 from Ambleside
to Coniston. Pub signed from bridge in village
Open: all day all week 11am-mdnt

L all wk 12-3 D all wk 6-9 **Facilities:** Parking Garden
Notes: ⊕ FREE HOUSE ⋔ ⋔

With a peaceful location at the foot of the mountains, The Sun Coniston offers a unique mix of bar, diner and inn, with the kind of comfortable informality and atmosphere that many attempt but few achieve. The 16th-century pub is a favourite with thirsty walkers and tourists seeking peace from the village below. It boasts a wealth of classic Lakeland features including stone bar, floors and walls, exposed beams and a working range. The newly created first floor Boat Room is an eating and drinking area, which is also home to an exhibition of rare Donald Campbell photographs. But at its heart is a very special bar with 8 guest real ales on hand-pull, 4 draft lagers, 20 plus malts and 30 plus wines. The menu has been created using locally sourced, seasonal ingredients to offer traditional British food as well as classic dishes with a twist. Depending on your mood, the freshly prepared food can be enjoyed in the bar, in the conservatory and outside on the front terrace.

Recommended in the area

Brantwood; Steam Yacht 'Gondola' (NT); Ravenglass & Eskdale Railway

The Punch Bowl Inn

★ ★ ★ ★ ★ ◉◉ INN

Address: CROSTHWAITE, Nr Kendal, LA8 8HR
Tel: 015395 68237
Fax: 015395 68875
Email: info@the-punchbowl.co.uk
Website: www.the-punchbowl.co.uk
Map ref: 6 SD49
Directions: M6 junct 36, A590 towards Barrow,
A5074 & follow signs for Crosthwaite. Pub by church on left
Open: all day all week 11am-mdnt
Rooms: 9 en suite **Facilities:** Parking Garden Wi-fi
Notes: ⊕ FREE HOUSE ♦♦ ♦♦ ♛ 14

The Punch Bowl is not only a bar and restaurant with excellent accommodation, it also serves as the village post office. The slate-floored bar, with open fires and original beams, is the perfect spot to enjoy a pint of Tag Lag from the Barngates Brewery. Leather chairs, gleaming wooden floors and a pale stone fireplace make for an elegant dining room. The award-winning menu features the local suppliers.

Recommended in the area

Sizergh Castle; Beatrix Potter country; Cartmel Race Course

Hadrian's Wall, Birdoswald

The Highland Drove Inn and Kyloes Restaurant

Address: GREAT SALKELD, Penrith, CA11 9NA
Tel: 01768 898349
Fax: 01768 898708
Email: highlanddroveinn@btinternet.com
Website: www.highland-drove.co.uk
Map ref: 6 NY53
Directions: Exit M6 junct 40, take A66 E'bound then A686 to Alston. After 4m, left onto B6412 for Great Salkeld & Lazonby
Open: all week noon-2 6-late (Closed Mon L) ▨ ﾖ L Tue-Sun 12-2 D all wk 6-9
Facilities: Parking Garden **Notes:** ⅰ ⼽ ⼦ 25

Father and son team Donald and Paul Newton have turned this 300-year-old country inn into the area's social hub. Deep in the lovely Eden Valley, it stands on the old drove road along which Kyloes, Highland cattle bred in the Western Isles, were once herded on their way to market. Maintaining its reputation for high quality food depends to some extent on the local game, meat and fish that goes into the traditional dishes and daily specials. Thus, typical main dishes might be salad of crispy fried squid and spring onion in sweet chilli sauce; wild salmon and mussel tagliatelle in white wine saffron cream sauce; and roast beef-tomato stuffed with savoury couscous topped with goat's cheese. Always popular are desserts such as vanilla crème brûlée with shortbread and fruits of the forest compote; and sticky toffee pudding with butterscotch sauce and Chantilly cream. Locals come here to enjoy a great wine list and the real ales are chosen by Paul, sourced from Cumbria's micro-breweries.

Recommended in the area

Lake District National Park; Hadrian's Wall; Pennine Way

The Queen's Head

★★★★ 🏵 INN

Address: Main Street, HAWKSHEAD, LA22 0NS
Tel: 015394 36271
Fax: 015394 36722
Email: enquiries@queensheadhotel.co.uk
Website: www.queensheadhotel.co.uk
Map ref: 5 SD39
Directions: M6 junct 36, A590 to Newby Bridge, 1st right, 8m to Hawkshead **Open:** all day all week 11am-11.45pm Sun 12-11.45 🍺 🍴 **L** 12-2.30 Sun 12-5 **D** all wk 6.15-9.30
Rooms: 13 en suite (2 GF) **Facilities:** Garden Wi-fi
Notes: ⊕ FREDERIC ROBINSON 🚶 🍷 16

This charming 16th-century inn sits in the heart of historic Hawkshead, the village where William Wordsworth went to school and Beatrix Potter created Peter Rabbit. Her husband William Heelis was the local solicitor and his old offices, now the Beatrix Potter Gallery, are full of her wonderful illustrations. The surrounding area is a haven for walkers, and Esthwaite Water is a stone's throw away. Inside, you'll find low oak-beamed ceilings, wood-panelled walls, an original slate floor and a welcoming fire. As well as a range of well-appointed en suite bedrooms and self-catering accommodation, the inn offers everything you could need for relaxed wining and dining. There's an extensive wine list with many available by the glass and a selection of well kept real ales, plus a full carte menu and an ever-changing specials board. Enjoy timeless pub classics along with a more up-to-date, hearty repertoire with plenty of local colour. Dishes draw from the wealth of quality produce on the doorstep - organic trout from Esthwaite Water, wild pheasant from Graythwaite, traditionally cured hams and Cumberland sausage from Waberthwaite, and slow-maturing Herdwick lamb.

Recommended in the area

Hill Top (NT); Go Ape at Grizedale Forest Park; Brantwood House and Gardens

Cumbria

The Horse & Farrier Inn

Address: Threlkeld Village, KESWICK, CA12 4SQ
Tel: 017687 79688
Fax: 017687 79823
Email: info@horseandfarrier.com
Website: www.horseandfarrier.com
Map ref: 5 NY22
Directions: M6 junct 40 follow Keswick (A66) signs, after 12m turn right signed Threlkeld. Pub in village centre
Open: all day all week 7.30am-mdnt 🍺 🍴 food served all day **Facilities:** Parking Garden Wi-fi **Notes:** ⊕ JENNINGS BROTHERS PLC ⛄ 🐕 🍷 10

Within its thick stone walls lies all you would expect from a traditional Lakeland inn. Built in 1688 beneath 868m Blencathra, and with views towards Skiddaw in the west and Helvellyn to the south, it has slate-flagged floors, beamed ceilings and open fires. For the last nine years, under Ian Court's ownership, The Horse & Farrier has received numerous awards and guide book recommendations, notably for its restaurant and accommodation. A typical dinner might start with terrine of wild boar and venison, or seared trio of Morecambe Bay scallops, and continue with pan-griddled duo of Cumberland sausages with butterbean and chive mash; fillet of sea bass with a cassolette of chorizo, haricot beans, mushrooms and pasta shells; or, in the bar, a home-made curry or Mediterranean vegetable lasagne. A house speciality is lamb shoulder slowly braised in Jennings Cumberland ale (this Cockermouth brewery's beers are a fixture in the bar, by the way) with chive mash and redcurrant and mint sauce. For dessert, a Swiss ice cream, perhaps, such as crunchy mint chocolate or parfait caramel. Stay overnight and enjoy a hearty Lakeland breakfast, then relax in the small beer garden and enjoy those magnificent mountain views.

Recommended in the area

Rheged Discovery Centre; Honister Slate Mine; Cumbria Way

57

The Kings Head

Address: Thirlspot, KESWICK, CA12 4TN
Tel: 017687 72393
Fax: 017687 72309
Email: stay@lakedistrictinns.co.uk
Website: www.lakedistrictinns.co.uk
Map ref: 5 NY22
Directions: From M6 take A66 to Keswick then A591, pub 4m S of Keswick
Open: all day all week ⓑ food served all day
❍ D all wk 7-8.30 **Facilities:** Parking Garden Wi-fi
Notes: ⊕ FREE HOUSE ⧫ ⌁ ☃ 9

With 950-metre Helvellyn rearing up behind this 17th-century former coaching inn, it is not hard to describe the views as anything but truly sublime. Take our word for it, they really are. On sunny days, the garden is the most sought-after place to enjoy a meal or drink, although the wooden beams and inglenook fireplaces of the bar, restaurant and lounge areas could make it a tough call. Dark, strong Sneck Lifter is one of the Jennings beers on draught brewed in nearby Cockermouth. Favourites from the bar menu include home-made beefburgers, Waberthwaite Cumberland sausage, and peach, Blengdale Blue cheese and rocket salad, while soups and bloomer bread sandwiches are available all day. The elegant St John's Restaurant menu offers dishes such as home-cured gravadlax with celeriac rémoulade, followed by rack of lamb with roasted root vegetables, or monkfish tail fettucine with steamed mussels. Those with a sweet tooth will find it hard to resist sticky toffee pudding, or vanilla pod crème brûlée. The Lakeland Speciality Shop is well worth a visit for home-made preserves, Emma Bridgewater pottery, and local ale gift packs.

Recommended in the area

Lake District National Park; Thirlmere; Aira Force Waterfall

Queen's Head

★★★★ ⇔ INN

Address: Townhead, TROUTBECK,
Windermere, LA23 1PW
Tel: 015394 32174 Fax: 015394 31938
Email: reservations@queensheadtroutbeck.co.uk
Website: www.queensheadtroutbeck.co.uk
Map ref: 6 NY40 Directions: M6 junct 36,
A590/591, towards Windermere, right at mini-rdbt
onto A592 for Penrith/Ullswater. Pub 2m on left Open:
all day 🍺 🍽 food served all day Rooms: 15 en suite
(2 GF) S £80-£90 D £130-£150 Facilities: Parking Wi-fi Notes: ⊕ FREDERIC ROBINSON 👬 🐕 🍷 8

A classic 17th-century coaching inn, the Queen's Head is situated in the valley of Troutbeck and offers
stunning views across the Garburn Pass. Just three miles from Windermere, this thriving pub continues
to provide sustenance and comfortable accommodation to its many visitors. The bars are full of nooks
and crannies, and there are open fires and carved settles. With Robinson's Brewery beers on the
pumps, and a reputation for good food all the day, it draws regulars and ramblers alike.

Recommended in the area

Brockhole National Park Visitor Centre; The World of Beatrix Potter; Lake Windermere

---

The Yanwath Gate Inn

Address: YANWATH, Penrith, CA10 2LF
Tel: 01768 862386
Email: enquiries@yanwathgate.com
Website: www.yanwathgate.com
Map ref: 6 NY52
Directions: Telephone for directions
Open: all day all week 🍺 🍽 L all wk 12-2.30
D all wk 6-9 Facilities: Parking Garden Wi-fi
Notes: ⊕ FREE HOUSE 👬 🐕 🍷 12

The delightful 17th-century inn takes its name from its original function as a tollgate. It has a growing
reputation for good food and has a beautiful garden with outdoor seating. At least three Cumbrian
ales are served here at any one time. For lunch the starter might be a bowl of mussels, soup of the
day or ham terrine followed by a main dish of fisherman's pie, venison burger or Cumberland sausage
with Yanwarth Gate black pudding. For dinner the mains include red bream, crisp belly pork, smoked
venison loin and an open lasagne of mushrooms and summer vegetables.

Recommended in the area

Rheged; Brougham Hall; steamer cruises on Ullswater

Buckland in the Moor, Dartmoor National Park

The Old Thatch Inn

Address: CHERITON BISHOP,
Nr Exeter, EX6 6HJ
Tel: 01647 24204
Email: mail@theoldthatchinn.f9.co.uk
Website: www.theoldthatchinn.com
Map ref: 2 SX79
Directions: 0.5m off A30, 7m SW of Exeter
Open: all week 11.30-3 6-11
Closed: 25-26 Dec, Sun eve
♨ ⊚| L Mon-Thu 12-2, Fri-Sat 12-2.30, Sun 12-3
D Mon-Thu 6.30-9, Fri-Sat 6.30-9.30
Facilities: Parking Garden **Notes:** ⊕ FREE HOUSE ♦♦ ⌂ ♀ 9

The Old Thatch Inn is a charming Grade II listed 16th-century free house located just inside the eastern borders of Dartmoor National Park, and half a mile off the A30. It once welcomed stagecoaches on the London to Penzance road and today it remains a popular halfway house for travellers on their way to and from Cornwall. For a time during its long history, the inn passed into private hands and then became a tea-room, before its licence was renewed in the early 1970s. Experienced owners David and head chef Serena London pride themselves on their high standards, especially when it comes to food, and all of the meals are prepared using fresh ingredients from the south-west, with seafood featuring strongly. Dishes change daily, depending on supplies, and examples include pan seared pigeon breast with a spinach mousse and mixed berry dressing; and baked fillet of seabass with a crayfish tail, lemon and thyme risotto. Diners can choose from a number of real ales and a good range of wines, with many available by the glass.

Recommended in the area

Castle Drogo (NT); Fingle Bridge, Dartmoor; Exeter

The Five Bells Inn

Address: CLYST HYDON, Cullompton, EX15 2NT
Tel: 01884 277288
Email: info@fivebellsclysthydon.co.uk
Website: www.fivebellsclysthydon.co.uk
Map ref: 2 ST00
Directions: B3181 towards Cullompton, right at
Hele Cross towards Clyst Hydon. 2m turn right, sharp
right at village sign Open: 11.30am-3 6.30-11pm
Closed: 25 Dec, Mon L ⅃ L Tue-Sun 11.30-2 D all
wk 6.30-9 Facilities: Parking Garden Notes: ⅃ ⅃ 8

Named after the number of bells in the village church, this beautiful white-painted, thatched former farmhouse is surrounded by rolling countryside. It became a pub around a century ago, and in recent years has become famous for its family-friendly atmosphere and the dedication to real ales and good food. The interior is welcoming, with old beams and an inglenook fireplace, gleaming copper and brass, with four eating areas. Choose from an interesting and well-balanced menu of traditional and modern British dishes based on fresh local ingredients such as prime West Country steaks and fresh fish.

Recommended in the area

Killerton Gardens; Exeter; Jurassic Coast World Heritage Site

The Two Moors Way, Castle Drogo

The New Inn

★★★★ INN

Address: COLEFORD, Crediton, EX17 5BZ
Tel: 01363 84242 **Fax:** 01363 85044
Email: enquiries@thenewinncoleford.co.uk
Website: www.thenewinncoleford.co.uk
Map ref: 2 SS70
Directions: From Exeter take A377, 1.5m after
Crediton turn left for Coleford, 1.5m to inn **Open:** all
week 12-3 6-11 (Sun 7-10.30 winter) **Closed:** 25-26
Dec ⓑ ⓘ **L** all wk 12-2 **D** all wk 6.30-9.30 **Rooms:**
6 en suite (1 GF) **S** £65 **D** £80-£89 **Facilities:** Parking Garden **Notes:** ⊕ FREE HOUSE ⓘⓘ ⏗ ⓘ 20

In a peaceful conservation village between Dartmoor and Exmoor stands this pretty 13th-century free house. The Cole stream flows past its well-tended gardens, guarded by a stately weeping willow, eventually to join the Exe. Once inside, you'll be welcomed by Captain, an Amazon blue parrot who has been greeting visitors with cheeky comments for 28 years. Your surroundings - oak beams, slate floors, wood burners, old carved chests and cushioned stone wall seats – will be just what you hoped for. In the bar you'll find real ales from Devon and Cornwall, and plenty of wines by the glass to accompany fresh fish from Brixham, and game, meats, cheeses and other produce from surrounding villages and farms. Sandwiches and ploughman's platters are available at lunchtime, while fuller meals might start with creamy mushroom pot topped with grilled Stilton, or pan-fried, shell-off king prawns with garlic butter. Main dishes include home-made steak and ale pie; lamb's liver, bacon and mash with onion gravy; and grilled salmon with smoked salmon filling. Finish with orange marmalade bread and butter pudding, or mascarpone cheesecake with blackcurrant compote. Comfortable overnight accommodation is guaranteed in the well-appointed bedrooms. Look out for the monthly hog roasts and live New Orleans jazz nights.
Recommended in the area
Castle Drogo (NT); City of Exeter; Tarka Trail

The Nobody Inn

★★★★ ⌒ INN

Address: DODDISCOMBSLEIGH, Exeter, EX6 7PS
Tel: 01647 252394 **Fax:** 01647 252978
Email: info@nobodyinn.co.uk
Website: www.nobodyinn.co.uk
Map ref: 2 SX88
Directions: 3m SW of Exeter Racecourse (A38)
Open: all day all week 11-11 (Sun 12-10.30)
Closed: 25-26 Dec, 1 Jan ⓑ **L** Mon-Sat 12-2, Sun
12-3 **D** Mon-Thu 6.30-9, Fri-Sat 6.30-9.30, Sun 7-9

⏺ **D** Mon-Thu 6.30-9, Fri-Sat 6.30-9.30, Sun 7-9 **Rooms:** 5 (4 en suite 1 pri fac) **S** £45-£70
D £60-£95 **Facilities:** Parking Garden Wi-fi **Notes:** ⊕ FREE HOUSE ♈ ⚑ 28

This 16th-century inn lies in rolling Devon countryside between the Haldon Hills and the Teign Valley. Although its history can be traced back to 1591, it was another two centuries before it became an inn and a further 160 years before it was renamed The No Body Inn, following an unfortunate episode involving a deceased landlord. You will be immediately transported back to the distant past by the low ceilings, blackened beams, inglenook and antique furniture, although in the interests of progress there have been some recent upgrades, mostly in the restaurant and guest rooms, and there's new seating in the pretty garden. Seasonal dishes, with fish delivered daily from Brixham, are served in the bar and restaurant, where typical starters include pan-fried pigeon breast with rocket and walnut dressing, and baked scallops in Devon Oke cheese sauce. Among the mains might appear roasted vegetable and Sharpham Brie pie in herb pastry; venison steak with mandarin and orange sauce; and kiln-roast salmon on bubble and squeak. You can sample over 250 wines, 230 whiskies in addition to an ever-changing range of real ales. Rooms are all beautifully decorated and with a welcoming decanter of sherry.

Recommended in the area

Dartmoor National Park; Dart Valley Railway; Ugbrooke House and Park

The Grove Inn

Address: KINGS NYMPTON, EX37 9ST
Tel: 01769 580406
Email: enquiry@thegroveinn.co.uk
Website: www.thegroveinn.co.uk
Map ref: 2 SS61
Directions: 2.5m from A377 (Exeter to Barnstaple rd) **Open:** all year noon-3 6-11 (BH noon-3)
Closed: Mon L ex BH ⊨ L Tue-Sat 12-2 ⏴⊙⏵ L Tue-Sun 12-2 D Tue-Sat 7-9 **Facilities:** Garden
Notes: ⊞ FREE HOUSE ⫝̸ ⏞ ⚐

Set in a beautiful conservation village in the Devon countryside, the award-winning Grove Inn has been working in partnership with local farmers and producers to bring a real taste of Devon to their guests since early 2003. Using quality produce, the menu offers top-notch dishes such as individual beef Wellington made with matured Devon beef from Lakehead Farm, luxury North Devon fish pie using fish landed at Clovelly and Appledore, or rare-breed sausages from Highland Farm, with a home-made dessert to finish. To drink there are West Country ales and ciders, and every wine and champagne is available by the glass.
Recommended in the area
RHS Rosemoor; South Molton Pannier Market; Exmoor and North Devon coast

Dartmoor National Park

Bickley Mill Inn

Address: KINGSKERSWELL,
Newton Abbot, TQ12 5LN
Tel: 01803 873201
Email: info@bickleymill.co.uk
Website: www.bickleymill.co.uk
Map ref: 2 SX86
Directions: From Newton Abbot on A380
towards Torquay. Right at Barn Owl Inn,
follow brown tourist signs
Open: all week Mon-Sat 11.30-3 6.30-11 (Sun
6-10.30) **Closed:** 27-28 Dec & 1 Jan ⅃ **L** Mon-Sat 12-2 (Sun 12-2.30) **D** Mon-Sat 6.30-9.15
(Sun 6-8.30) ⅃ **L** Mon-Sat 12-2 (Sun 12-2.30) **D** all wk 6.30-9.15 **Facilities:** Parking Garden Wi-fi
Notes: ⊕ FREE HOUSE ♦♦ ⊁ ⊉ 9

Once a flour mill and dating back to the 13th century, Bickley Mill Inn is a family-run free house.
Located in the beautiful wooded Stoneycombe Valley, it is within convenient reach of Torquay, Newton
Abbot and Totnes. The mill was bought by David and Patricia Smith and reopened after a thorough
refurbishment, which blends old and new in a fresh contemporary style. An 18th-century former barn,
the Millers Room, has been transformed into a function room catering for groups of 25 - 125 guests.
In the restaurant, quality produce from the south-west is transformed by chef Bill Gott into a range of
British dishes with an international influence. The seasonally changing menu might include crispy pork
belly with smashed parsnips and apples; grilled sea bream fillets with roast vegetables and tomato
sauce; and sweet potato and aubergine rogan josh, all accompanied by wine from a well-chosen list.
Fresh fish is delivered every day from neighbouring Brixham. In the cosy bar, roaring log fires and
comfortable sofas make it easy to relax over one of the locally brewed ales.

Recommended in the area

Dartmoor National Park; Paignton Zoo; Compton Castle (NT)

California Country Inn

Address: California Cross, MODBURY, Ivybridge, PL21 0SG
Tel: 01548 821449
Fax: 01548 821566
Email: enquiries@californiacountryinn.co.uk
Website: www.californiacountryinn.co.uk
Map ref: 2 SX65
Directions: Near Modbury on B3392, follow brown tourist signs
for California Cross **Open:** all day all week
⌂ **L** Mon-Sat 12-2, Sun 12-2.30 **D** Mon-Sat 6-9, Sun 6-8.30
⏣ **L** Sun 12-2 **D** Wed-Sun 6-9 **Facilities:** Parking Garden Wi-fi
Notes: ⏣ FREE HOUSE ⛼ ⛾

An award-winning 14th-century country inn, locally noted for its
food. Painted a rich cream outside, its atmospheric interior features exposed dry stone walls and old
beams, with a dining room full of photos, fresh flowers, prints and brasswork. As a supporter of local
food, the kitchen sources most of its produce from the fields of the South Hams and the local waters. At
lunchtime or in the evening enjoy a bar meal from the extensive menu and specials board, with classics
like lamb's liver on mustard mash with crispy onions and gravy; chargrilled pork loin with sautéed
potatoes, Stilton and mushroom cream sauce; and beer-battered cod. For those preferring the polished
cutlery, glassware and table cloths of the dining room, the Modern British cooking includes three-way
Woolston pork (crispy belly, Parma ham and black pudding) with pear, Devon Blue cheese and sherry
vinegar dressing, or roasted red pepper as a starter; followed by medley of monkfish, salmon, scallops
and king prawns with chive pommes purée and white wine cream sauce; sticky honey and lemon
chicken; or wild mushroom and asparagus risotto. In the summer months, enjoy a well-kept local real
ale in the delightful landscaped garden.

Recommended in the area

South West Coast Path; Kitley Caves; Dartmoor Zoological Park

The Ship Inn

Address: NOSS MAYO, Plymouth, PL8 1EW
Tel: 01752 872387
Fax: 01752 873294
Email: ship@nossmayo.com
Website: www.nossmayo.com
Map ref: 2 SX54
Directions: 5m S of Yealmpton on River
Yealm estuary
Open: all day all week 🍴 ⏺ Mon-Sat 12-9.30,
Sun 12-9 **Facilities:** Parking Garden
Notes: ⊕ FREE HOUSE ♦♦ 🐾 🍷 13

Reclaimed English oak and local stone characterise this beautifully renovated 16th-century free house on the Yealm (sometimes pronounced Yam, apparently) estuary. The waterside location makes it an excellent walking and sailing destination - you can tie up your boat outside. Deceptively spacious inside, yet it remains cosy, thanks to the wooden floors, old bookcases, log fires and dozens of local pictures. From Dartmoor Brewery in Princetown, home of the prison, comes the whimsically named Jail Ale, plus Proper Job, Tribute Dartmoor and guest ales. Sit anywhere from the panelled library to a waterside table for a home-made snack or meal from the daily-changing bar or carte menus. A starter like leek and potato soup, or traditional crayfish tail cocktail with Marie Rose sauce, could be followed by pan-fried duck breast on potato rosti with plum sauce; Thai green chicken curry with rice; Cajun salmon fillet on creamed potatoes with roasted vine tomatoes; or pumpkin and pea risotto. Don't fall at the final hurdle by forgoing apple and berry crumble and custard; or chocolate mousse with shortbread. Interesting global wines, a decent list of malts, liqueurs and hot drinks complete the menu, which you can study while enjoying the great views from the waterside garden.

Recommended in the area

Saltram House (NT); Dartmoor Wildlife Park; National Shire Horse Centre

Saltram House, Plympton (NT)

The Harris Arms

Address: PORTGATE, Lewdown, EX20 4PZ
Tel: 01566 783331
Fax: 01566 783359
Email: info@theharrisarms.co.uk
Website: www.theharrisarms.co.uk
Map ref: 1 SX48
Directions: From A30 at Broadwoodwidger/Roadford Lake exit follow signs to Lifton then for Portgate
Open: Tue-Sun L **Closed:** Mon & Sun eve
🍴 🍽 L Tue-Sun 12-2 **D** Tue-Sat 6.30-9
Facilities: Parking Garden
Notes: ⊕ FREE HOUSE ♟♦ ♞ ♟ 20

A 16th-century inn with wonderful views to Brent Tor, this establishment lives up to its promotional strapline: 'Eat Real Food and Drink Real Wine'. Located on the old A30 close to the boundary between Devon and Cornwall, it's an accessible spot for honest food with substance and style, plus real ales and excellent wines. Owners Rowena and Andy Whiteman have previously run vineyards in France and New Zealand, so their wine list, with over 150 wines, is both eclectic and extensive; twenty are served by the glass. The pub's excellent reputation, which reaches far beyond the local area, is built on exact cooking and locally-sourced, quality ingredients. Example of a starter is roast breast of pigeon with beetroot risotto and red wine sauce, and main courses might include slow-roasted pork belly with spinach, apple sauce and black pudding and potato croquette; and pub classics such as home-cooked ham with eggs and chips. A children's menu is available. In warmer weather, enjoy a glass of Sharp's Doom Bar, Otter Ale or Bays Best or a meal outside on the decked patio that overlooks amazing countryside.

Recommended in the area

Dartmoor National Park; Lydford Gorge; Lawrence House Museum, Launceston

Jack in the Green Inn

◎◎

Address: London Road, ROCKBEARE, Nr Exeter, EX5 2EE
Tel: 01404 822240 **Fax:** 01404 823445
Email: info@jackinthegreen.uk.com
Website: www.jackinthegreen.uk.com
Map ref: 2 SY09 **Directions:** From M5 take old A30 towards
Honiton, signed Rockbeare **Open:** all week 11-3 5.30-11 (Sun
noon-11) **Closed:** 25 Dec-5 Jan ﬞ ◎ **L** Mon-Sat 12-2, Sun 12-9
D Mon-Sat 6-9.30, Sun 12-9 **Facilities:** Parking Garden Wi-fi
Notes: ⊕ FREE HOUSE ⦁¶ ⚑ 12

There has been an inn on this site for several centuries,
but since Paul Parnell took over some 20 years ago, it has
become an award-winning beacon of good food in a contemporary and relaxed atmosphere. Within its
whitewashed walls is a lounge bar furnished with comfy seating and dark wood tables, and a smart
restaurant. The simple philosophy here is to serve real food to real people, with a firm commitment
from the kitchen to sourcing the best and freshest local produce and preparing it to a consistently high
standard. Typical dishes on the bar menu include home-made chicken liver parfait with redcurrant
jelly; 'Posh' prawn cocktail with 'Bloody Mary' sauce; braised faggots, creamed potato and onion
gravy; confit Creedy Carver duck leg with creamed haricot beans. Throughout 2011 the inn is offering
a 'Totally Devon' 3-course menu experience. Current cask ales include Otter Ale, Doom Bar and
Butcombe Bitter plus three Devon ciders including St George's Temptation and Yarde Real Cider.
Perfect for the summer months is the alfresco eating area for up to 80 people with full menu table
service, and jazz fans should seek out the Friday night events. Dogs are welcome outside, with water
provided and a field for walking them.

Recommended in the area

Bicton Park; Escot Park; Crealy Adventure Park

The Blue Ball

★ ★ ★ ★ INN

Address: Stevens Cross, Sidford,
SIDMOUTH, EX10 9QL

Tel: 01395 514062

Fax: 01395 519584

Email: rogernewton@blueballinn.net

Website: www.blueballinnsidford.co.uk

Map ref: 2 SY18

Directions: M5 junct 30 exit to A3052. Through Sidford towards Lyme Regis, on left after village,

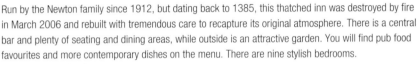

approx 13m **Open:** all day all week **Closed:** 25 Dec eve ⬛ ⵘ◯ **L** all wk 12-2.30 **D** all wk 6-9 **Rooms:** 9 en suite (1 GF) **S** £60 **D** £95 **Facilities:** Parking Garden **Notes:** ⊕ PUNCH TAVERNS ⭥ ⛭ ⚐ 13

Run by the Newton family since 1912, but dating back to 1385, this thatched inn was destroyed by fire in March 2006 and rebuilt with tremendous care to recapture its original atmosphere. There is a central bar and plenty of seating and dining areas, while outside is an attractive garden. You will find pub food favourites and more contemporary dishes on the menu. There are nine stylish bedrooms.

Recommended in the area

Crealy Adventure Park; Seaton Tramway; South West Coast Path

Sidmouth

Dukes

★★★★ 🛏 INN

Address: The Esplanade, SIDMOUTH, EX10 8AR
Tel: 01395 513320
Fax: 01395 519318
Email: dukes@hotels-sidmouth.co.uk
Website: www.hotels-sidmouth.co.uk
Map ref: 2 SY18
Directions: M5 junct 30 onto A3052, take 1st exit to Sidmouth on right then left onto Esplanade
Open: all day all week 🛏 🍴 Sun-Thu 12-9, Fri-Sat 12-9.30 **Rooms:** 13 en suite S £37-£52 D £74-£124
Facilities: Parking Garden Wi-fi **Notes:** ⊕ FREE HOUSE 🎎 🐾 🍷 20

Situated at the heart of Sidmouth town centre on the Regency Esplanade, Dukes is a contemporary inn that successfully combines traditional values with an informal atmosphere. The interior is stylish and lively, with a relaxed continental feel in the bar and public areas, and there are comfortable en suite bedrooms to stay in, most of which have sea views and come with a range of home comforts, including Wi-fi. In fine weather, the patio garden overlooking the sea is the perfect place to bask in the sun with a smoothie or freshly ground mid-morning coffee and home-baked pastry, or to enjoy a pint and plate of your choice at lunchtime. Branscombe and O'Hanlons are among the real ale choices on offer, and about 20 wines are served by the glass. Traditional English-style dishes vie with the specials board, where seafood from Brixham and Lyme Bay, and prime meats from West Country farms will be found. The head chef and his team aim to produce dishes that will suit all tastes: potted crab, crispy duck confit and home-made banoffee pie are typical examples.

Recommended in the area

Jurassic Coast; Crealy Great Adventure Parks; Exeter Cathedral

The Tower Inn

Address: Church Road, SLAPTON, Kingsbridge, TQ7 2PN
Tel: 01548 580216
Email: towerinn@slapton.org
Website: www.thetowerinn.com
Map ref: 2 SX84
Directions: Off A379 S of Dartmouth, turn left at Slapton Sands
Open: 12-3 6-11 **Closed:** 1st 2wks Jan, Mon winter
🛏 🍴 L all wk 12-2 **D** all wk 7-9 **Facilities:** Parking Garden
Wi-fi **Notes:** ⊕ FREE HOUSE ♦ ⁴ 🐾

The Tower is a 14th-century inn set in an historic village in Devon's lovely South Hams, approached down a narrow lane. Its name comes from the ruined tower overlooking the pub's walled garden. Inside are interconnecting rooms, with stone walls, beams, pillars and pews, flagstone floors, scrubbed oak tables and log fires. Food at lunchtime ranges from sandwiches to full meals, and a separate evening menu is served by candlelight. Food is sourced locally where possible, including fish landed at Start Bay. There is an excellent range of traditional beers, plus local cider and mulled wine in winter.

Recommended in the area

Slapton Sands; Slapton Ley Nature Reserve; Cookworthy Museum of Rural Life

Exeter Cathedral

The Golden Lion Inn

Address: TIPTON ST JOHN, Sidmouth, EX10 0AA
Tel: 01404 812881
Email: info@goldenliontipton.co.uk
Website: www.goldenliontipton.co.uk
Map ref: 2 SY09
Directions: Telephone for directions
Open: all wk 12-2.30 (Sat-Sun 12-3.30) 6-11
(Sun 7-10.30)  L all wk 12-2 **D** Mon-Sat 6.30-8.30,
Sun 7-8.30 **Facilities:** Parking Garden
Notes: ♥ ♟ 12

Francois (Franky) and Michelle Teissier have been running their
inviting village pub for quite a while now. It manages to retain
that traditional pub feel with low wooden beams, stone interior walls and a blazing log fire
and charmingly eclectic décor of Art Deco prints, Tiffany lamps and paintings by Devon and Cornwall
artists. Franky and Michelle welcome customers with their extensive menu comprising the highest
quality British, Mediterranean and rustic French cooking, such as lunchtime smoked duck salad with
onion marmalade; home-cooked ham, egg and chips; and mussels, french fries and crusty bread.
Dinner could begin with escargots de Bourgogne, or grilled goat's cheese crouton with Italian ham.
To follow, try breast of chicken with light sherry and cream sauce; marinated lamb kebab in garlic
and rosemary; or a blackboard special featuring fresh fish or seafood landed at nearby Sidmouth,
such as sea bass stuffed with cream cheese and sage; monkfish kebabs; lobster in garlic butter;
and Lyme Bay crab. Outside, a grassy beer garden shares the sun with a terracotta-walled terrace
and tumbling grapevines. A pint of locally brewed Otter or a glass of cold Chablis tastes good in either
on a warm day.

Recommended in the area
Cadhay Elizabethan Manor House; South West Coast Path; Exeter Cathedral

The Durant Arms

★★★★ ⇔ INN

Address: Ashprington, TOTNES, TQ9 7UP
Tel: 01803 732240
Website: www.durantarms.co.uk
Map ref: 2 SX86
Directions: Exit A38 at Totnes junct, to Dartington & Totnes, at 1st lights right for Kingsbridge on A381, in 1m left for Ashprington **Open:** all week Sat-Sun all day ⓑ ⊚ **L** all wk 12-2 **D** all wk 7-9.15
Rooms: 8 en suite (2 GF) **S** £50-£55 **D** £80-£85
Facilities: Parking Garden Wi-fi **Notes:** ⊕ FREE HOUSE ⦁† ⚲ ♟ 10

A locally renowned dining pub set in a pretty South Hams village, The Durant Arms dates from the 18th century and was originally the counting house for the neighbouring 500-acre Sharpham Estate. Sharpham wines and cheese are among the culinary delights, offered alongside a choice of real ales and excellent dishes cooked to order, using local produce where possible. There are eight comfortably furnished and attractively decorated bedrooms if you would like to stay over.
Recommended in the area
Sharpham Vineyard & Cheese Dairy; Elizabethan town of Totnes; River Dart

River Dart, Totnes

The White Hart

Address: Dartington Hall, TOTNES, TQ9 6EL
Tel: 01803 847111 **Fax:** 01803 847107
Email: bookings@dartingtonhall.com
Website: www.dartingtonhall.com
Map ref: 2 SX86
Directions: On A384, 2 miles from Totnes and close to A38 **Open:** all day all week (Mon-Sat 10am-11pm, Sun 10am-10.30pm) **Closed:** 24-29 Dec 🛏 🍽 **L** all wk 12-2.30 **D** all wk 6-9 **Facilities:** Parking Garden
Notes: ⊕ FREE HOUSE 👬 ♟ 14

The White Hart is tucked away in the courtyard of 14th-century Dartington Hall, now famed for its association with the arts. The gardens in the surrounding 1200-acre estate are among the finest in the country, and contain several sculptural features, including a reclining figure by Henry Moore. The restaurant, originally the hall's kitchen, retains its historic architecture, original tapestry and huge open fireplace, although a recent makeover now provides a more contemporary, yet still atmospheric, environment. How well it complements the chunky beams, roughcast walls, flagstone floor, limed-oak settles and log fire of the informal bar. The same menu serves both areas, relying heavily on locally sourced and seasonal produce, such as cured ham, single-suckled beef, grass-reared lamb, additive-free and free-range chickens and eggs, fish selected daily at the local fish market, and interesting speciality cheeses. Typical main dishes include mussels marinière with french fries; chargrilled pork loin with wholegrain mustard, butter beans, roast squash and port reduction; and root vegetable, courgette and cannellini bean stew, gremolata and herb dumplings. At weekends soup and baguettes are served between 15.00 and 17.30. Enjoy the range of West Country real ales, and choose wine from a list that classifies bottles by taste.

Recommended in the area

Dartington Cider Press Centre; Buckfast Abbey; Dart Valley Railway

Cridford Inn

Address: TRUSHAM, Newton Abbot, TQ13 0NR
Tel: 01626 853694
Email: reservations@vanillapod-cridfordinn.com
Website: www.vanillapod-cridfordinn.com
Map ref: 2 SX88
Directions: A38 take junct for Teign Valley,
turn right follow signs Trusham for 4m
Open: all week 11-3 6-11 (Sat 11am-11pm Sun
noon-10.30) ⚑ **L** all wk 12-2.30 **D** all wk 7-9.30
⚑ **L** Sun 12-1 **D** Mon-Sat 7-9.30
Facilities: Parking Garden **Notes:** ⊕ FREE HOUSE ♦♟ 10

Award-winning chef Ian Nixon and his wife, Tracey, run this ancient bar and the Vanilla Pod restaurant, which stands where a smallholding mentioned in the Domesday Book used to be. Built as a Devon longhouse, the beamed bar contains what is thought to be the country's earliest domestic medieval window frame, as well as a good selection of local ales, wines, traditional pub grub and specials. The fine-dining restaurant menu uses the finest, seasonal Devonshire ingredients.

Recommended in the area

Canonteign Falls; Belvedere Castle; Haldon Forest and Go Ape

Powderham Castle

The Digger's Rest

Address: WOODBURY SALTERTON, EX5 1PQ
Tel: 01395 232375
Fax: 01395 232711
Email: bar@diggersrest.co.uk
Website: www.diggersrest.co.uk
Map ref: 2 SY08
Directions: 2.5m from A3052. Signed from Westpoint
Open: all week 11-3 5.30-11 (Sun 12-3.30 5.30-10.30)
🍴 L Mon-Sat 11-2.15, Sun 12-2.15
D Mon-Sat 6.30-9.30, Sun 6.30-9
Facilities: Parking Garden Wi-fi
Notes: FREE HOUSE 13

The Digger's Rest is everything you would expect of a cosy country free house. Originally a Devon cider house, this 500-year-old building has thick walls of stone and cob with heavy beams under a thatched roof and a real log fire. The menu features simple fresh food expertly prepared to order. The emphasis here is on using fresh fish and local meats, supporting good farming husbandry and buying local and West Country organic produce where available. The menu, which includes pub classics, changes to reflect seasonal availability of raw ingredients and there is also a specials board and children's menu with proper food which kids actually like. Real ales feature Otter Bitter from Devon and guest appearances from other local and award-winning brewers. Wines are from the renowned wine merchant, Tanners of Shrewsbury, and for those looking for something non-alcoholic there is a range of interesting soft drinks. Whether you want a pint, coffee, glass of wine, snack or a full meal, you will find a warm welcome at The Digger's Rest.

Recommended in the area

Jurassic Coast; Powderham Castle; Fairlynch Museum

Rose & Crown

Address: Market Street, YEALMPTON, PL8 2EB
Tel: 01752 880223
Fax: 01752 881058
Email: info@theroseandcrown.co.uk
Website: www.theroseandcrown.co.uk
Map ref: 2 SX55
Directions: Telephone for directions
Open: all week
L all wk 12-2.30 **D** all wk 6.30-9.30
Facilities: Parking Garden Wi-fi
Notes: FREE HOUSE

Just a ten minute drive from Plymouth city centre is this very stylish village pub for eating and drinking, under new ownership since December 2009. The decor includes an attractive mix of tables and old dining chairs, with some good quality sofas, and a large fire place. The absence of curtains and other soft furnishings mean the acoustics are generally lively. This pub has a sensibly thought through balance between the contemporary and the traditional. The terraced garden, with a charming fountain, is a lovely spot in the warmer months. There is a good range of wines, but real ales are taken seriously too. The food on offer is a smart mix of modern pub food with restaurant presentation and quality. The regular-changing à la carte menu tends to include fish, game, meat and vegetarian dishes – all sourced as locally as possible. A 2-course set lunch for £10 (3 courses for £13) is always popular. There is a function room opposite – suitable for wedding receptions, other celebrations, meeting room etc.

Recommended in the area

Kitley Caves; South West Coast Path; Dartmoor National Park

DORSET

Clavell's Tower overlooking Kimmeridge Bay

The Anchor Inn

Address: High Street, BURTON BRADSTOCK, DT6 4QF
Tel: 01308 897228
Email: info@dorset-seafood-restaurant.co.uk
Website: www.dorset-seafood-restaurant.co.uk
Map ref: 2 SY48
Directions: 2m SE of Bridport on B3157 in centre of
Burton Bradstock **Open:** all week 11.30-3 5.30-12
(Sat-Sun 11.30am-mdnt) ⓑ ⑩ L all wk 12-2 D all
wk 6-9.30 **Facilities:** Parking Wi-fi **Notes:** ⓦ PUNCH
TAVERNS ⑪ ⚞ ⚑ 10

This 300-year-old coaching inn is just inland from a stretch of the Jurassic Coast World Heritage Site,
and near the amazing shingle feature known as Chesil Beach. In keeping with its name, the pub is full
of marine memorabilia, fishing tools and shellfish adorning the walls. The house speciality is fish and
seafood, and there are 20 main fish courses on offer, plus Catch of the Day. Look out for whole crab,
lobster, mussels and dived scallops plus plaice, skate wing, Dover sole and halibut. Meat dishes include
a range of chargrilled steaks and roasted crispy duck. There is a selection of fine wines available.
Recommended in the area
Coastline from Chesil Beach to Lyme Regis; West Bay Harbour; Abbotsbury Sub-Tropical Gardens

The Cock & Bottle

Address: EAST MORDEN, Wareham, BH20 7DL
Tel: 01929 459238
Map ref: 2 SY99
Directions: From A35 W of Poole turn right B3075,
pub 0.5m on left
Open: all week 11.30-2.30 6-11
(Sun noon-3 7-10.30) ⓑ ⑩ L all wk 12-2
D Mon-Sat 6-9 (Sun 7-9) **Facilities:** Parking Garden
Notes: ⓦ HALL & WOODHOUSE ⑪ ⚞

Once a cob-walled Dorset longhouse, this now popular dining pub acquired a brick skin around 1800.
Interiors are comfortably rustic with low-beamed ceilings, lots of nooks and crannies around the log
fires and attractive paintings. A good range of real ales and wines is complemented by bar, light lunch
and specials menus that recognise the breadth of the average palate, a fact that chef John works
tirelessly to reflect with locally sourced seasonal game, lamb shanks, steak and kidney pudding, pigeon
pie and chicken curry. Fish fans will appreciate fresh deliveries daily, including sea bass, haddock,
salmon and skate wing.
Recommended in the area
Corfe Castle; Tank Museum, Bovington; Hardy's Cottage (NT)

The Acorn Inn

★★★★ ◉ INN

Address: EVERSHOT, Dorchester, DT2 0JW
Tel: 01935 83228
Fax: 01935 83707
Email: stay@acorn-inn.co.uk
Website: www.acorn-inn.co.uk
Map ref: 2 ST50
Directions: A303 to Yeovil, Dorchester Rd, on A37 right to Evershot **Open:** all day all week 11-11.30pm ⓦ ⓘ **L** all wk 12-2 **D** all wk 7-9 **Rooms:** 10 en suite **S** £65-£130 **D** £95-£130 **Facilities:** Parking Garden Wi-fi **Notes:** ⊕ FREE HOUSE ♦♦ ♦

Thomas Hardy immortalised this 16th-century, stone-built coaching inn as the 'Sow and Acorn' in *Tess of the d'Urbervilles*, and in later years notorious 'hanging' Judge Jeffreys is thought to have used the main hall to hold court. The inn is set in the pretty village of Evershot (Hardy's Evershead) in a designated Area of Outstanding Natural Beauty. There are two oak-panelled bars, and log fires blaze in carved Hamstone fireplaces. Meals and drinks can be taken in the bar, restaurant, outside on the patio or in the garden. Three of the bedrooms feature four-poster beds, and two are suitable for families. All rooms have refurbished, en suite bathrooms and are equipped with satellite TV, Wi-fi and facilities for making hot drinks. All food is sourced locally whenever possible from sustainable sources and responsible suppliers, allowing the inn to take full advantage of the fantastic seafood, game and vegetables on their doorstep. The varied carte menu in the restaurant changes frequently according to the seasonally available ingredients, and the bar menu offers hearty wholesome dishes to accompany the real ales and ciders; there's also the daily-changing special board. The award-winning Evershot Village Bakery supplies the excellent breads.

Recommended in the area

Mapperton House and Gardens; Jurassic Coast World Heritage Site; Dorchester

The Cricketers

Address: IWERNE COURTNEY OR SHROTON,
Blandford Forum, DT11 8QD
Tel: 01258 860421
Fax: 01258 861800
Email: cricketers@heartstoneinns.co.uk
Website: heartstoneinns.co.uk
Map ref: 2 ST81
Directions: 7m S of Shaftesbury on A350,
turn right after Iwerne Minster. 5m N of Blandford
Forum on A360, past Stourpaine, in 2m left into Shroton.
Pub in village centre
Open: all week 11-3 6-11 (Sat-Sun 11-11 summer only)
🍴 ⏺ L all wk 12-2.30 D Mon-Sat 6-9.30
Facilities: Parking Garden **Notes:** ⊕ FREE HOUSE ♦♦

The Cricketers lies at the foot of Hambledon Hill in the heart of the beautiful Dorset countryside, with The Wessex Ridgeway nearby. At The Cricketers you will find great pub food, a selection of real ales, and a warm welcome from hosts Andy and Natasha and their team. Daily deliveries of fresh fish, meat and local produce, combined with a choice of well kept real ales, mean that The Cricketers is the perfect choice for food or just to enjoy a quiet pint. Although proud of their food, The Cricketers is a real village pub and customers are equally welcome to drop by for a pint of real ale or a glass of wine. The pub lies between the cricket pitch and the village green. A right of way passes through the pub garden which provides a delightful spot for weary walkers to take refreshment. Andy and Natasha are proud of their long association with Shroton Cricket Club from which the pub takes its name.

Recommended in the area

Cavalcade of Costume Museum; Gold Hill Museum and Garden; Royal Signals Museum

The Bottle Inn

Address: MARSHWOOD, Bridport, DT6 5QJ
Tel: 01297 678254
Email: thebottleinn@googlemail.com
Website: www.bottleinn.co.uk
Map ref: 2 SY39
Directions: On B3165 (Crewkerne to Lyme Regis rd) 5m from Hunters Lodge **Open:** all week Mon-Fri noon-3 6-11, Sat-Sun noon-11 🛏 ❄️ **L** all wk 12-2.30 **D** Mon-Sat 6.30-9, Sun 6.30-8.30
Facilities: Parking Garden **Notes:** ⊕ FREE HOUSE 🛉

Standing at the top of the Marshwood Vale, under the shadow of Lamberts Castle, this little thatched pub famously holds the World Nettle Eating Championships, an annual event now some 12 years old. Apparently, back in the 18th century, it was the first pub in the area to serve bottled beer rather than beer from the jug - hence the name. Its rustic interior has simple wooden settles, scrubbed tables and a warming wood-burner. Bar snacks are served at lunch times, while an extensive carte takes over in the evenings. Tuesday night is steak night, while Wednesdays feature the carvery.

Recommended in the area

West Dorset Heritage Coast; Forde Abbey and Gardens; Seaton Tramway

Rose & Crown Trent

Address: TRENT, Sherborne, DT9 4SL
Tel/fax: 01935 850776
Email: hkirkie@hotmail.com
Website: www.roseandcrowntrent.com
Map ref: 2 ST51 **Directions:** Just off A30 between Sherborne & Yeovil **Open:** 12-3 6-11 (Sat-Sun 12-11) **Closed:** Mon 🛏 ❄️ **L** Tue-Sun 12-3 **D** Tue-Sat 6-9 **Facilities:** Parking Garden
Notes: ⊕ WADWORTH 🛉 🐾 🍷 8

Heather Kirk is well into her stride at this picturesque rural gem. Built in the 14th century for the builders of the village church spire, its rustic charm is now due in no small measure to its thatched roof, beams, large fireplaces and flagstone floors. The Trent Barrow Room is the perfect place to retire once the drinks have been brought. Quality local produce is the key to tempting light bites and tapas, or more substantial offerings such as chargrilled sirloin steak with fondant potatoes and roast vine tomato or sun-blushed tomato, wild mushroom and spinach tartlet. There is an Early Doors menu at £8.95 between 6-7pm, Tuesday to Friday. Alfresco dining can be enjoyed in the beer garden.

Recommended in the area

Fleet Air Arm Museum, Yeovilton; Montacute House; (NT); Tintinhull House & Garden (NT)

Ruins of Barnard Castle by Castle Bridge

Rose & Crown

★★ ◎◎ HOTEL
Address: ROMALDKIRK, Barnard Castle, DL12 9EB
Tel: 01833 650213 **Fax:** 01833 650828
Email: hotel@rose-and-crown.co.uk
Website: www.rose-and-crown.co.uk
Map ref: 7 NY92 **Directions:** 6m NW from Barnard Castle
on B6277 **Open:** all week 11-11 **Closed:** 23-27 Dec
L all wk 12-1.30 D all wk 6.30-9.30 L Sun 12-1.30
D all wk 7.30-8.45 **Rooms:** 12 (5 GF) S £92-£120 D £140-
£180 **Facilities:** Parking Wi-fi **Notes:** FREE HOUSE 14

An 18th-century coaching inn overlooking one of three village
greens, the stocks and pump. Next door is the Saxon church
known as The Cathedral of the Dale. Dine in the bar, with open fire, carriage lamps, old settle and
prints; the candlelit oak-panelled restaurant is all white linen and silver cutlery; or in the brasserie with
its warm red walls. You will find impressive classic British fare with modern and regional influences on
the menu. Why not stay over in one of the beautifully furnished bedrooms.

Recommended in the area

Yorkshire Dales National Park; Cauldron Snout Waterfall; Hamsterley Forest

Romaldkirk countryside

Red-brick windmill, Thaxted

Axe & Compasses

Address: High St, ARKESDEN, CB11 4EX
Tel: 01799 550272
Fax: 01799 550906
Map ref: 3 TL43
Directions: From Buntingford take B1038 towards Newport. Then left for Arkesden
Open: all week noon-2.30 6-11 (Sun noon-3 7-10.30) 🍺 🍽 L all wk 12-2 D all wk 6.45-9.30
Facilities: Parking Garden
Notes: ⊕ GREENE KING 🍷 14

Picture postcard perfect, this historic inn is located in the narrow main street of a beautiful village. A stream called Wicken Water runs alongside, criss-crossed by footbridges leading to white, cream and pink colour-washed thatched cottages. The central section of the inn – the thatched part – dates from 1650, but the building has since been extended to utilise the old stable block, which accommodated horses until the 1920s, and into a 19th-century addition that now houses the public bar. The beamed interior is full of character and includes the welcoming bar, a comfortable and softly lit restaurant, and a cosy lounge furnished with antiques, and displaying horse brasses and old agricultural implements. During winter there may well be a warming fire blazing in the hearth, and in summer there is further seating outside on the patio. Beer lovers will enjoy the real ales on tap, which include Greene King IPA, Abbot Ale and Old Speckled Hen. For those who prefer the juice of the vine, there is a wine list that's split almost evenly between France and the rest of the world. The restaurant offers a full carte, while an extensive blackboard menu is available in either the lounge or bar. Dishes include pan-fried duck breast with black cherries and cherry brandy; whole grilled lemon sole; medallions of beef fillet and rösti potato with soft green peppercorns, brandy and cream.

Recommended in the area

Audley End House & Gardens; Imperial War Museum Duxford; Mountfitchet Castle

The Bell Inn

Address: Saint James Street, CASTLE HEDINGHAM,
Halstead, CO9 3EJ
Tel: 01787 460350
Email: bell-castle@hotmail.co.uk
Website: www.hedinghambell.co.uk
Map ref: 4 TL73
Directions: On A1124 N of Halstead, right to Castle
Hedingham **Open:** all week 11.45-3 6-11 (Fri-Sat
noon-mdnt Sun noon-11) **Closed:** 25 Dec eve
🛏 L Mon-Fri 12-2, Sat-Sun 12-2.30 D Sun-Mon
7-9, Tue-Sat 7-9.30 **Facilities:** Parking Garden Wi-fi **Notes:** ⊕ GRAYS ♦♦ 🐾

Scratch the imposing Georgian façade of the award-winning Bell and inside you'll find exposed beams
and wattle and daub walling, evidence of its 15th-century origins as a hall house. The Fergusons have
run this unspoilt, unpretentious pub for more than 40 years, so they know all about serving excellent
real ales and good food. Using local produce, expect steak and ale pie, bangers and mash, daily Turkish
specials and Mediterranean barbecued fish. Look out for live music on Fridays and regular beer festivals.
Recommended in the area
Hedingham Castle; Colne Valley Steam Railway; Melford Hall (NT)

The Cricketers

Address: CLAVERING, Saffron Walden, CB11 4QT
Tel: 01799 550442 **Fax:** 01799 550882
Email: info@thecricketers.co.uk
Website: www.thecricketers.co.uk
Map ref: 4 TL43
Directions: From M11 junct 10, A505 E.
Then A1301, B1383. At Newport take B1038
Open: all day all week **Closed:** 25-26 Dec
🛏 ⏿ L all wk 12-2 D all wk 6.30-9.30 **Facilities:**
Parking Garden Wi-fi **Notes:** ⊕ FREE HOUSE ♦♦ ⊊ 17

A 16th-century country inn run by Sally and Trevor Oliver since 1976. Look no further than the nearby
cricket pitch for the reason behind the pub's name and the cricketing memorabilia in the beamed,
log fire-warmed bar and restaurant. Seasonal menus and daily specials include lots of fresh fish,
properly hung meats and, for children, organic salmon and free-range chicken breast. Famous son
Jamie supplies vegetables, herbs and leaves from his certified organic garden. The extensive wine list
changes regularly. In warmer weather, head outside to the pretty terrace at the front of the pub.
Recommended in the area
Audley End House; Imperial War Museum Duxford; Cambridge

The Swan at Felsted

Address: Station Road, FELSTED,
Dunmow, CM6 3DG
Tel: 01371 820245
Fax: 01371 821393
Email: info@theswanatfelsted.co.uk
Website: www.thegreatpubcompany.co.uk
Map ref: 4 TL62
Directions: Exit M11 junct 8 onto A120 signed
Felsted. Pub in village centre
Open: all week 11.30-3 5-11

🛅 🍽 **L** Mon-Sat 12-2.30, Sun 12-4 **D** Mon-Sat 5.30-9.30 **Facilities:** Parking Garden
Notes: ⊕ GREENE KING ♦♦ 🚶 🍷 14

Ideally situated for exploring the stunning north Essex countryside, and only a short drive from Stansted Airport, The Swan is an imposing building and was for many years the village bank. It was rebuilt after a disastrous fire in the early 20th century, and the interior decoration has a fresh, contemporary feel. A pretty courtyard garden to the rear provides a tranquil, sheltered eating area overlooked by the village church, and during winter a roaring log fire greets guests as they cross the threshold. The kitchen has a great commitment to quality local produce, with dishes ranging from pork sausages, creamy mash and red onion gravy, or Swan bacon and cheese burger, to slow roasted lamb neck in a port, mushroom and baby onion sauce with dauphinoise potatoes or oven roasted cod, olive oil mash, local asparagus and nut brown butter. Fine wines, including a good selection by the glass, and well-kept cask ales also help to achieve a fine balance between the traditional English pub and a high quality restaurant. A stylish function room with its own entrance and bespoke menus is available for private parties of up to 18 people.

Recommended in the area

Hatfield Forest National Nature Reserve; Mountfitchet Castle Experience; Paycockes House

The Compasses at Pattiswick

Address: Compasses Road, PATTISWICK, Braintree, CM77 8BG

Tel: 01376 561322

Fax: 01376 564343

Email: info@thecompassesatpattiswick.co.uk

Website: www.thegreatpubcompany.co.uk

Map ref: 4 TL82

Directions: From Braintree take A120 E towards Colchester. After Bradwell 1st left to Pattiswick

Open: all week 11.30-3 5.30-11 (Fri and Sat 5.30-mdnt, Sun noon-10.30) 🚬 **L** all wk 12-3 **D** Mon-Thu 5.30-9.30, Fri-Sat 5.30-9.45 🍽 **L** Mon-Sat 12-3, Sun 12-3.30 **D** Mon-Thu 5.30-9.30, Fri-Sat 5.30-9.45 Sun 5.30-9.00 **Facilities:** Parking Garden Wi-fi **Notes:** 🌐 FREE HOUSE 👨 🐕 🍷 13

Tucked away in delightful countryside, this renovated gastro-pub offers a contemporary take on country style, with a flagstone floor in the bar, an open fire and rustic furniture. The menu of light bar meals and à la carte dishes is packed with quality produce, including a rich selection of game from the surrounding woods. Dishes range from traditional pub classics, such as beer battered fish and chips, to leg of lamb steak with creamy roasted garlic mash and red wine jus, along with daily specials. Similarly, the children's menu concentrates on simple classics popular with younger guests. The balance between bar, restaurant and private dining room enables The Compasses to cater for any occasion, and it is popular with locals, walkers and cyclists as well as those willing to travel in search of quality. Outside, extensive patios offer separate areas allowing families a clear view of the children's play area, while locals can enjoy the glorious Pattiswick sunsets with a well-kept pint of Woodforde's Wherry, from Norfolk, or one of a range of local ales from Nethergate Brewery.

Recommended in the area

Paycockes House; Beth Chatto Gardens; Colchester Zoo

Westonbirt Arboretum

The Old Passage Inn

★ ★ ★ ★ ⊛⊛ ♨ RESTAURANT WITH ROOMS
Address: Passage Road, ARLINGHAM, GL2 7JR
Tel: 01452 740547
Fax: 01452 741871
Email: oldpassage@ukonline.co.uk
Website: www.theoldpassage.com
Map ref: 2 SO71
Directions: 5m from A38 adjacent M5 junct 13
Open: 11-3 6-finish (all day Etr-Sep) **Closed:** 25 Dec, Sun eve
& Mon ⅋⊖ **L** Tue-Sat 12-2.30, Sun 12-3 **D** Tue-Sat 6-9
Rooms: 3 en suite **S** £40-£130 **D** £60-£130 **Facilities:** Parking
Garden Wi-fi **Notes:** ⊕ FREE HOUSE ⅋ ⅋ ⅋ 12

The 'old passage' in the name refers to the ford and later ferry service that crossed the River Severn here. The rich harvest of salmon and elvers that once came from the river is now sadly depleted, but chef Mark Redwood's seafood menu features local, sustainable ingredients, such as freshwater crayfish, whenever possible. Fresh lobster from Pembrokeshire (sometimes from Cornwall) is always available from the tank, and freshly shucked oysters and Fruits de Mer are specialities. The simple but innovative menus often change daily to reflect what is available, but might include such dishes as roast tranche of turbot served with parsley new potatoes and hollandaise. The large dining room has a fresh and airy appeal, and in summer you can eat out on the garden terrace, with views across a bend in the river towards Newnham-on-Severn and the distant Forest of Dean. The three stunning en suite bedrooms enjoy the same views and enable guests to enjoy not only an exceptional breakfast, but also take full advantage of the excellent wine list at dinner, which includes plenty of half bottles and wines by the glass, and features wines from the Three Choirs Vineyard at Newent.

Recommended in the area

Wildfowl and Wetlands Trust, Slimbridge; Owlpen Manor; Berkeley Castle

The Queens Arms

Address: The Village, ASHLEWORTH, GL19 4HT
Tel: 01452 700395
Website: www.queensarmsashleworth.co.uk
Map ref: 2 SO82 **Directions:** From Gloucester N
on A417 for 5m. At Hartpury, opp Royal Exchange
turn right at Broad St to Ashleworth. Pub 100yds past
village green **Open:** noon-3 7-11 **Closed:** 25-26 Dec
& 1 Jan, Sun eve (ex BH wknds) ﹩ ﾔﾙ L all wk 12-2
D Mon-Sat 7-9 **Facilities:** Parking Garden
Notes: ⊕ FREE HOUSE ﹢﹟ ﾔ 14

Hailing from South Africa, experienced restaurateurs Tony and Gill Burreddu bought The Queens
Arms in 1998. They have created a warm, homely atmosphere with the emphasis on imaginative,
locally sourced food, well kept ales and an excellent wine list. All the food is home made including the
delicious desserts. Alongside traditional favourites such as steak and kidney pie and salmon fishcakes,
specialities might include slow roasted belly of pork, lamb noisettes with wild mushroom sauce, fresh
halibut with asparagus and beurre blanc, and South African dishes of Bobotie and Tomato Bredie.
Recommended in the area
Ashleworth Tithe Barn; Gloucester Docks and Museum; Slimbridge Wildfowl & Wetlands Trust

Eight Bells

Address: Church Street, CHIPPING
CAMPDEN, GL55 6JG
Tel: 01386 840371
Fax: 01386 841669
Email: neilhargreaves@bellinn.fsnet.co.uk
Website: www.eightbellsinn.co.uk
Map ref: 3 SP13
Directions: 8m from Stratford-upon-Avon,
M40 junct 15
Open: all day all week noon-12 (Sun noon-10.30)
Closed: 25 Dec ﹩ ﾔﾙ L Mon-Thu 12-2, Fri-Sun 12-2.30 **D** Mon-Thu 6.30-9, Fri-Sat 6.30-9.30,
Sun 6.30-8.45 **Facilities:** Garden Wi-fi **Notes:** ⊕ FREE HOUSE ﹢﹟ ﾔﾖ ﾔ 9

This beautiful 14th-century Cotswold stone inn was built to house stonemasons working on the nearby
church and to store the eight church bells. There is an atmospheric bar and a candlelit dining room with
oak beams, open fires and a priest's hole. Traditional ales and ciders are served and there's a daily-
changing menu of freshly prepared local food. Outside is a courtyard garden and a terrace.
Recommended in the area
The Cotswold Way; Hidcote Manor (NT); Stratford-upon-Avon

The Tunnel House Inn

Address: Tarlton Road, COATES, Cirencester, GL7 6PW
Tel: 01285 770280 **Fax:** 01285 700040
Email: info@tunnelhouse.com
Website: www.tunnelhouse.com
Map ref: 2 SO90
Directions: From Cirencester on A433 towards Tetbury, in 2m turn right towards Coates, follow brown signs to Canal Tunnel & Inn **Open:** all week Noon-Late **Closed:** 25 Dec
🛏 †◎ Noon-9.30 **Facilities:** Parking Garden Wi-fi
Notes: ⊕ FREE HOUSE ♦♦ ♗

In a glorious rural location down a very bumpy track, this old Cotswolds pub by Sapperton Tunnel once provided accommodation for the navvies building the Thames and Severn Canal. The enjoyably cluttered bar is festooned with pictures, prints, posters and advertising signs, so there's plenty to read over a pint, or head outside to the garden and enjoy the views across the fields. Log fires provide comfort when it's cold. Open all day for food, the menu alters monthly according to seasonal changes in local produce. Eat lightly with a tomato, mozzarella and pesto sandwich or a ploughman's, or choose something more filling such as 8oz English rump or rib-eye steaks with beurre Café de Paris, chips, mixed leaves and peppercorn sauce; monkfish wrapped in prosciutto on a lentil cassoulet; or cannelloni filled with roasted chunky ratatouille topped with three-cheese sauce. There are pub classics too, including Wiltshire honey-roast ham and eggs, and beer-battered cod and chips. For dessert, check out the individual blackberry cheesecake, or profiteroles topped with rich coffee, chocolate and hazelnut sauce. Children will probably opt for their usual favourites to eat, following which they can let off steam in their own play area.

Recommended in the area

Westonbirt Arboretum; Cotswold Water Park; Cirencester; South Cerney Lakes

The Green Dragon Inn

★★★★ ⊜ INN

Address: Cockleford, COWLEY,
Cheltenham, GL53 9NW
Tel: 01242 870271 **Fax:** 01242 870171
Email: green-dragon@buccaneer.co.uk
Website: www.green-dragon-inn.co.uk
Map ref: 2 SO91
Directions: Telephone for directions
Open: all day all week ▦ ▯ **L** Mon-Fri 12-2.30, Sat
12-3, Sun 12-3.30 **D** all wk 6-10 **Rooms:** 9 en suite

(4 GF) **S** £70 **D** £95-£150 **Facilities:** Parking Garden Wi-fi **Notes:** ⊕ BUCCANEER ⋔ ⅓

A handsome stone-built inn dating from the 17th century, the Green Dragon is located in the hamlet of Cockleford at the heart of the picturesque Cotswolds. It is a popular retreat for those who appreciate good food, fine wine and real ales. The fittings and furniture are the work of Robert Thompson, the Mouse Man of Kilburn (so-called for his trademark mouse) who lends his name to the Mouse Bar, with its stone-flagged floors, beamed ceilings and crackling log fires. Nine cottage-style, en suite bedrooms are available, including a suite. All rooms are equipped with direct dial telephones and TVs, and breakfast is included, along with the newspaper of your choice. The menu takes in lunchtime sandwiches, children's favourites, and starters/light meals such as baked field mushroom with spinach, Cerney goat's cheese and cranberry relish, warm Thai chicken noodle salad and Caesar salad. The daily specials board might offer grilled brill fillet with an orange, watercress and fennel salad or roasted pork loin steak with pear and leek stuffing and cider gravy. The choice of real ales includes Battledown Premium, Directors and Butcombe. Additional features are the heated dining terrace and the function room/skittle alley.

Recommended in the area

Holst Birthplace Museum; Gloucester Cathedral; Witcombe Roman Villa

The Inn at Fossebridge

★★★★ ⇔ INN

Address: FOSSEBRIDGE, nr Cheltenham, GL54 3JS
Tel: 01285 720721 **Fax:** 01285 720793
Email: info@fossebridgeinn.co.uk
Website: www.fossebridgeinn.co.uk
Map ref: 3 SP01
Directions: From M4 junct 15, A419 towards
Cirencester, then A429 towards Stow. Pub approx
6m on left in dip **Open:** all day all week noon-11
≜ ⦿ **L** 12-2.30, Sat 12-3, Sun 12-3.30 **D** all wk

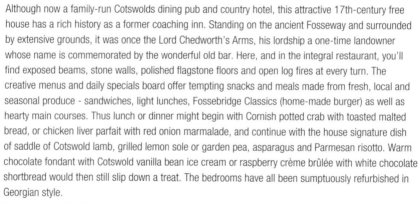

6-9 **Rooms:** 8 **S** £110-£135 **D** £120-£160 **Facilities:** Parking Garden **Notes:** ⊕ FREE HOUSE ♠ ⌁

Although now a family-run Cotswolds dining pub and country hotel, this attractive 17th-century free house has a rich history as a former coaching inn. Standing on the ancient Fosseway and surrounded by extensive grounds, it was once the Lord Chedworth's Arms, his lordship a one-time landowner whose name is commemorated by the wonderful old bar. Here, and in the integral restaurant, you'll find exposed beams, stone walls, polished flagstone floors and open log fires at every turn. The creative menus and daily specials board offer tempting snacks and meals made from fresh, local and seasonal produce - sandwiches, light lunches, Fossebridge Classics (home-made burger) as well as hearty main courses. Thus lunch or dinner might begin with Cornish potted crab with toasted malted bread, or chicken liver parfait with red onion marmalade, and continue with the house signature dish of saddle of Cotswold lamb, grilled lemon sole or garden pea, asparagus and Parmesan risotto. Warm chocolate fondant with Cotswold vanilla bean ice cream or raspberry crème brûlée with white chocolate shortbread would then still slip down a treat. The bedrooms have all been sumptuously refurbished in Georgian style.

Recommended in the area

Chedworth Roman Villa (NT); Keith Harding's World of Mechanical Music; Bibury Trout Farm

The Weighbridge Inn

Address: MINCHINHAMPTON, GL6 9AL
Tel: 01453 832520
Fax: 01453 835903
Email: enquiries@2in1pub.co.uk
Website: www.2in1pub.co.uk
Map ref: 2 SO80
Directions: Between Nailsworth & Avening on B4014
Open: all day all week noon-11 (Sun noon-10.30)
Closed: 25 Dec ⓑ ⓘ food served all wk 12-9.30
Facilities: Parking Garden
Notes: ⊕ FREE HOUSE ⸬ ⌇ ⸰ 15

By the side of the old packhorse road to Bristol, now a footpath and bridleway, stands this part-17th century classic Cotswold inn. The weighbridge that once was here used to serve the local woollen mills, weighing the raw materials on arrival, and again when the finished cloth left for markets in Bristol, Bath and London. An illustration on the cover of the restaurant menu shows how it looked when the horsedrawn vehicles lined up to have their cargoes weighed, while memorabilia from the mills themselves and rural artefacts from the area are displayed around the pub. In the bar and restaurant you'll find a good choice of real ales, wines and traditional home-prepared hearty fare, including the inn's 'famous 2-in-1' pies. First produced here more than 30 years ago, these double delights contain a filling of your choice, such as salmon in a creamy sauce, or steak and kidney, in one half, while the other can be packed with cauliflower cheese, broccoli mornay or root vegetables to give a variety of combinations. Other main courses include lamb shank, seafood bake, chicken Maryland, and spinach and mushroom lasagne. Outside, the patios and sheltered landscaped gardens offer good views of the Cotswolds.

Recommended in the area

Westonbirt Arboretum; Woodchester Mansion; Chavenage House

The Ostrich Inn

Address: NEWLAND, nr Coleford, GL16 8NP
Tel: 01594 833260
Email: kathryn@theostrichinn.com
Website: www.theostrichinn.com
Map ref: 2 SO50
Directions: Follow Monmouth signs from Chepstow (A466), Newland signed from Redbrook
Open: all week 12-3 (Mon-Sat 6-11.30 Sun 6-10.30) **Facilities:** Garden
Notes: ⊕ FREE HOUSE ♦♦ ♠

A 13th-century free house in a pretty village close to two Areas of Outstanding Natural Beauty, the Forest of Dean and the Wye Valley. It was constructed for the workmen who built All Saints church opposite, known locally as the Cathedral of the Forest. The pub's name probably came from the ostrich emblem used by the Probyn family, one-time local landowners. An unusual feature is the priest hole, alongside the more predictable wooden beams and log fire warming the large lounge bar, where landlady Kathryn Horton serves up to eight regular and guest real ales. You eat in the small, intimate restaurant, the larger bar, the walled garden or on the patio, choosing dishes such as freshly prepared rack of Welsh lamb with merguez sausage and smoked belly pork in rich Madeira sauce; monkfish and tiger prawns in rich chive butter cream sauce, Gruyère mashed potato and dressed salad leaves; or creamy wild mushroom and wilted rocket risotto, lemon and white truffle oil and wild mushroom scented pepper. In the bar expect 'fulfilling' soup, pastas, sizzling ribs, and three cheese 'certainly not a quiche' tart. With a reference to an affordable wine list, The Ostrich can rest its case.

Recommended in the area

Clearwell Caves; Dick Whittington Family Leisure Park; National Diving and Activity Centre, Chepstow

Cotswold Water Park

The Bell at Sapperton

Address: SAPPERTON, Cirencester, GL7 6LE
Tel: 01285 760298
Fax: 01285 760761
Email: thebell@sapperton66.freeserve.co.uk
Website: www.foodatthebell.co.uk
Map ref: 2 SO90
Directions: From A419 halfway between Cirencester & Stroud follow signs for Sapperton. Pub in village centre near church
Open: all week 11-2.30 6.30-11 (Sun 12-10.30)
Closed: 25 Dec ▙ ▐◎▌ L all wk 12-2.15 D all wk 7-9.15
Facilities: Parking Garden **Notes:** ⊕ FREE HOUSE ⌁ ♟ 20

Regular diners come to this restored Cotswold pub, located in an idyllic and historic village close to the source of the River Thames, for Paul Davidson and Pat LeJeune's regularly-changing menus. These are based on produce from an impressive line up of West Country and Welsh Borders suppliers. If you want just a drink, there are plenty of wines by the glass, while Paul's passion for real ales ensures his Uley Old Spot and Otter Bitter are always in tip-top condition. Although The Bell could hardly be further from the sea, it enjoys a reputation for the freshest fish and seafood, so check the chalkboards for the day's catch, which might include wild salmon, turbot, brill, and scallops (a wider selection is offered at weekends). The daily changing lunchtime menu features both light dishes, such as grilled sardines on red peppers with olive oil dressing, and more substantial ones, such as bacon chop with free-range fried egg and Butts Farm black pudding. Evening choices are home-cured salt cod croquette with pickled chicory, tomato and tarragon dressing; chargrilled Hereford rib-eye steak with roast tomato and mushrooms; and butternut and mascarpone risotto infused with truffle oil and salad leaves.

Recommended in the area

Cotswold Water Park; Westonbirt Arboretum; The Cotswolds

The Swan at Southrop

@@@

Address: SOUTHROP, Nr Lechlade, GL7 3NU
Tel: 01367 850205
Fax: 01367 850517
Email: info@theswanatsouthrop.co.uk
Website: www.theswanatsouthrop.co.uk
Map ref: 3 SP10
Directions: Off A361 between Lechlade & Burford
Open: all week **Closed:** 25th Dec 🏠 🍴 **L** all wk 12-3
D Mon-Sat 6-10 **Facilities: Notes:** ⊕ FREE HOUSE ⚏ 🐾

The early 17th-century, creeper-clad Swan sits almost smugly on the green in this trim Cotswolds village, as indeed it has every right to. Re-opened in 2008 by Sebastian and Lana Snow, and managed by Dom and Joelle Abbott, this much-accoladed free house has fast gained an enviable reputation, and two AA Rosettes, for excellent, locally sourced 'turf to table' food and attentive, friendly service. The interior - bar, snug and restaurant - is surprisingly light for such an historic building, but homely too, especially with the open fires burning. Seasonal ingredients from the immediate area often feature on the menu, such as crayfish from the old gravel pits in Lechlade, partridge from the Hatherop estate, and pork from Kelmscott (try slow-roasted pork belly with apples, cannellini beans and sage). Other possibilities are stuffed saddle of rabbit, prunes, spiced couscous and chickpeas; teriyaki of salmon, king prawns and oriental vegetable spaghetti; and wild mushroom risotto. As well as an extensive wine list are the beers - Swan Bitter, Hook Norton and a monthly local guest. An old-fashioned skittle alley doubles up as a delightful private room for larger parties, while accommodation is available in delightful cottages on Southrop Manor Estate. There is also a newly opened cookery school – Thyme at Southrop.

Recommended in the area

Bibury; Minster Lovell Hall; Buscot Park (NT)

Bear of Rodborough Hotel

★★★ 79% HOTEL

Address: Rodborough Common, STROUD, GL5 5DE
Tel:　　01453 878522
Fax:　　01453 872523
Email:　info@bearofrodborough.co.uk
Website: www.cotswold-inns-hotels.co.uk/bear
Map ref: 2 SO80
Directions: From M5 junct 13 follow signs for
Stonehouse then Rodborough
Open: all day all week ❧ L all wk 12-2.30 D all wk
6.30-10 ⏺ D all wk 7-10 **Rooms:** 46 en suite **S** £75-£85 **D** £120-£130 **Facilities:** Parking Garden
Notes: ⊕ FREE HOUSE ♦♦ ᴙ ☗ 10

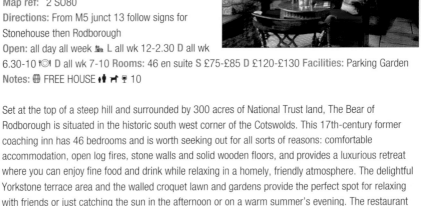

Set at the top of a steep hill and surrounded by 300 acres of National Trust land, The Bear of
Rodborough is situated in the historic south west corner of the Cotswolds. This 17th-century former
coaching inn has 46 bedrooms and is worth seeking out for all sorts of reasons: comfortable
accommodation, open log fires, stone walls and solid wooden floors, and provides a luxurious retreat
where you can enjoy fine food and drink while relaxing in a homely, friendly atmosphere. The delightful
Yorkstone terrace area and the walled croquet lawn and gardens provide the perfect spot for relaxing
with friends or just catching the sun in the afternoon or on a warm summer's evening. The restaurant
with its stone-arched dining room is a great setting for the contemporary English cuisine with strong
traditional influences, which uses the finest fresh ingredients, many produced locally. The seasonal
menu might include caramelised loin of Old Spot pork wrapped in Parma ham or roasted pumpkin and
parmesan risotto. Enjoy fine traditional British ales in the Grizzly Bar, where there is an extensive menu
if you wish to lunch or dine in a more relaxed atmosphere.

Recommended in the area

Owlpen Manor; Westonbirt Arboretum; Stroud House Gallery

Gumstool Inn

Address: Calcot Manor, TETBURY, GL8 8YJ
Tel: 01666 890391 **Fax:** 01666 890394
Email: reception@calcotmanor.co.uk
Website: www.calcotmanor.co.uk
Map ref: 2 ST89
Directions: 3m W of Tetbury **Open:** all week
11.30-2.30 5.30-11 ⓑ L all wk 11.30-2 **D** Mon-
Sat 7-9.30, Sun 7-9 ⓘⓞⓘ L all wk 12-2 **D** Mon-Sat
7-9.30, Sun 7-9 **Facilities:** Parking Garden Wi-fi
Notes: ⊕ FREE HOUSE ⲓ↑ 🍷 21

The cheerful and cosy Gumstool is part of Calcot Manor Hotel, set in 220 acres of Cotswold countryside. As a free house, The Gumstool Inn stocks a good selection of real ales, mostly from the West Country, and an excellent choice of wines. The food is top-notch gastro-pub quality – no wonder, as it is meticulously supervised by Executive Chef Director Michael Croft, as is the hotel's Conservatory Restaurant. There is a pretty sun terrace outside, while dark winter evenings are warmed with log fires.

Recommended in the area

Westonbirt Arboretum; Slimbridge Wetlands Centre; Tetbury

The Trouble House

Address: Cirencester Road, TETBURY, GL8 8SG
Tel: 01666 502206
Website: www.troublehousetetbury.co.uk
Map ref: 2 ST89
Directions: On A433 between Tetbury & Cirencester
Open: 11.30-3 7-11 **Closed:** 2 weeks in Jan, Sun
eve, Mon ⓑ L Tue-Fri 12-2 ⓘⓞⓘ L Tue-Sun 12-2
D Tue-Sat 7-9.30 **Facilities:** Parking Garden
Notes: ⊕ WADWORTH ⲓ↑ 🐾 🍷 12

This cosy pub witnessed Civil War conflicts and agricultural riots, so it is aptly named. By the roadside yes, but step inside to another world, one of ancient beams, fireplaces and a charmingly crooked ceiling, to see what English country pubs are all about. Wadworth real ales are served in the relaxed atmosphere of the bar. There is a regularly changing specials board in the restaurant where food is simply prepared from the finest quality produce in season. Don't miss rib of beef for two, roasted in hay, with duck-fat chips and confit shallots, or grilled Lydney Park venison.

Recommended in the area

Westonbirt Arboretum; Malmesbury Abbey and Gardens; Tetbury

Acers, Westonbirt Arboretum

The Farriers Arms

Address: Main Street, TODENHAM,
Moreton-in-Marsh, GL56 9PF
Tel: 01608 650901
Email: info@farriersarms.com
Website: www.farriersarms.com
Map ref: 3 SP23
Directions: Right to Todenham at N end of Moreton-in-Marsh. 2.5m from Shipston on Stour
Open: all week noon-3 6-11 (Sun 6.30-11) 🍽 🍴
L Mon-Sat 12-2, Sun 12-2.30 **D** Mon-Sat 6-9, Sun
6.30-9 **Facilities:** Parking Garden **Notes:** ⊕ FREE HOUSE 🐕 🏠 🍷 10

Leave Stratford-upon-Avon to the tourists for a while and take a 20-minute drive to this picturesque Cotswold village and its 17th-century pub. It was built as a church house in 1650, then became an ironworks, finally acquiring a beer licence in 1840. All the features you'd associate with a country local are here: polished flagstone floors, exposed stone walls, hop-hung beams and a large inglenook fireplace, while outside, a suntrap patio garden offers views of the church. The menu in the bar and refurbished restaurant changes regularly to offer a good range of freshly prepared, award-winning dishes using local produce, including village-reared meats and seasonal game. Chicken breast is served with sweet potato and Parmesan mash and mango salsa; venison haunch steak comes with roast onion-crushed potatoes, parsnip crisps and port and juniper sauce; and whole grilled lemon sole is accompanied by caper and lemon butter. For vegetarians, goat's cheese and roast vegetable cannelloni should fit the bill. If you're not into any of the well-kept local real ales, maybe you'd prefer the Cotswold-brewed lager; there's also a comprehensive wine list. Groups of up to a dozen may dine in the secluded library, surrounded by a collection of interesting old books.

Recommended in the area

Batsford Arboretum; Cotswold Farm Park; Blenheim Palace

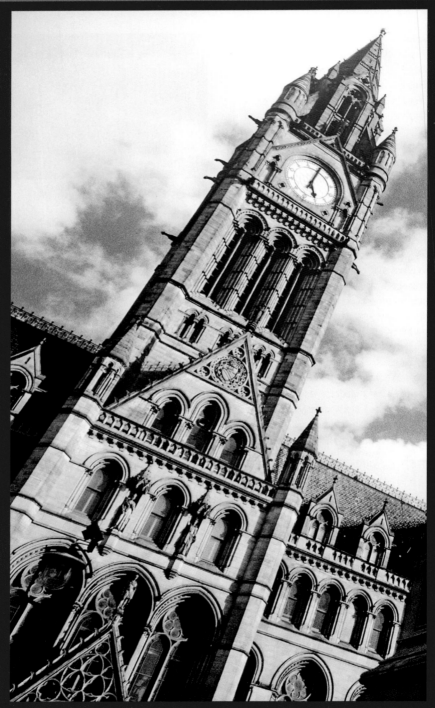

Manchester town hall, Albert Square

The Victoria

Address: Stamford Street, ALTRINCHAM, WA14 1EX
Tel: 0161 613 1855
Email: the.victoria@yahoo.co.uk
Map ref: 6 SJ78
Directions: From rail station, cross main road, turn right.
2nd left onto Stamford St
Open: all day all week noon-11 (Sun noon-6)
Closed: 26 Dec & 1 Jan ⓑ L Mon-Sat 12-3 D Mon-Sat 5.30-9
⍣ L Mon-Sat 12-3, Sun 12-4 D Mon-Sat 5.30-9
Notes: ⌖ FREE HOUSE ♦♦ ♟ 10

Situated in the Stamford quarter of Altrincham, tucked away
behind the main shopping street, The Victoria has been carefully
restored as a traditional food-led tavern. This small, one-roomed pub now offers a wood-panelled
dining area to one side, and a more casual bar area on the other. As well as the main menu, which
changes every six to eight weeks according to seasonal availability and majors on locally sourced
ingredients, there's a lighter lunch menu. Starters might include Morecambe Bay brown shrimp
and battered prawn cocktail; Bury black pudding Scotch egg topped with locally smoked bacon; or
Blacksticks Blue cheese and broad bean rice pudding. Among the main courses may be naturally raised
Cumbrian pink veal and mushroom steamed pudding; and oven-roasted monkfish on a bed of pease
pudding. On Sunday, a traditional roast is also available, usually including locally raised rib of beef. The
wine list features over 30 carefully chosen bottles, while there are a range of handpulled cask ales,
as well as many non-alcoholic drinks from the temperance bar, such as Dandelion and Burdock. The
search is on for products no longer seen on menus, and future delights may include dishes such as
tripe, smoked eel and pressed tongue.

Recommended in the area

Dunham Massey Hall Park and Garden (NT); Altrincham Market; Altrincham Ice Dome

HAMPSHIRE

Lymington harbour

The Anchor Inn

★★★★ ◉◉ INN

Address: Lower Froyle, ALTON, GU34 4NA
Tel: 01420 23261 **Fax:** 01420 520467
Email: info@anchorinnatlowerfroyle.co.uk
Website: www.anchorinnatlowerfroyle.co.uk
Map ref: 3 SU73
Directions: A31 signed Bentley, follow brown tourist signs to Anchor Inn **Open:** all day all week
⚒ L all wk 12-2.30 D all wk 6.30-9.30
🍽 L Mon-Sat 12.30-2.30, Sun 12-4 D Mon-Fri

6.30-9.30, Sat 6.30-10, Sun 7-9 **Rooms:** 5 en suite **S** £90-£140 **D** £90-£140
Facilities: Parking Garden Wi-fi **Notes:** ⊞ THE MILLERS COLLECTION ⋆ ⋆ ⋆ 9

The Anchor belongs to Miller's Collection, a group of sensitively restored old inns that evoke the feel of a bygone England. The decor in this classically furnished dining pub is influenced by WWI and WWII with rooms named after war poets. Thus, you may have a pint of Hampshire-brewed real ale while enjoying a meal and listening to cricket on a Robert's radio. As much produce as possible is sourced within a tight radius, so at the bar you might meet the farmer who produces the beef, or the keen shot who supplied the pheasant. The principally traditional British menu with occasional European influences should therefore be no surprise, nor should the two AA Rosettes. Begin with hand-picked Portland crab mayonnaise, chilli and lime, avocado purée and brown crab pâté on toast. Mains are typified by roast pheasant breasts, pan haggerty, cabbage and bacon, Puy lentils; free-range chicken Kiev with sun-dried tomato salad; and fillet of wild turbot with sauté potatoes, spinach and beef shin sauce. Unashamedly supporting country sports, the inn can organise local fishing or shooting. Overnight guests enjoy luxurious, individually designed rooms. Every Armistice Day there's a fund-raising lunch for the Royal British Legion.

Recommended in the area

Jane Austen's House; Birdworld; North Downs Way

The Wellington Arms

Address: Baughurst Road, BAUGHURST, RG26 5LP
Tel: 0118 982 0110
Email: hello@thewellingtonarms.com
Website: www.thewellingtonarms.com
Map ref: 3 SU56 **Directions:** M4 junct 12 follow
Newbury signs on A4. At rdbt left signed Aldermaston.
Through Aldermaston. Up hill, at next rdbt 2nd exit,
left at T-junct, pub 1m on left **Open:** 12-3.30 6-11
Closed: Sun eve 📇 🍽 L all wk from noon **D** Mon-
Thu from 7pm, Fri-Sat from 6pm **Facilities:** Parking Garden Wi-fi **Notes:** ⊕ FREE HOUSE ♦♦ 🐾 ♟ 11

The Wellington Arms is an exceptionally pretty white-washed building, set amid well tended gardens, surrounded by fields and woodland. After five years Jason King and Simon Page's gastro-pub is well reputed for its elegantly furnished dining room, impressive daily changing menus and very good value lunches. The board is chalked up daily with many of the pub's home-grown favourites; crispy fried, home-grown courgette flowers stuffed with ricotta, parmesan and lemon zest on home-grown leaves; roast rack of home-reared Tamworth pork with crackling, sticky red cabbage and roast new potatoes; jelly made from their own elderflower cordial with home-grown strawberries and organic raspberry sorbet. Further evidence of the commitment to quality are the pub's three Langstroth beehives, 150 free-range, rare breed hens, four pedigree saddleback and Tamworth pigs, working poly tunnel, herb and vegetable gardens, home-made jams, chutneys and pickles together with careful sourcing of organic and home-grown produce. Fish is delivered direct from the market in Brixham and English meat comes from Vicars family butchers in Reading. From Australia comes a range of Aesop soaps and hand cream, Husk herbal teas and pink salt flakes from the Murray River area, all exclusively available here.

Recommended in the area

The Vyne (NT); Basing House; Roman Silchester

The Sun Inn

Address: Sun Hill, BENTWORTH,
Alton, GU34 5JT
Tel: 01420 562338
Map ref: 3 SU64
Directions: Telephone for directions
Open: all week 12-3 6-11 (Sun 12-10.30)
 L all wk 12-2 D all wk 7-9.30
Facilities: Parking Garden
Notes: ⊕ FREE HOUSE ♦♦ ♛ ☻ 12

This delightful, flower-adorned, 17th-century pub stands at one end of Bentworth, just after you think you've passed the last cottage in the village. Full of character, little has changed over the years. There are three interconnecting, beamed, brick- and wood-floored rooms, each with its own inglenook fireplace, scrubbed pine tables with candles, oak benches, sparkling brassware and old pictures. Adding to this heady atmosphere are fresh flowers and plants, daily newspapers and magazines, and helpful cheery staff. It's a big hit with beer drinkers - as a thriving free house, it offers eight hand-pumped real ales, among them Ringwood Best, Hogs Back TEA and Andwell Resolute, all Hampshire brewed. There's an extensive menu of tempting home-prepared food, examples being steak and ale pie; beef stew with dumplings; calf's liver and bacon; giant filled Yorkshire pudding; half shoulder of lamb; avocado and Stilton bake; crispy beer-battered cod; venison cooked in Guinness; and pheasant casserole. Popular desserts are banoffee pie, warm chocolate brownie and apple and raspberry crumble. Outside at the front (don't worry, there's little passing traffic) is a row of tables with umbrellas and there's a small, pretty garden.

Recommended in the area

Gilbert White's House and the Oates Museum; Watercress Line; Basing House

The Red Lion

Address: Rope Hill, BOLDRE, Lymington, SO41 8NE
Tel: 01590 673177 **Fax:** 01590 674036
Website: www.theredlionboldre.co.uk
Map ref: 3 SZ39
Directions: 1m from Lymington off A337. From M27
junct 1 through Lyndhurst & Brockenhurst towards
Lymington, follow signs for Boldre **Open:** all week
11-3 5.30-11 (Winter Sun noon-4 6-10.30, Summer
Sat 11-11 Sun noon-10.30) ☕ ✹ **L** Mon-Sat 12-
2.30, Sun 12-3.30 (Summer Sat 12-9.30, Sun 12-9)
D Mon-Sat 6-9.30, Sun 6-9 (Summer Sat 12-9.30, Sun 12-9) **Facilities:** Parking Garden
Notes: ⊕ FREE HOUSE ♦♦ ↸ ☗ 17

Is the Red Lion old? Well, yes, if a mention in the Domesday Book counts for anything, although today's building dates from the comparatively recent 15th century, when it evolved from a stable and two cottages. It remains the quintessential dog- and horse-friendly New Forest pub, with a rambling interior of cosy, beamed rooms packed with rural memorabilia. Home-made dishes are based on Hampshire's excellent bounty (the pub is a member of The New Forest Marque for use of local produce) such as wild venison, a by-product of the Forest's deer management policy, and sustainable fish from local catches. The seasonal menus are so full of appealing possibilities that selection of a few representative dishes isn't easy, but give thought to these: the famous steak and Ringwood Ale pie; home-cooked Hampshire ham with New Forest free-range fried eggs; pan-fried crab and spring onion fishcakes, with a hint of fresh chilli; and home-made beef Wellington with home-made New Forest venison pâté. Check the pub's website and book early for the monthly 'Pie & Pudding' evenings. Whenever you go, always drive slowly through the New Forest because animals not only wander across roads, they sometimes lie down on them.

Recommended in the area

Buckler's Hard: Exbury Gardens; Beaulieu Motor Museum

Carnarvon Arms

Address: Winchester Road, BURGHCLERE,
Newbury, RG20 9LE
Tel: 01635 278222 **Fax:** 01635 278444
Email: info@carnarvonarms.com
Website: www.carnarvonarms.com
Map ref: 3 SU46
Directions: M4 junct 13, A34 S to Winchester. Exit
A34 at Tothill Services, follow Highclere Castle signs.
Pub on right **Open:** all day all week ⓑ L all wk 12-
2.30 D all wk 6.30-9 ⓘ L all wk 12-2.30 D all wk
6.30-9.30 **Facilities:** Parking Garden Wi-fi **Notes:** ⓘ ⌁ ⓟ 15

The 5th Earl of Carnarvon, who famously excavated Tutankhamun's tomb in 1922, is buried on Beacon
Hill, a mile away from this one-time coaching inn. The family seat was neighbouring Highclere Castle, star
of TV's *Downton Abbey*, and it was at the Carnarvon Arms that castle visitors would alight. Today it's a
modern country inn offering excellent food, stylish bedrooms and sensible prices. The warm and friendly
bar, decorated in fresh natural colours and furnished with rich leather upholstery, offers sandwiches,
salads and dishes such as pan-fried calf's liver with mash and shallot sauce; and oven-roasted sausages
with creamed potato, fine beans and shallot jus. The dining room is quite remarkable, with Egyptian-
inspired wall carvings that pay homage to those long-ago excavations. Its Modern British seasonal
menu offers marinated yellow-fin tuna with avocado salsa, and roasted peppers with tomato velouté as
starters; and mains that include roasted fillet of beef with boulangère potatoes; pan-fried Barbary duck
with fondant potato, red onion marmalade and carrot purée; and roasted pork tenderloin with rösti potato,
braised red cabbage and confit shallot jus. English raspberry parfait with champagne and white chocolate
sauce is a typical pudding, and there's an excellent cheeseboard with home-made chutney.

Recommended in the area

Newbury Racecourse; Sandham Memorial Chapel; Watership Down

The East End Arms

Address: Main Road, EAST END,
nr Lymington, SO41 5SY
Tel/Fax: 01590 626223
Email: manager@eastendarms.co.uk
Website: www.eastendarms.co.uk
Map ref: 3 SZ39
Directions: From Lymington towards Beaulieu
(past Isle of Wight ferry), 3m to East End Open: all
week ¶♥ L all wk 12-2.30 D Mon-Sat 7-9.30
Facilities: Parking Garden Notes: ⊕ FREE HOUSE ♦♦ ♂

The East End Arms Pub and Restaurant cleverly combines serious food with local tradition.
The emphasis is on fresh local ingredients and a varied menu which is changed daily. There is an
abundance of charm and character with roaring log fires in the winter and a pretty courtyard garden
for the summer. A recent addition to the pub is five en suite bedrooms. This traditional New Forest
pub is owned by the former Dire Straits bass guitarist, John Illsley, and is idyllically situated between
Lymington and Beaulieu.

Recommended in the area

Bucklers Hard; Hurst Castle; Beaulieu Motor Museum

The Chestnut Horse

Address: EASTON, Winchester, SO21 1EG
Tel: 01962 779257
Fax: 01962 779037
Email: info@thechestnuthorse.com
Website: www.thechestnuthorse.com
Map ref: 3 SU53
Directions: From M3 junct 9 take A33 towards
Basingstoke, then B3047. Take 2nd right, then 1st left
Open: all week noon-3.30 5.30-11 (Sun eve closed
winter) ⓑ L all wk 12-2.30 D Mon-Sat 6-9.30
¶♥ L all wk 12-2 D Mon-Sat 6-9.30 Facilities: Parking Garden Notes: ⊕ HALL & WOODHOUSE ♦♦ ♂ ♥

This 16th-century dining pub has a well-earned local reputation for the quality of its food. Old tankards
and teapots hang from the low-beamed ceilings in the two bar areas, where a large open fire is the central
focus in winter. The candlelit restaurants are equally inviting: the light, panelled Green Room, and the
darker low-beamed Red Room with a wood-burning stove. Menus might include pork tenderloin, garlic
roast potatoes, purées of beetroot and orange, or Bombay crusted hake fillet and lemon confit potatoes.

Recommended in the area

Watercress Steam Railway; River Itchen (walking, fishing); Intech Science Museum

The Bugle

Address: High Street, HAMBLE-LE-RICE, SO31 4HA
Tel: 023 8045 3000
Fax: 023 8045 3051
Email: manager@buglehamble.co.uk
Website: www.buglehamble.co.uk
Map ref: 3 SU40
Directions: M27 junct 8, follow signs to Hamble. In village centre turn right at mini-rdbt into one-way cobbled street, pub at end **Open:** all day all week
L Mon-Thu 12-2.30, Fri 12-3, Sat 12-10, Sun 12-9 D Mon-Thu 6-9.30, Fri 6-10, Sat 12-10, Sun 12-9 **Facilities:** Wi-fi **Notes:** FREE HOUSE 10

The Bugle is at the heart of village life with its charming waterside location and river views. The Grade II listed building features natural flagstone floors, exposed beams and brickwork, a solid oak bar and real open fires. In addition to the restaurant area, a private dining room, the Captain's Table, is available upstairs, accommodating up to 12 guests. The seasonal menu is based on fresh, top quality ingredients, using local produce wherever possible, with meals served alongside well-kept local real ales, wine and speciality rums. The menu offers a good range of bar bites such as salt 'n' pepper squid and devilled whitebait. For something a bit more substantial, there's Hampshire free-range beef burger, relish and skinny chips, or south coast day boat sole with lemon and parsley butter and new potatoes. Fresh seafood and other home-made dishes are offered from the daily specials board, and there's a tempting range of desserts. At weekends, The Bugle's traditional roasts are popular. Alfresco dining with river views is possible, plus there are heated umbrellas if the weather's not quite at its best. Regular events at The Bugle include wine club, and quiz and live music nights.

Recommended in the area

Hamble River boat trips; Royal Victoria Country Park; Netley Abbey

The Vine at Hannington

Address: HANNINGTON, Tadley, RG26 5TX
Tel: 01635 298525
Fax: 01635 298027
Email: info@thevineathannington.co.uk
Website: www.thevineathannington.co.uk
Map ref: 3 SU55
Directions: Hannington signed from A339 between Basingstoke & Newbury
Open: 12-3 6-11 (Sat-Sun all day) **Closed:** 25 Dec, Sun eve & Mon in winter ⓑ ⓘ L Mon-Fri 12-2, Sat-Sun 12-2.30 D all wk 6-9 **Facilities:** Parking Garden Wi-fi **Notes:** ⊕ FREE HOUSE ⦿ ⚲ ⚱ 11

This traditional village pub sits high up on the beautiful Hampshire Downs – a delightful establishment where visitors can enjoy a warm welcome and delicious home-made food. The menu changes with the seasons and includes daily specials. Many of the ingredients come from the pub's own large garden, and typical dishes are home-made steak and ale pie or locally reared Aberdeen Angus steak. From the specials board come roast pheasant and grilled skate wing.

Recommended in the area

Highclere Castle; The Wayfarers Walk; Milestones Museum, Basingstoke

The Plough Inn

Address: LONGPARISH, Andover, SP11 6PB
Tel: 01264 720358
Email: eat@theploughinn.info
Website: www.theploughinn.info
Map ref: 3 SU44 **Directions:** M3 junct 8, A303 towards Andover. In approx 6m take B3048 towards Longparish **Open:** Mon-Sat 12-2.30 6-9.30 (Sun 12-8) **Closed:** Sun eve in winter ⓑ ⓘ L 12-2.30 D 6-9.30 **Facilities:** Parking Garden Wi-fi **Notes:** ⊕ ENTERPRISE INNS ⦿ ⚲

This charming 18th-century inn stands on the beautiful Test Way, literally - it cuts through the car park. The Test itself is actually so close that ducks waddle over to be fed, and the landlord can catch his own trout. The comfortable, flagstone- and oak-floored interior of this warm and inviting inn is furnished with leather chairs and warmed by open fires, along with fishing and local game shooting memorabilia and bric-a-brac. Hampshire-sourcing drives the fish specials, pub classics and main menus, which provide, for example, seafood paella; pan-fried calves' liver and bacon; or local saddle of venison.

Recommended in the area

Winchester Cathedral; Stonehenge; Mottisfont Abbey (NT)

The Wayfarers Walk, Tichborne

The Fox

Address: NORTH WALTHAM,
Basingstoke, RG25 2BE
Tel: 01256 397288
Email: info@thefox.org
Website: www.thefox.org
Map ref: 3 SU54
Directions: M3 junct 7, A30 towards Winchester.
North Waltham signed on right. Take 2nd signed road
Open: all day all week 11-11 ⓑ ⓘ L all wk 12-2.30
D all wk 6-9.30 **Facilities:** Parking Garden
Notes: ⊕ FREE HOUSE ⓮ ⓶ ⓹ 14

It is well worth leaving the tedium of the M3 for this free house and restaurant in a country lane just off the motorway's junction 7. It was once three 17th-century farm cottages, as becomes evident when you see the exposed beams and open fires. In the restaurant the fresh flowers look lovely, while in the cosy Village Bar are beers from Brakspear, Ringwood and Wychwood Hobgoblin, at least ten bottled ciders, and fourteen wines by the glass. Not for consumption, though, is the collection of miniatures - more than 1,100 so far and counting (further contributions are always welcome). The bar and monthly changing restaurant menus and daily blackboard specials make full use of local game and other produce, including vegetable and herbs from the garden and daily deliveries of fresh fish from the coast. Specialities include a superb cheese soufflé and main courses of Shetland mussels steamed in white wine and garlic; pork tenderloin medallions; halibut fillet stuffed with salmon mousseline; and wild mushroom Stroganoff. Regular 'special menu' evenings – Burns Supper and St George's Day, for example – are always popular. Meals can be served in the large garden, which includes a children's play area.

Recommended in the area

The Vyne; Winchester Cathedral; Stonehenge

The Bush

Address: OVINGTON, Alresford, SO24 0RE
Tel: 01962 732764
Fax: 01962 735130
Email: thebushinn@wadworth.co.uk
Website: www.wadworth.co.uk
Map ref: 3 SU53
Directions: A31 from Winchester, E to Alton &
Farnham, approx 6m turn left off dual carriageway
to Ovington. 0.5m to pub
Open: all day all week ⅃ L 12-2.30 D 7-9
Facilities: Parking Garden **Notes:** ⊞ WADWORTH ⅋ ↑

A rose-covered vision of a bygone age, The Bush is as delightful as it is hard to find, tucked away just off a meandering lane and overhung by trees. Once a refreshment stop on the Pilgrim's Way linking Winchester and Canterbury, these days the pub is more likely to attract walkers exploring the Itchen Way. A gentle riverside stroll along the Itchen, which flows past the pretty garden, will certainly set you up for a leisurely drink or a lingering meal. The pub's interior is dark and atmospheric; there's a central wooden bar, high backed seats and pews, stuffed animals on the wall and a real fire. Ales on offer include Wadworth 6X, IPA and Malt & Hops, JCB, Horizon, Old Timer and guest beers. The regularly-changing menu makes good use of local produce. Choices range from bar snacks, sandwiches and ploughman's lunches through to satisfying gastro-pub meals, taking in the likes of organic smoked trout mousse with warm toast, and slow-roasted belly pork on braised Savoy cabbage with organic cider jus. Finish with a traditional pudding such as Eton mess or rhubarb crumble. Not surprisingly, film crews love this location.

Recommended in the area

Avington Park; Winchester Cathedral; Mid-Hants Railways

The Rose & Thistle

Address: ROCKBOURNE, Fordingbridge, SP6 3NL
Tel: 01725 518236
Email: enquiries@roseandthistle.co.uk
Website: www.roseandthistle.co.uk
Map ref: 3 SU11
Directions: Follow Rockbourne signs from A354 (Salisbury to Blandford Forum road), or from A338 at Fordingbridge follow signs to Rockbourne **Open:** all week Mon-Sat 11-3 6-11 (Sun 12-8) ᴸ L all wk 12-2.30 D Mon-Sat 7-9.30
Facilities: Parking Garden Wi-fi **Notes:** ⊞ FREE HOUSE ⁙ ⁙ ⁙ 12

Nestling in one of the most picturesque villages in the county, on the edge of the New Forest, The Rose & Thistle has everything

you'd expect from the quintessential English pub: a tranquil setting, flowers around the door and a beautiful old building dating back to the 16th century. It has a welcoming low-ceilinged interior with oak beams and furniture, fresh flowers, magazines and an open fireplace. In summer, you can enjoy the delightful country garden. Well-kept real ales – Fuller's London Pride, Timothy Taylor Landlord and Palmers Copper Ale – are on offer, along with Scrumpy (cider), a carefully selected wine list and other drinks. Fresh seasonal food is cooked to order and includes fish such as skate, turbot and Cornish crab when available. The restaurant menu, available at lunch and dinner, offers dishes such as venison steak with sloe gin and blackberries, pork belly with crab apple gravy, and tagliatelle with feta, spinach and sun blush tomatoes. Lighter lunch choices might include scrambled eggs with crispy proscuitto, locally-made pork and sausages with wholegrain mustard mash, and chickpea and butternut squash crumble; the Sunday lunch of rare roast sirloin of beef is also very popular. Desserts are all home made and an extensive local cheeseboard is delicious.

Recommended in the area

Rockbourne Roman Villa and Trout Fishery; Breamore House; Salisbury

The Plough Inn

Address: Main Road, SPARSHOLT, Nr Winchester, SO21 2NW
Tel: 01962 776353
Fax: 01962 776400
Map ref: 3 SU43
Directions: From Winchester take B3049 (A272) W, left to Sparsholt, Inn 1m
Open: all week Mon-Sat 11-3 6-11 (Sun 12-3 6-10.30)
Closed: 25 Dec ⓑ L all wk 12-2 D Sun-Thu 6-9, Fri-Sat 6-9.30
†◎¹ L Mon-Sun 12-2 D Sun-Thu 6-9, Fri-Sat 6-9.30
Facilities: Parking Garden **Notes:** ⊕ WADWORTH †† ↿↾ ☻ 15

Set in beautiful countryside, just a stone's throw from Winchester, this inn is a great place to refresh yourself after a walk in the nearby Farley Mount Country Park. Owners Richard and Kathryn Crawford have a simple philosophy: to serve customers with good quality food and drink in a friendly atmosphere. The Plough was built about 200 years ago as a coach house for Sparsholt Manor, but within 50 years it had already become an alehouse. Since then it has been much extended, yet from the inside it all blends together very well, helped by the farmhouse-style furniture and the adornment with agricultural implements, stone jars and dried hops. The Wadworth brewery supplies all of the real ales, and there's a good wine selection. The left-hand dining area is served by a blackboard menu offering such light dishes as feta and spinach filo parcels with a Thai pesto dressing or a beef, ale and mushroom pie with vegetables. To the right, a separate board offers meals that reflect a more serious approach – perhaps breast of chicken filled with mushrooms on a garlic and bacon sauce; lamb shank with braised red cabbage and rosemary jus; and several fish dishes. Booking is always advisable.

Recommended in the area

Winchester Cathedral; Mottisfont Abbey (NT); Sir Harold Hillier Gardens and Arboretum

HEREFORDSHIRE

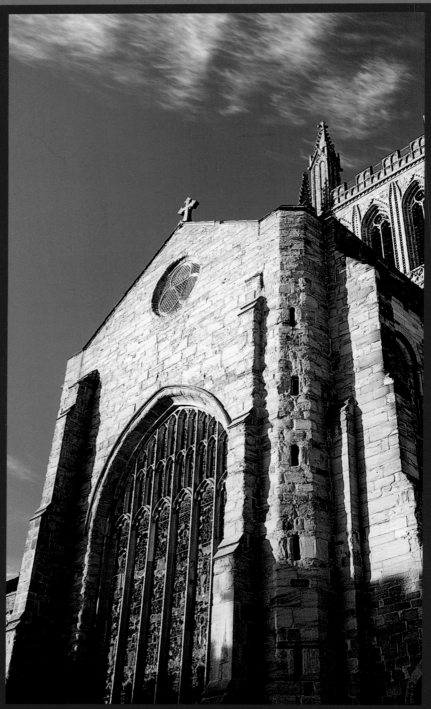

Hereford Cathedral

The Penny Farthing Inn

Address: ASTON CREWS, Ross-on-Wye, HR9 7LW
Tel/fax: 01989 750366
Email: thepennyfarthinginn@hotmail.co.uk
Map ref: 2 SO62
Directions: 5m E of Ross-on-Wye
Open: Mon-Thu 12-3 6-11 (Sun 12-3)
Closed: Mon in winter ♿ ⚅ L Tue-Sun 12-3
D Tue-Sat 6.30-9 **Facilities:** Parking Garden Wi-fi
Notes: ⊞ PUBFOLIO ♦♦ 🐾

This 17th-century blacksmith's shop and coaching inn sits high above the Wye Valley with stunning views of the Black Mountains and the Malvern Hills. Inside there is plenty of character with oak beams, antiques and warming log fires. The menu uses a wealth of local produce and some of the best meat in the country; why not try home-made steak and ale pie or maybe whole lemon sole with garlic butter from the daily specials. Follow with one of the sumptuous home-made desserts, such as sticky toffee pudding or vanilla and raspberry crème brûlée. Footpaths radiate from the front door of this traditional British country pub.

Recommended in the area

International Centre for Birds of Prey; Goodrich Castle; Symonds Yat

Stockton Cross Inn

Address: KIMBOLTON, Leominster, HR6 0HD
Tel: 01568 612509
Fax: 01568 620238
Email: mb@ecolots.co.uk
Website: www.stocktoncrossinn.co.uk
Map ref: 2 SO56
Directions: On A4112, 0.5m off A49, between
Leominster & Ludlow
Open: 12-3 7-11 **Closed:** Sun eve & Mon
♿ ⚅ L Tue-Sun 12-2 D Tue-Sat 7-9
Facilities: Parking Garden Wi-fi **Notes:** ⊞ FREE HOUSE ♦♦ ♟ 8

Stockton Cross is a 16th-century drovers' inn whose picturesque black and white exterior is regularly photographed by tourists and for calendars etc. Its peace and beauty are belied by the historical fact that alleged witches were once hanged here. There is a serious interest in good food, with much produce locally sourced to provide an interesting and varied menu. The relaxed and friendly atmosphere, cosy log fires, real ales and fine wines add to the charm, and there is also a pretty country garden.

Recommended in the area

Hergest Croft Gardens; Croft Castle; Berrington Hall (NT)

The Saracens Head Inn

★★★★ INN

Address: SYMONDS YAT [EAST], HR9 6JL
Tel: 01600 890435
Email: contact@saracensheadinn.co.uk
Website: www.saracensheadinn.co.uk
Map ref: 2 SO51
Directions: From Ross-on-Wye take A40 to
Monmouth. In 4m take Symonds Yat East turn. 1st
right before bridge. Right in 0.5m. Right in 1m
Open: all day all week **Closed:** 25 Dec
L all wk 12-2.30 D all wk 6.30-9
Rooms: 10 en suite (1 GF) S £55-£75 D £79-£130
Facilities: Parking Garden Wi-fi
Notes: FREE HOUSE 10

Symonds Yat is a spectacular natural attraction, and The Saracens Head is located in an Area of
Outstanding Natural Beauty on the east bank of the Wye where the river meets the Royal Forest of
Dean. Formerly a cider mill, the 17th-century inn is just over a mile from the Welsh border and makes
a convenient base for exploring an area ideal for walking and cycling. An ancient hand ferry carries
passengers across the Wye as it has for many years. The inn's atmosphere is informal and relaxed,
with two eating areas inside and two riverside terraces outside, with views of the Wye Valley. A great
choice of food majors on popular bar fare and restaurant main courses, including many traditional
home-made dishes with modern touches. Old Speckled Hen and ales from Theakstons and the Wye
Valley Brewery are served in the flagstoned bar. Eight standard bedrooms are offered in the main house
and two superior rooms are available in the boathouse annexe.

Recommended in the area

Goodrich Castle; Symonds Yat Rock; Forest of Dean

The Mill Race

Address: WALFORD, Ross-on-Wye, HR9 5QS
Tel: 01989 562891
Email: enquiries@millrace.info
Website: www.millrace.info
Map ref: 2 SO52
Directions: From Ross-on-Wye take B4234 to
Walford. Pub 3m on right after village hall
Open: all week 11-3 5-11 (Sat-Sun all day)
🏠 🍽 L Mon-Fri 12-2, Sat-Sun 12-2.30 D Mon-Sat
6-9.30, Sun 6-9 **Facilities:** Parking Garden Wi-fi
Notes: ⊕ FREE HOUSE 🚻 ☂ 14

In the beautiful Wye Valley, the award-winning Mill Race is a friendly village gastro-pub whose original
stone floors and Welsh slate floor are well complemented by a modern interior. The blazing fire literally
ensures a warm welcome, while the large terrace offers outdoor dining and views towards Goodrich
Castle. The bar serves a selection of local ales and ciders, and the extensive wine list offers fourteen
by the glass. An environmentally responsible approach to local food sourcing, including from the pub's
own farm 2 miles away and Bishopswood Shoot, lies behind a regularly changing menu of simple,
well-prepared food. The menu carefully combines traditional pub classics such as venison burger with
red cabbage pickle and chips; game pie with seasonal vegetables; and beer-battered pollack and chips,
with brasserie style dishes such as spiced fig tart with goat's cheese; crayfish and avocado cocktail with
lemon jelly; ricotta and squash rotollo with tomato and herb sauce; and seared duck breast with shallot
Tatin. Suppliers Nights such as Chase Vodka Night and Wye Valley Ale Night promote the wonderful local
produce and give customers the opportunity to meet the suppliers. The pub makes a good base for local
walks, including the one-mile Woodland Walk, which partly follows a disused railway line.

Recommended in the area

Symonds Yat; International Centre for Birds of Prey; Hereford Cathedral

Hoecroft Lane, Little Hadham

The Bricklayers Arms

Address: Hogpits Bottom, FLAUNDEN,
Nr Hemel Hempstead, HP3 0PH
Tel: 01442 833322
Fax: 01442 834841
Email: goodfood@bricklayersarms.com
Website: www.bricklayersarms.com
Map ref: 3 TL00
Directions: M25 junct 18 onto A404 (Amersham road).
Right at Chenies for Flaunden **Open:** all day all week 12-11.30
(25 Dec 12-3) 🍺 🍽 L Mon-Sat 12-2.30, Sun 12-3.30 D Mon-
Sat 6.30-9.30, Sun 6.30-8.30 **Facilities:** Parking Garden Wi-fi
Notes: 🌐 FREE HOUSE 🍴 🐕 🍷 16

This picturesque, 18th-century listed country pub is an ivy-clad, flint building situated in a lovely village at the end of winding lanes that snake between Chipperfield and Latimer. The interior has low wooden beams, exposed brickwork and real log fires, and a warm welcome from Alvin and Sally Michaels is guaranteed. Over the past seven years, The Bricklayers Arms has gained an excellent reputation for its traditional English and French fusion menu created by the highly trained and award-winning chef, Claude Paillet. The same menu can be enjoyed throughout the restaurant and pub seven days a week, with dishes including the famous, home-smoked fish plate; home-made terrines; traditional Tring Ale battered cod; 21-day aged fillet steak, and fillet of locally reared Worcestershire Black Spot pork. There's always a choice of fresh fish dishes and vegetarian options on the menu plus tantalising specials of the day. A carefully selected wine list of over 140 varieties to suit all budgets and tastes is available, as well as beers and local ales on tap. If you're thinking of calling in for the ever popular Sunday lunch, be sure to book in advance.

Recommended in the area

Chenies Manor House; Berkhamsted Castle; Ashridge Estate (NT)

Alford Arms

Address: Frithsden, HEMEL HEMPSTEAD, HP1 3DD
Tel: 01442 864480
Fax: 01422 876893
Email: info@alfordarmsfrithsden.co.uk
Website: www.alfordarmsfrithsden.co.uk
Map ref: 3 TL00
Directions: From Hemel Hempstead on A4146 take 2nd left at Water End. In 1m left at T-junct, right after 0.75m. Pub 100yds on right
Open: all day all week 11-11 (Sun 12-10.30)

Closed: 26 Dec ☕ ⓘ **L** Mon-Fri 12-2.30, Sat 12-3, Sun 12-4 **D** Mon-Thu 6.30-9.30, Fri-Sat 6.30-10, Sun 7-9.30 **Facilities:** Parking Garden Wi-fi **Notes:** ⊕ SALISBURY PUBS LTD ᛀ ᛗ ᛩ 20

An attractive Victorian pub in the unruffled hamlet of Frithsden, surrounded by National Trust woodland. The flower-filled garden overlooks the village green, and historic Ashridge Forest is nearby. Cross the threshold and in the dining room and bar you'll pick up on the warm and lively atmosphere, derived partly from the buzz of conversation, partly from the discreet background jazz, and partly from the rich colours and eclectic mixture of old furniture and pictures, mostly acquired from Tring salerooms. The seasonal menu and daily specials balance modern British with more traditional fare, mostly prepared from fresh, local produce. A good choice of 'small plates' ranges from rustic breads with roast garlic and olive oil, to oak-smoked bacon on bubble and squeak with hollandaise sauce and poached egg. Main meals with a similarly imaginative approach include Moroccan spiced lamb shank on sweet potato mash, pan juices and cumin yoghurt; Cornish fish stew with saffron potatoes, rouille and gruyère; and pumpkin gnocchi with roast beetroot, porcini, watercress and walnut pesto. Puddings are interestingly tweaked too, such as crispy banana and almond spring roll with lemongrass caramel.

Recommended in the area

Berkhamsted Castle; Walter Rothschild Zoological Museum; Whipsnade Wild Animal Park

The Fox and Hounds

Address: 2 High Street, HUNSDON, SG12 8NH
Tel: 01279 843999
Fax: 01279 841092
Email: info@foxandhounds-hunsdon.co.uk
Website: www.foxandhounds-hunsdon.co.uk
Map ref: 3 TL41 **Directions:** From A414 between
Ware & Harlow take B180 in Stanstead Abbotts N to
Hunsdon **Open:** noon-4 6-11 **Closed:** 26 Dec, Sun
eve, Mon & BHs eve (Tue after BHs) ⓑ L Tue-Sun
12-3 D Tue-Sat 6.30-9.30 ⓘ L Sun 12-3.30
D Fri-Sat 7-9.30 **Facilities:** Parking Garden Wi-fi **Notes:** ⊕ FREE HOUSE ⁉ 🐾 ⚑ 9

This welcoming pub is set in a pretty village surrounded by Hertfordshire countryside. It has a comfy, laid-back bar featuring a log fire, leather sofas and local ales. There's a large separate dining room and an outside terrace in the large garden. Chef owner James Rix, who trained under some of the industry's top chefs, has quickly made a name for himself at this family-run establishment, with a seasonal menu that combines classics with modern touches, and changes twice a day.

Recommended in the area

Henry Moore Foundation; Paradise Wildlife Park; Lee Valley Park

Ruins of Berkhamsted Castle

Exmoor pony on the Saxon Shore Way

Castle Inn

Address: CHIDDINGSTONE, TN8 7AH
Tel: 01892 870247
Email: info@castleinn-kent.co.uk
Website: www.castleinn-kent.co.uk
Map ref: 4 TQ54
Directions: 1.5m S of B2027 between Tonbridge & Edenbridge **Open:** all day all week 11-11 (Sun 12-10.30) **Food:** L Mon-Fri 12-2, Sat-Sun 12-4 D Mon-Sat 7-9.30
Facilities: Garden **Notes:** 🛢 FREE HOUSE ⇊ 🐕 ⌾ 9

The building was first mentioned in 1420, although three more centuries elapsed before anyone sold ale here. Situated in a National Trust village, it forms part of a particularly fine row of timber-framed houses, and has an interior full of original oak beams, mullioned windows and big fireplaces. As well as a public bar, where you can play traditional pub games, there is a saloon bar and areas for more private dining, plus a private dining room. Outside is the vine-hung courtyard and Garden Bar, while across a bridge lies a lawn and beautifully tended flowerbeds. The owner is John McManus, previously of Le Gavroche, who arrived in early 2010, with Andy Wilson as head chef and a team that shares John's passion for the highest standards and attention to detail. The bar menu offers snacks like home-made focaccia, as well as the more substantial potato gnocchi; chicken Caesar salad; cottage pie; and braised Kentish lamb. In addition, there is a children's menu, and cream teas are served all day. In the evening you're more likely to find poached lemon sole; 42-day aged beef sirloin; poached and roasted leg of chicken; and pithiviers of provençale vegetables; with desserts such as treacle tart with almond and Chantilly cream, and Bramley apple crumble. There is a well chosen, modern wine list together with real ales, brewed in the village at the acclaimed Larkins Brewery, just 400 yards from the pub.

Recommended in the area

Hever Castle; Penshurst Place; Chartwell

Griffins Head

Address: CHILLENDEN, Canterbury, CT3 1PS
Tel: 01304 840325
Fax: 01304 841290
Map ref: 4 TR25
Directions: A2 from Canterbury towards Dover, then B2046. Village on right
Open: all week **Closed:** Sun pm 🍽 L all wk 12-2
D Mon-Sat 7-9.30 **Facilities:** Parking Garden
Notes: ⊕ SHEPHERD NEAME ♆ 10

Dating from 1286, this Kentish Wealden hall has great historical character, with beamed bars and inglenook fireplaces. Fine Kentish ales from Shepherd Neame and home-made food have helped the old inn to make its mark with visitors as well as locals, among them Kent's cricketing fraternity. The menu is typically English and specialises in game from local estates in season and locally caught fish when possible. Outside there's a very pretty garden where drinkers can linger at their leisure, and a bat and trap pitch (an ancient relative of cricket, still popular in Kent). A vintage car club meets here on the first Sunday of every month.

Recommended in the area

Goodnestone Park Gardens; Howletts Wild Animal Park; Dover Castle

Dover Castle

The Plough at Ivy Hatch

Address: High Cross Road, IVY HATCH, TN15 0NL
Tel: 01732 810100
Email: info@theploughivyhatch.co.uk
Website: www.theploughivyhatch.co.uk
Map ref: 4 TQ55
Directions: Off A25 between Borough Green &
Sevenoaks, follow signs to Ightham Mote
Open: all week noon-3 6-11 (Sat noon-11 Sun 10-6)
Closed: 1 Jan 🍽 🍴 L Mon-Sat 12-2.45, Sun 12-6
D Mon-Sat 6-9.30 **Facilities:** Parking Garden Wi-fi
Notes: ⊕ FREE HOUSE ♦♦ ☐ 10

Deep in the countryside, this tile-hung village pub is a perfect spot for a lingering lunch or supper. The aim of Miles and Anna is to make it the centre of the community; their driving passion is to source the best locally produced farm products and present them as classic dishes on a British- and European-influenced menu that they update daily, all home made. Typical starters are beetroot-cured salmon with blinis and dill crème fraîche or chicken liver parfait. Main courses include pan-fried guinea fowl breast with roasted butternut squash and blackberry jus, or pan-fried fillet of grey mullet with herb-crushed new potatoes. For a lighter meal or bar snack try a crayfish tail and lemon mayonnaise or roast beef and horseradish cream sandwich, or maybe local sausages or honey roast ham with hand-cut chips and their own free range eggs. There is also a sweet and savoury pancake menu. Desserts include seasonal fruit crumbles or tarts, sticky chocolate pudding and treacle tart, plus local cheeses. Ales are mainly from Royal Tunbridge Wells Brewing Company, with guest ales from Larkins, Westerham and Hogs Back breweries. The back gardens are surrounded by cobnut trees and living amongst them is Maya and Ellie, the pet pigs who, with chickens, dog and cat, keep The Plough full of life and entertainment.

Recommended in the area

Ightham Mote; Knole House and Park; Oldbury Hill & Styants Wood

The Bottle House Inn

Address: Coldharbour Road, PENSHURST,
Tonbridge, TN11 8ET
Tel: 01892 870306 **Fax:** 01892 871094
Email: info@thebottlehouseinnpenshurst.co.uk
Website: www.thebottlehouseinnpenshurst.co.uk
Map ref: 4 TQ54
Directions: From Tunbridge Wells take A264 W, then
B2188 N. After Fordcombe left towards Edenbridge
& Hever. Pub 500yds after staggered x-rds **Open:** all
day all week 11-11 (Sun 11-10.30) **Closed:** 25 Dec

🍴 ⚑ food served all day **Facilities:** Parking Garden **Notes:** ⊕ FREE HOUSE ❉ ⚐ ♟ 11

A well-regarded dining pub, The Bottle House was built as a farmhouse in 1492, and in 1806 a licence
was obtained to sell ales and ciders. It was registered as an alehouse at each subsequent change of
hands, at a time when hop-growing was the major local industry. The pub was said to be the originator
of the ploughman's lunch, made with bread from the old bakery next door and cheese donated by
Canadian soldiers billeted nearby. The building was completely refurbished in 1938 and granted a
full licence; it was reputedly named after all the old bottles discovered during these works. Today,
low beams and a copper-topped counter give the bar a warm, welcoming atmosphere. Choose from
the range of Harveys and Larkins hand-pumped beers and eleven wines by the glass. The menu has
something for everyone, starting with ham hock, cornichon and parsley terrine or pan-seared scallops
with sautéed black pudding, hot sweetcorn purée and crispy pancetta. Lighter meals and shares are
also available and may include garlic and chilli grilled crevettes with rustic bread or home-made soup
with half sandwich of the day. For main courses enjoy slow-roasted belly of pork with a light cider
sauce and creamed Savoy cabbage with bacon, or cornfed chicken breast with tarragon cream sauce.
Recommended in the area

Hever Castle; Royal Tunbridge Wells; Penshurst Place & Gardens

The Beacon

★★★★ ⇔ INN

Address: Tea Garden Lane, Rusthall,
nr ROYAL TUNBRIDGE WELLS, TN3 9JH
Tel: 01892 524252 **Fax:** 01892 534288
Email: beaconhotel@btopenworld.com
Website: www.the-beacon.co.uk
Map ref: 4 TQ53
Directions: From Tunbridge Wells take A264
towards East Grinstead. Pub 1m on left
Open: all day all week 11-11 (Sun 12-10.30) ⓑ

🍴 **L** Mon-Thu 12-2.30, Fri-Sun 12-9.30 **D** Mon-Thu 6.30-9.30, Fri-Sun 12-9.30 **Rooms:** 3 en suite
Facilities: Parking Garden **Notes:** ⊕ FREE HOUSE ⚬ ⚏ 12

High up on a sandstone outcrop just 1.5 miles from Tunbridge Wells, The Beacon has one of the best
views in southeast England. Formerly a grand country home, it retains impressive architectural features,
including stained glass, moulded ceilings and an oak-panelled bar in which you can select from a fine
range of beers and wine to complement the food. As members of Kentish Fare, the proprietors are
strongly committed to using county-produced ingredients, and in the restaurant you can choose from
starters such as local pork terrine with apple chutney and crisp sage, or pressed English goat's cheese
and eggplant with piquant tomato relish. Your meal could continue with slow-roasted shoulder of
English mutton, fondant potato and caper and parsley sauce, or crisp line-caught fillet of sea bass with
ginger and soy, ribbon courgettes and lemony rice. Try to save room for dessert, notably natural yogurt
and rose water panacotta with rhubarb compote, or brioche bread and butter pudding with Baileys and
chocolate. Walk off your meal in the 17 acres of grounds, which include lakes, woodland paths and a
chalybeate spring. There's also a lovely terrace and spacious, comfortable accommodation.

Recommended in the area

Royal Tunbridge Wells; Penshurst Place & Gardens; Spa Valley Railway

The Coastguard

Address: St Margaret's Bay,
ST MARGARET'S AT CLIFFE, CT15 6DY
Tel: 01304 853176
Email: thecoastguard@talk21.com
Website: www.thecoastguard.co.uk
Map ref: 4 TR34 **Directions:** 2m off A258 between Dover
& Deal, follow St Margaret's at Cliffe signs. Through village
towards sea **Open:** all day all week 11-11 (Sun 11-10.30)
🍴 **L** all wk 12.30-2.45 **D** all wk 6.30-8.45
Facilities: Parking Garden Wi-fi **Notes:** ⊕ FREE HOUSE ♦♦ 🐕

Britain's 'nearest pub to France' stands a stone's throw from the
English Channel, with the White Cliffs of Dover as its backdrop.
The extensive bar stocks real ales from local micro-breweries, British and European bottled beers, wines
from Kent and a range of single malts. The menu changes daily depending upon the weather and what's
available. For that reason you will only find a sample menu on the website, if you look before you leave
home, when you arrive you are sure to find locally caught fish and seafood, and beef from a local farm.
Recommended in the area
Dover Castle; Walmer Castle; South Foreland Heritage Coast

The gardens of Penshurst Place

Forest of Bowland at Whitewell

Clog and Billycock

Address: Billinge End Road, Pleasington, BLACKBURN, BB2 6QB
Tel: 01254 201163
Email: enquiries@theclogandbillycock.com
Website: www.theclogandbillycock.com
Map ref: 6 SD62
Directions: M6 junct 29 onto M65 junct 3, follow signs for Pleasington
Open: all week noon-11 (Sun noon-10.30) **Closed:** 25 Dec
L Mon-Sat 12-2, Sun 12-8.30 (afternoon bites Mon-Sat 2-5.30) D Mon-Fri 6-9, Sat 5.30-9, Sun 12-8.30 L Mon-Sat 12-2, Sun 12-8.30 D Mon-Fri 6-9, Sat 5.30-9, Sun 12-8.30
Facilities: Parking Garden **Notes:** FREE HOUSE

The Clog and Billycock has been part of Pleasington's history for over 150 years, although this venture opened only in 2008. Its name comes from the attire of an early landlord (a billycock is black felt hat, a predecessor of the bowler). Set in the quaint village of Pleasington, the building has undergone an expensive renovation, and the result is a warm and relaxing pub in which to enjoy Thwaites ales, draught ciders, fine wines and superb food. Winnie Swarbricks Goosnargh cornfed chicken liver pâté makes an excellent light lunch, while the ploughman's highlights the pub's real food objectives, consisting of an impressive plate of Garstang Blue, Leagrams Tasty Lancashire, York hand-raised pork pie, pickled onion, pickled white cabbage, piccalilli and bread. Hot options from chef Nigel Haworth's locally sourced menu may include breadcrumbed breast of Goosnargh chicken with scallop potatoes, cabbage and wilted spinach and garlic and herb butter; Simpson's Dairy rice pudding could complete a meal to remember. Children are welcomed with fun educational sheets and competitions, as well as equally well thought-out children's meals.

Recommended in the area

Pleasington Priory; Pleasington Old Hall Wood and Wildlife Garden; Witton Country Park

The Highwayman

Address: BURROW, Nr Kirkby Lonsdale, LA6 2RJ
Tel: 01524 273338
Email: enquiries@highwaymaninn.co.uk
Website: www.highwaymaninn.co.uk
Map ref: 6 SD67
Directions: M6 junct 36, A65 to Kirkby Lonsdale.
Then A683 S. Burrow approx 2m
Open: all week noon-11 (Sun noon-10.30)
Closed: 25 Dec ⓛ L Mon-Sat 12-2, Sun 12-8.30
D Mon-Fri 6-9, Sat 5.30-9, Sun 12-8.30
Facilities: Parking Garden **Notes:** ⊕ RIBBLE VALLEY INNS ⋔ ⛫ ⛾ 13

Starting life as a coaching inn during the 18th century, a legend surrounds this establishment regarding its use as a midnight haunt of notorious Lancashire highwaymen. The inn is set in a delightful country area close to the historic market town of Kirkby Lonsdale, popular for its pretty cottages, quaint streets and attractive shops and tea rooms. The refurbished Highwayman has a stone-floored interior with solid wood furniture and welcoming open fires. There is also a beautifully landscaped terraced garden. Thwaites cask ales, ciders and guest beers are served alongside a list of fine wines, and the menus are a tribute to regional specialities and local producers and suppliers. Typical dishes are Port of Lancaster Smokehouse kipper fillet, with boiled egg and watercress salad; Herdwick mutton pudding, capers, parsley mash and black peas; and Cartmel sticky toffee pudding with butterscotch sauce and vanilla ice cream. Don't miss the tri-counties cheeseboard, with the best from Lancashire, Yorkshire and Cumbria. The children's menu offers real food in smaller portions, and seasonal fun sheets are available to keep younger customers amused.

Recommended in the area

Sizergh Castle; Levens Hall; White Scar Caves

The Assheton Arms

Address: Downham, CLITHEROE, BB7 4BJ
Tel: 01200 441227
Fax: 01200 440581
Email: asshetonarms@aol.com
Website: www.assheton-arms.co.uk
Map ref: 6 SD74
Directions: A59 to Chatburn, then follow Downham signs
Open: all week Mon-Fri 12-3 6-11 (Sat-Sun noon-11pm) ⓑ ⓞ L Mon-Sat 12-2, Sun 12-9 D all wk 6-9 **Facilities:** Parking **Notes:** ⊕ FREE HOUSE ⅰⅼ ⅻ ♈ 20

Pendle Hill looms over the village, whose houses, thanks to the Assheton family who owns it, are delightfully free of TV aerials and dormer windows; there aren't any village name road signs either. Even the original stocks remain, so imagine how TV drama producers love it as a location. The stone-built pub was renamed in 1950 after Ralph Assheton, who became Lord Clitheroe in 1955 in recognition of his contribution during the Second World War. The family coat of arms on the sign above the door features a man holding a scythe incorrectly; the reason involves the English Civil War - any local will tell you the tale. In the single bar and sectioned rooms you'll find solid oak tables, wingback settees, the original 1765 fireplace, and a large blackboard listing the daily specials. Be pleasantly surprised this far from the coast by the range of seafood (according to season), including oysters, mussels, scallops, lobster, monkfish and sea bream. Other dishes are Mrs Whelan's Burnley black pudding with piccalilli and mustard; bacon and cranberry casserole; traditional fish and chips; and, the one that in this neck of the woods would be conspicuous by its absence, Lancashire hot pot.

Recommended in the area

Forest of Bowland; Samlesbury Hall; Yorkshire Dales National Park

Cartford Country Inn & Hotel

Address: Little Eccleston, PRESTON, PR3 0YP
Tel: 01995 670166
Email: info@thecartfordinn.co.uk
Website: www.thecartfordinn.co.uk
Map ref: 6 SD52
Directions: Off A586
Open: all day **Closed:** 25 Dec, Mon L
🍽 L Tue-Sat 12-2, Sun 12-8 **D** Mon-Thu 5-9,
Fri-Sat 5-10 **Facilities:** Parking Garden Wi-fi
Notes: ⊕ FREE HOUSE ♦♦

A 17th-century farmhouse that after a couple of centuries became a coaching inn. Today this pleasantly rambling, three-storey building stands sentinel by the toll bridge over the tidal River Wyre, a few miles from its estuary and the Irish Sea. Owners Patrick and Julie Beaume have successfully combined traditional and contemporary elements, with a log fire in the winter grate, and positively up-to-date polished wood floors and chunky dining furniture. Established for many years now as a welcoming, real ale pub, it maintains four cask beers, at the time of writing Theakston's Old Peculier, Pride of Pendle from Moorhouse, Lakeland Gold from Hawkshead and Bowland's Hen Harrier. The restaurant provides an extensive menu of creative dishes using fresh local produce. Starters might include venison sausage casserole with horseradish dumpling; skewer of tempura king prawns; wood platters of antipasti, Fleetwood-landed seafood or organic crudités; and main courses of papillote of fresh sea bass and salmon mousseline; roast Goosnargh duck breast; and field and wild mushroom Stroganoff. There's a beer garden for alfresco dining with river views and the Trough of Bowland as a backdrop, and live music some Friday nights. Overnight accommodation is available.

Recommended in the area

Blackpool Tower; Samlesbury Hall; Martin Mere Wetland Centre

The Norman keep of Clitheroe Castle

The Three Fishes

Address: Mitton Road, Mitton, WHALLEY, BB7 9PQ
Tel: 01254 826888
Fax: 01254 826026
Email: enquiries@thethreefishes.com
Website: www.thethreefishes.com
Map ref: 6 SD73
Directions: M6 junct 31, A59 to Clitheroe. Follow signs for Whalley, take B6246 for 2m
Open: all day all week **Closed:** 25 Dec ⓑ ⓘ **L** Mon-

Sat 12-2, Sun 12-8.30 **D** Mon-Fri 6-9, Sat 5.30-9, Sun 12-8.30 **Facilities:** Parking Garden
Notes: ⓫ FREE HOUSE ⓦ ⚑ ⓪ 13

The Three Fishes is over 400 years old and has been a pub for most of that time, providing refreshment to travellers on the old road from the 16th-century bridge at Lower Hodder and the ferry at Mitton. The place was supposedly named after the three fishes pendant in the coat of arms of John Paslew, last abbot of nearby Whalley Abbey (look above the entrance to see them carved in stone). The tiny hamlet of Mitton is set on a limestone rise above the River Ribble and is surrounded by beautiful countryside. The pub prides itself on its genuine Lancashire hospitality, real ales, and the best food ever in its long history. The menu demonstrates a passionate commitment to regional food, with dishes such as Morecambe Bay shrimps, served with blade mace butter and toasted muffin; heather reared Lonk lamb Lancashire hotpot; and Lake District farmers 10oz sirloin steak with proper chips. You might finish your meal with Bramley apple crumble with Simpsons double cream, or the excellent Lancashire cheese board with biscuits and fireside chutney. Photographs of local 'food hero' producers and suppliers line the walls, in tribute to their contribution to the success of The Three Fishes.

Recommended in the area

Stonyhurst College; Clitheroe Castle; All Hallows Medieval Church

The Inn at Whitewell

★★★★★ ◉ INN

Address: Forest of Bowland, WHITEWELL,
Nr Clitheroe, BB7 3AT
Tel: 01200 448222
Fax: 01200 448298
Email: reception@innatwhitewell.com
Website: www.innatwhitewell.com
Map ref: 6 SD64
Directions: From B6243 follow Whitewell signs
Open: all week 10am-1am 🍺 L all wk 12-2 D all wk
7.30-9.30 🍽 D all wk 7.30-9.30 **Rooms:** 23 en suite (2 GF) **S** £83-£177 **D** £113-£218
Facilities: Parking Garden Wi-fi **Notes:** ⊕ FREE HOUSE 👫 🐾 🍷 16

Commanding wonderful views this delightful 16th-century inn, a former deer keeper's cottage, is set high up on the banks of the River Hodder in the Forest of Bowland. The bar – just one area where the family passion for antiques is evident – serves local real ales, and organic beers and ciders, and impressive food at lunchtime and evening. For formal dining, try the riverside restaurant. Richly furnished rooms available.

Recommended in the area

Ribchester Roman Museum; Browsholme Hall; Yorkshire Dales National Park

River Hodden, Whitewell

Battlefield Steam Railway

The Queen's Head

★★★★  RESTAURANT WITH ROOMS

Address: 2 Long Street, BELTON, Loughborough, LE12 9TP
Tel: 01530 222359
Fax: 01530 224860
Email: enquiries@thequeenshead.org
Website: www.thequeenshead.org
Map ref: 8 SK42
Directions: On B5324 between Coalville & Loughborough
Open: all day all week
Closed: 25-26 Dec **Rooms:** 6 en suite **S** £70 **D** £80-£100
Facilities: Parking Garden **Notes:** ♦♦ ♍ ♟ 14

A stunning contemporary gastro-pub with individually-designed
bedrooms, located in the very heart of the East Midlands. Whether you just want to enjoy a drink in
the stylish bar area with its leather seating or try the culinary creations of head chef David Ferguson in
the award-winning restaurant, The Queen's Head has all round appeal. Modern British food is skilfully
cooked and presented with style using fresh local produce.

Recommended in the area

National Forest; Conkers; The Great Central Railway

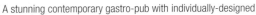

Great Central Railway, Loughborough

LONDON

Neal's Yard, Covent Garden

North Pole Bar & Restaurant

Address: 131 Greenwich High Road, Greenwich,
LONDON, SE10 8JA
Tel: 020 8853 3020
Fax: 020 8853 3501
Email: natalie@northpolegreenwich.com
Website: www.northpolegreenwich.com
Map ref: 3 TQ38
Directions: From Greenwich rail station, turn right,
pass Novotel. Pub on right (2 min walk)
Open: all day all week noon-2am 🍴 L all wk 12-10
D all wk 12-10 🍽 L Sat-Sun 12-5 D all wk 6-10.30 **Facilities:** Garden Wi-fi
Notes: ⊕ FREE HOUSE ♦ ⌀ ♟ 9

Drinking, dining, dancing – you can do it all at this grand old corner pub, which offers a complete
night out under one roof. Start with a cocktail in the bar, then, if you're there on a Thursday to Sunday
evening, head upstairs to the stylish Piano Restaurant, where the resident pianist will entertain
you. Look up and you'll see goldfish swimming around in the chandeliers, but don't worry, they're
for real and nothing to do with that earlier cocktail. An extensive bar menu is available all day, with
choices including chorizo risotto, swordfish steak, and oriental platter. The cooking style in the Piano
Restaurant's grand green room and elegant red room is modern European, typified by prosciutto salad;
Asian-style crab and noodle salad; lamb shank tagine; pan-fried sea bream; twice cooked Asian pork
belly; veal escalopes; and roasted spicy squash risotto. Desserts include ice peach soufflé with mixed
berries, and chocolate nemesis with crème fraîche and strawberries. In the basement is the South Pole
club, where you can dance until 2am. Sunday is the day for live jazz, funk and Latin music. To complete
the picture there's a terrace, an ideal spot for a Pimms on a summer evening.

Recommended in the area

Maritime Greenwich; Royal Observatory; Eltham Palace

The Bountiful Cow

Address: 51 Eagle Street, Holborn, LONDON, WC1R 4AP
Tel: 020 7404 0200 **Fax:** 020 7404 8737
Email: manager@roxybeaujolais.com
Website: www.thebountifulcow.co.uk
Map ref: 3 TQ38
Directions: 230mtrs NE from Holborn tube station, via Procter St. Walk through 2 arches into Eagle St. Pub between High Holborn & Red Lion Square **Open:** all day **Closed:** BHs Sun 🍽 food served all day **Facilities:** Wi-fi **Notes:** ⊕ FREE HOUSE 🚻 ⚱ 14

Roxy Beaujolais, proprietor of the ancient Seven Stars in WC2 overleaf, found a 1960s pub between Red Lion Square and High Holborn and turned it into The Bountiful Cow, 'a public house devoted to beef'. You enter below green waterfalls of periwinkles to find two floor levels that feel neatly halfway between a funky bistro and a stylish saloon. Walls are bedecked with pictures of cows, bullfights, cowgirls, meat cuts diagrams and cow-themed films, presided over by a colourful poster for Cattle Queen of Montana starring Barbara Stanwyck and a former president of the United States. The house seats 70 diners; the music is jazzy but discreet. Head Cook Roxy is author of the pub cookbook *Home From the Inn Contented* and was a presenter of the BBC's *Full On Food*. Her menu, based on beef sourced at Smithfield Market and aged in-house, features exceptionally large and well-made hamburgers and big steaks (rib-eye, sirloin, T-bone, filet, onglet) destined to be accurately cooked by the grill chef, alongside cask-conditioned ales and wines. Lunches are of particularly notable value: the pub pays homage to the Free Lunch tradition of US pre-prohibition days with an Almost Free Lunch. Memorable choices are offered at 'nugatory', i.e. low prices, with the customer requested to also buy a drink (it could be a soft drink). The sights and tourist destinations are a short walk away.

Recommended in the area

British Museum; Dr Johnson's House; Dickens House Museum; Sir John Soame's Museum

The Seven Stars

Address: 53 Carey Street, LONDON, WC2A 2JB
Tel: 020 7242 8521
Email: roxy@roxybeaujolais.com
Map ref: 3 TQ38 **Directions:** From Temple N via The Strand &
Bell Yard to Carey St. From Holborn SE via Lincoln's Inn Fields &
Searle St to Carey St **Open:** all day all week 11-11 (Sat noon-11,
Sun noon-10.30) **Closed:** 25-26 Dec, 1 Jan, Good Fri, Etr Sun
🍴 🍽 L Mon-Fri 12-3, Sat-Sun 12-9 **D** Mon-Fri 5.30-9, Sat-
Sun 12-9 **Facilities:** Wi-fi **Notes:** ⊕ FREE HOUSE

Built in 1602, this charming little pub at the back of the Royal
Courts of Justice is presided over by the celebrated 'alewife'
(as she calls herself) Roxy Beaujolais, cookbook author and TV
food show presenter. Since she took it over it has had a subtle freshening and has expanded into the
former legal wig shop next door—wigs are still displayed—to now provide 28 covers at green chequed
oilcloth-covered tables, in case you are diffident about sitting at the bar on Lloyd Loom stools. The
improvements were managed with such Grade II discretion by Roxy's architect husband that some
think his glazed, mahogany-mullioned dumbwaiter is ancient. Roxy and her assistants cook simple
dishes seven days a week that are, famously, slightly revisionist. A blackboard reveals what the market
provides, which might include a meat, fowl or game pie; cockle bisque; paella with mixed sausages;
linguine with chestnuts and truffle oil. Real ales from Adnams, Dark Star, Fullers and others are served,
and a few good wines. The venerable pub cat Tom Paine wears a chorister's ruff, to the delight of
customers - many of them barristers from across the road. The chalkboard outside lists frequently
changing rules such as 'no querulousness', 'no apostrophe mistakes' and 'no dogs except Archie'.
Even if you don't need the loo, try the narrow and ridiculously steep Elizabethan stairs.

Recommended in the area

The Soane Museum; The Hunterian Museum; Lincoln's Inn

NORFOLK

A field of lavender, West Newton

Kings Head

Address: Harts Lane, BAWBURGH, NR9 3LS
Tel: 01603 744977
Email: anton@kingshead-bawburgh.co.uk
Website: www.kingshead-bawburgh.co.uk
Map ref: 4 TG10
Directions: From A47 W of Norwich take B1108 W
Open: all day **Closed:** 25-27 Dec eve,
1 Jan eve 🍴 L Mon-Sat 12-2, Sun 12-4
D Mon-Sat 5.30-9 **Facilities:** Parking Garden Wi-fi
Notes: ⊕ FREE HOUSE 🏠 ⚲ 14

A peaceful setting by the banks of the River Yare is perfect for visitors who want to head out of Norwich and enjoy the relaxing atmosphere of a genuine village pub, complete with heavy timbers and bulging walls. Standing opposite the village green, the pub is big on traditional charm, with wooden floors, log fires and comfy leather seating. The monthly changing carte menu and daily changing specials board include pub classics with imaginative and local twists. Fresh bread is hand-made every day and the range of puddings is based on locally grown seasonal fruits, hand-made ice creams and local cheeses.

Recommended in the area

Norwich Cathedral; Norfolk Broads; Norwich Theatre Royal

Norwich Cathedral

The Blakeney White Horse

Address: 4 High Street, BLAKENEY, NR25 7AL
Tel: 01263 740574
Fax: 01263 741303
Email: info@blakeneywhitehorse.co.uk
Website: www.blakeneywhitehorse.co.uk
Map ref: 4 TG04
Directions: From A148 (Cromer to King's Lynn road) onto A149 signed to Blakeney
Open: all day all week 10.30am-11pm
Closed: 25 Dec ⛔ ⏹ L all wk 12-2.15 D Sun-Thu 6-9, Fri-Sat 6-9.30 **Facilities:** Parking Garden Wi-fi
Notes: ⊕ FREE HOUSE 🚹 🐾 ♈ 35

Blakeney is a gem of a coastal village. Narrow streets of flint-built fishermen's cottages wind their way to a small tidal harbour, beyond which vast marshes surround the creeks and estuary. Dominating the horizon is the shingle ridge of Blakeney Point. Norfolk doesn't often do steep, but it does here, at least from the quayside to the 17th-century White Horse, formerly a coaching inn, and run by the same team for many years. There are two eating areas – the bar which is informal and bustling and the light and airy conservatory. Lobster, crab and mussels come from local fishermen as the seasons dictate; butchers, graziers and Norfolk estates supply meat and game; soft fruit, salads, asparagus and free-range eggs come from local smallholders. Lunchtime snacks include granary bread sandwiches, fish pie and Binham Blue ploughman's. A daily changing à la carte dinner menu offers Holkham estate venison bourguignon with steamed herb dumplings; Cley sea bass, pommes Anna, provençale vegetables and gremolata; fricassée of chanterelles, pumpkin and spinach with sage gnocchi. An 80-bin wine list with 35 available by the glass and four regional real ales complete the picture.

Recommended in the area

North Norfolk Heritage Coast; Wells & Walsingham Light Railway; Holkham Hall

The Hoste Arms

★★★ 87% ⊛⊛ HOTEL

Address: The Green, BURNHAM MARKET, PE31 8HD
Tel: 01328 738777
Fax: 01328 730103
Email: reception@hostearms.co.uk
Website: www.hostearms.co.uk
Map ref: 4 TF84
Directions: Signed off B1155, 5m W of Wells-next-the-Sea **Open:** all week ⓑ ⑩ L all wk 12-2 D all wk 6-9 **Rooms:** 34 (7 GF) **S** £118-£191 **D** £145-£234
Facilities: Parking Garden Wi-fi **Notes:** ⊕ FREE HOUSE ⑪ ⟲ ⚑ 16

The late Paul Whittome's 17th-century coaching inn is very much the social hub of Burnham Market, famed for its fabulous shops and galleries. The traditional front bar, with its log fire and great atmosphere, is popular with locals and visitors alike. The stylish eating areas include a panelled dining room, a conservatory, and the canopied Moroccan Garden. The chefs pride themselves on serving imaginative food, and source local and seasonal ingredients. The 35 bedrooms are individually styled.

Recommended in the area

Titchwell Bird Reserve; Holkham Hall; The Sandringham Estate

The Lord Nelson

Address: Walsingham Road, BURNHAM THORPE,
King's Lynn, PE31 8HN
Tel/Fax: 01328 738241
Email: simon@nelsonslocal.co.uk
Website: www.nelsonslocal.co.uk
Map ref: 4 TF84
Directions: B1355 (Burnham Market to Fakenham road), 1.75m from Burnham Market. Pub near church
Open: noon-3 6-11 (Jul-Aug noon-11pm)
Closed: Mon eve (ex school hols) ⓑ ⑩ L all wk 12-2.30 D Tue-Sun 6-9 **Facilities:** Parking Garden Wi-fi **Notes:** ⊕ GREENE KING ⑪ ⟲ ⚑ 14

Dating back 400 years, this pub is in the village where Lord Nelson was born, and the great Admiral used to eat and drink here, hosting a farewell meal for the whole village here in 1793. There is no bar — all drinks are served from the tap room, and the pub is famous for its real ales, direct from the cask. It also has a popular menu of freshly prepared food. Outside, the massive garden has seating, a barbecue, and wooden play equipment. Dogs are allowed, except in the restaurant.

Recommended in the area

Holkham Hall; Titchwell Nature Reserve; Sandringham House

Chequers Inn

Address: Griston Road, THOMPSON,
Thetford, IP24 1PX
Tel: 01953 483360 **Fax:** 01953 488092
Email: richard@thompsonchequers.co.uk
Website: www.thompsonchequers.co.uk
Map ref: 4 TL99
Directions: Between Watton & Thetford off A1075
Open: all week 11.30-3 6.30-11 ⅃ ⅃◎⅃ **L** all wk
12-2 **D** all wk 6.30-9 **Rooms:** 3 en suite (3 GF)
S £45 **D** £65 **Facilities:** Parking Garden
Notes: ⊕ FREE HOUSE ⅃⅃ ⅃ ⅃ 8

With its low-slung thatched roof, and hidden among the trees in the heart of Breckland, this 17th-century free house was where manor courts, dealing with rents, land lettings and small crimes were once held. Original features include exposed beams and timbers and old farming implements hang from the walls. It's all very unpretentious, which means that there's something for everyone, including light bites in the bar, and a lunchtime menu offering a 2 course set lunch for £6.95, as well as traditional fayre such as deep-fried breaded scampi, burgers and steak and kidney pudding. In the evening the menu stays along the traditional line, with old favourites like grilled rump, sirloin and gammon steaks. There is an extensive specials board where fresh fish dishes such as baked whole sea bream and freshly prepared game dishes (when in season) such as venison medallions and pigeon breast can be found. Dogs are welcome in the large rear beer garden, where there are also picnic tables. Purpose-built guest accommodation offers everything for the modern traveller. Nearby is the eight-mile Pingo Trail, host to glacially formed swamping depressions in the ground and the Peddars Way footpath where many uncommon and protected wildlife live.

Recommended in the area

Thompson Water; Peddars Way; Thetford Forest

Wiveton Bell

Address: Blakeney Road, WIVETON, Holt, NR25 7TL
Tel: 01263 740101
Email: enquiries@wivetonbell.co.uk
Website: www.wivetonbell.com
Map ref: 4 TG04
Directions: 1m from Blakeney. Wiveton Rd off A149
Open: all day all week **Closed:** 25 Dec ⊨ ⅠⓄⅠ L all
wk 12-2.15 **D** all wk 6-9 **Facilities:** Parking Garden
Wi-fi **Notes:** ⊕ FREE HOUSE ⦁⦁ ⅋ ♛ 17

This pretty, 17th-century inn overlooks the village green just a mile from Blakeney on Norfolk's beautiful north coast. Inside, an inglenook fireplace, settles, scrubbed wooden tables and oil paintings create a relaxed atmosphere where customers are just as likely to be walkers with muddy boots (and muddy dogs) as members of the area's business community. The award-winning restaurant is strong on local produce such as mussels, crabs, oysters and lobster, as well as game from the Holkham Hall Estate. Other dishes might include slow-roast Norfolk pork belly or braised oxtail with venison faggots. At lunchtime, lighter dishes are on offer, including chicken and bacon bruschetta, omelette Arnold Bennett, or a fine steak sandwich. Some of the Norfolk beers come from neighbouring brewery Yetmans, whose owner regards the Bell as his brewery taproom. In summer, the sheltered gardens, with their fine views of the village church and countryside, come into their own. Nice touches are the wind-up torches and umbrellas left in the bus shelter on the green for customers to use on the way to and from their cars. For those who wish to stay in the area, the Bell has four well-equipped rooms and a tastefully restored fisherman's cottage.

Recommended in the area

Holkham Beach; seal-watching trips to Blakeney Point; Wells Beach

St Mary and All Saints Collegiate Church by the River Nene, Fotheringhay

George and Dragon

Address: Silver St, CHACOMBE,
nr Banbury, OX17 2JR
Tel: 01295 711500 **Fax:** 01295 710516
Email: georgeanddragonchacombe@
googlemail.com
Map ref: 3 SP44 **Directions:** M40 junct 11, A361
(Daventry road). Chacombe 1st right **Open:** all day
all week noon-11 🍴 🍽 Mon-Thu 12-9, Fri-Sat
12-9.30, Sun 12-7 **Facilities:** Parking Garden Wi-fi
Notes: ⊕ EVERARDS ♦♦

On the edge of a peaceful and picturesque village, this 17th-century stone pub features a copper-topped bar, low beams, wooden chairs and settees, stone-flagged floor, wood-burning stoves, sun terrace and a well. Freshly prepared food served from a seasonal menu throughout the day, every day, is listed on blackboards and includes a range of starters and light mains — examples are corned beef hash cakes; bangers and mash; braised pork belly; seared duck breast; smoked haddock rarebit; and spaghetti carbonara.

Recommended in the area

Sulgrave Manor; Silverstone Circuit; Broughton Castle

The Falcon Inn

◉

Address: FOTHERINGHAY, Nr Oundle, PE8 5HZ
Tel: 01832 226254 **Fax:** 01832 226046
Email: info@thefalcon-inn.co.uk
Website: www.thefalcon-inn.co.uk
Map ref: 3 TL09
Directions: N of A605 between Peterborough
& Oundle **Open:** all day all week noon-11
🍴 🍽 L Mon-Sat 12-2.15, Sun 12-3 D Mon-Sat
6.15-9.15, Sun 6.15-8.30 **Facilities:** Parking
Garden Wi-fi **Notes:** ⊕ FREE HOUSE ♦♦ 🐾 🍷 14

Mary, Queen of Scots, ended her days in this pretty, stone-built village, home of this highly regarded, award-winning dining pub. With a warm welcome and friendly service, the inn's great character stems partly from the beautiful, peaceful garden and the conservatory restaurant overlooking the splendid church. The two bars offer real ales and warming log fires in winter. Traditional, wholesome bar food and the frequently-changing impressive à la carte European menu rely extensively on local produce.

Recommended in the area

Fotheringhay Castle; Burghley House; Nene Valley railway

The Red Lion

Address: 43 Welland Rise, SIBBERTOFT, Nr Market Harborough, Leicester, LE16 9UD
Tel: 01858 880011
Email: andrew@redlionwinepub.co.uk
Website: www.redlionwinepub.co.uk
Map ref: 3 SP68
Directions: From Market Harborough take A4304, through Lubenham, left through Marston Trussell to Sibbertoft
Open: noon-2 6.30-11 **Closed:** Mon & Tue L, Sun eve 🍴 L Wed-Sun 12-2 **D** Mon-Sat 6.30-9.30 🍴 L Wed-Sun 12-2 **D** Mon-Sat 6.30-9.30
Facilities: Parking Garden Wi-fi **Notes:** 🍺 FREE HOUSE ♦♦ 🍷 20

Wine is the special passion of owner Andrew Banks at this friendly 300-year-old free house. Over 200 bins appear on the ever-growing wine list, and twenty are served by the glass. Additionally all the wines can be bought at take-home prices – so having tasted a wine you can avoid the guesswork in a supermarket. When choosing a wine for dinner, allow time to absorb the useful guidelines on twinning food types with grape varieties; you'll also enjoy the humorous quotations, which reveal truths every wine lover will recognise. "The list is my passion and I will always be around to discuss it with you," says Andrew. He is also developing fun and informative dinners during which his customers can listen to wine makers and suppliers. The pub offers an appealing blend of contemporary and classic décor, with oak beams, leather upholstery and a smartly turned-out dining room. In fine weather, meals are served in the quiet garden, which is a favourite with local walkers and cyclists; there's also an outdoor play area for children. The same monthly-changing menu is served in all the pub's eating areas; local and seasonal produce is used wherever possible, including meat from nearby farms.
Recommended in the area
Coton Manor; Mallory Park; Rutland Water

The Crown

Address: Helmdon Road, WESTON, nr Towcester, NN12 8PX
Tel/Fax: 01295 760310
Email: info@thecrownweston.co.uk
Website: www.thecrownweston.co.uk
Map ref: 3 SP54
Directions: Accessed from A43 or B4525
Open: all week 6-11.30 (Fri-Sat noon-3.30 6-11.30 Sun noon-
3.30 7-11) **Closed:** 25 Dec 🍺 🍴 **L** Fri-Sun 12-2.30 **D** Tue-Sat
6-9.30 **Facilities:** Parking Garden **Notes:** ⊕ FREE HOUSE 👫 🐕

This is a place that's oozing with history: a hostelry since the
reign of Elizabeth I, the first documented evidence of The Crown
pins the year down to 1593 and the first recorded owner was All
Souls College, Oxford. Current owner Robert Grover has more recently completed a refurbishment of
the building and brought renown to the pub for its excellent food, all prepared from fresh ingredients.
A typical menu might start with goats' cheese and sun-dried tomato tart; or moules marinière and
French bread. Mains range from the simple Charolais minute steak and caramelised onion baguette; or
shepherd's pie with steamed vegetables; to lamb casserole with mint and apricots, vegetables and herb
mash; wild mushroom risotto; or breast of duck with potato, Savoy cabbage, bacon rösti and kumquat
sauce. Desserts take in a selection of ice creams and sorbets, as well as raspberry crème brûlée;
lemon curd and ginger sponge pudding; and spiced apple pie with custard. A 45-bin wine list has been
carefully selected to complement the food, and beer drinkers are rewarded with Greene King IPA, Hook
Norton Best, Black Sheep, Landlord and other fine ales.
Recommended in the area
Sulgrave Manor; Silverstone; Canons Ashby House (NT)

The Wollaston Inn

Address: 87 London Road,
WOLLASTON, NN29 7QS
Tel: 01933 663161
Email: info@wollaston-inn.co.uk
Website: www.wollaston-inn.co.uk
Map ref: 3 SP96
Directions: From Wellingborough, onto A509 towards Wollaston. After 2m, over rdbt, then immediately left. Inn at top of hill
Open: all day all week ⓑ ⓞ food served all day
Facilities: Parking Garden **Notes:** ⊕ FREE HOUSE ♟ 12

Chris Spencer took over this historical pub, once the Sunday night venue of the late DJ John Peel, in 2003, reinventing it as a restaurant within a pub and giving it a new name. His loving restoration of the 350-year-old building's original features sits comfortably with the Italian leather sofas and casual tables and chairs. A commitment to please both formal and casual diners is reflected in the reasonably priced set lunch menus (available until 7pm), and an evening carte of seasonal dishes, with everything from the bread and infused oils to the ice creams and dark chocolate truffles made in the kitchen. Daily changing selections, with ingredients coming from regional suppliers, might include venison haunch steak; Thai red chicken curry; slow roasted pork belly with pancetta and cannellini bean cassoulet; and Mediterranean vegetable and buffalo mozzarella stack. There are lots of fresh fish and seafood too, such as lobster and monkfish thermidor; baked mackerel, sunblush tomato and courgette risotto; and organic sustainable cod, braised oxtail and caramelised apple. The traditional Sunday roast is very popular. Service is attentive wherever you eat – choose from the bar, restaurant, patio or garden – and there is a good selection of real ales and an extensive wine list.

Recommended in the area

Summer Leys Nature Reserve; Santa Pod Raceway; Silverstone

Allendale

The Pheasant Inn

★★★★ INN

Address: Stannersburn, FALSTONE, NE48 1DD
Tel/Fax: 01434 240382
Email: enquiries@thepheasantinn.com
Website: www.thepheasantinn.com
Map ref: 6 NY78
Directions: A69, B6079, B6320, follow signs for Kielder Water
Open: 12-3 6.30-11 **Closed:** 25-27 Dec, Mon-Tue (Nov-Mar) ⅃ L Mon-Sat noon-2.30 ⍔ L Mon-Sat 12-2.30 **D** Mon-Sat 6.30-8.30 **Rooms:** 8 en suite (5 GF) S £50-£55 D £90-£95
Facilities: Parking Garden **Notes:** ⊕ FREE HOUSE ⅋ ⅋

Set close by the magnificent Kielder Water, this classic country inn, built in 1624, has exposed stone walls, original beams, low ceilings, open fires and a display of old farm implements in the bar. Run by the welcoming Kershaw family since 1985, the inn was originally a farmhouse and has been refurbished to a very high standard. The bright, modern en suite bedrooms, some with their own entrances, are all contained in stone buildings adjoining the inn and are set round a pretty courtyard. All the rooms, including one family room, are spotless, well equipped, and have tea- and coffee-making facilities, hairdryer, TV and radio alarm clock; all enjoy delightful country views. Delicious home-cooked breakfasts and evening meals are served in the bar or in the attractive dining room, or may be taken in the pretty garden courtyard if the weather permits. Irene and her son Robin are responsible for the traditional home cooking using local produce and featuring delights such as game pie and roast Northumbrian lamb, as well as imaginative vegetarian choices. Drying and laundry facilities are available and, for energetic guests, cycle hire can be arranged.

Recommended in the area

Hadrian's Wall; Scottish Borders; Northumbrian castles and stately homes

Battlesteads Hotel & Restaurant

Address: Wark, HEXHAM, NE48 3LS
Tel: 01434 230209
Fax: 01434 230039
Email: info@battlesteads.com
Website: www.battlesteads.com
Map ref: 7 NY96
Directions: 10m N of Hexham on B6320 (Kielder road)
Open: all day all week 🛏 🍽 **L** all wk 12-3 **D** all wk 6.30-9.30 **Facilities:** Parking Garden Wi-fi
Notes: ⊕ FREE HOUSE 👪 🐕

Originally built in 1747, this traditional award-winning Northumbrian inn and restaurant features a cosy bar with wood-burning stove, sunny conservatory and secret walled garden, excellent bar meals and à la carte menus (including vegetarian) using fresh, local produce, plus a choice of 20 wines (including a range of organic and bio-dynamic wines) and five cask ales. Taken over some six years ago by Richard and Dee Slade, Battlesteads has quickly gained a reputation for its character and warm welcome as a friendly, family run establishment. Chefs source the best of local ingredients (from within a 25 mile radius) to ensure freshness and flavour – including top quality Northumbrian lamb, beef and seasonal game. Fish and seafood is sourced from North Shields Fish Quay, and smoked fish and game from Bywell Smokery. Fresh vegetables and herbs are grown in the hotel garden, and vegetarian choices are always offered. Locally reared beef, lamb and pork are available at the popular Sunday lunch carvery, and all at set prices. Leave room for desserts like sticky toffee pudding or the award-winning whisky and marmalade bread and butter pudding. Battlesteads has 17 en suite rooms.

Recommended in the Area

Hadrian's Wall; Kielder Forest and Lake; Alnwick Castle

The Anglers Arms

Address: Weldon Bridge, LONGFRAMLINGTON,
Morpeth, NE65 8AX
Tel: 01665 570271 & 570655
Email: johnyoung@anglersarms.fsnet.co.uk
Website: www.anglersarms.com
Map ref: 10 NU10
Directions: From N, 9m S of Alnwick right
Weldon Bridge sign. From S, A1 to by-pass Morpeth,
left onto A697 for Wooler & Coldstream. 7m, left to
Weldon Bridge
Open: all day all week 11-11 (Sun 12-10.30) 🍽 food served all day **Facilities:** Parking Garden
Notes: ⊕ FREE HOUSE ♦♦

A 1760s coaching inn, now traditional pub and restaurant, overlooking the picturesque Weldon Bridge across the River Coquet. Your hosts here are John and Julie Young, who have created a bar that derives some of its warmth and friendliness from a collection of nice little touches - ornaments, antiques, quaint pieces of bric-a-brac, including some interesting hand-painted wall tiles, and fishing memorabilia. Meals in here are typified by mixed grill; home-made steak and ale pie; grilled salmon; oriental sizzling platter; and vegetable stew. As an unusual experience, dine in style in the Pullman railway carriage, where your choice might be a starter of garlic king prawns; scallop and bacon salad; or twice-cooked belly pork with honey-spiced apples, followed by a main course of tournedos Flodden, a prime fillet stuffed with Applewood cheese in bacon with garlic sauce; Borders rack of lamb; pan-fried breast of duck with honey-roasted parsnips, sweet potatoes and Cumberland glaze; or oven-baked peppers. Lighter meals include sandwiches and fresh garden leaf salads. The desserts board changes daily. Children will probably head outside for the playground.

Recommended in the Area
Bamburgh Castle; Brinkburn Priory; Hadrian's Wall

Statue of Robin Hood and Little John, Sherwood Forest Visitor Centre

The Martin's Arms

Address: School Lane,
COLSTON BASSETT, NG12 3FD
Tel: 01949 81361
Fax: 01949 81039
Email: martins_arms@hotmail.co.uk
Website: www.themartinsarmsinn.co.uk
Map ref: 8 SK73
Directions: Off A46 between Leicester & Newark
Open: all week noon-3.30 6-11
Closed: 25 Dec eve ⓑ L Mon-Sat 12-2, Sun 12-

2.30 D Mon-Sat 7-9.30 ⓘ L all wk 12-2 D Mon-Sat 7-9.30 **Facilities:** Parking Garden **Notes:** ⓲

So popular is this award-winning inn that it has made appearances on both regional and national television. It is a listed 18th-century building, set close to the old market cross in this stunning village in the Vale of Belvoir, an area that is renowned for its Stilton cheese. The interior has a real country house feel to it, with period furnishings, traditional hunting prints and seasonal fires in the Jacobean fireplace. Outside there is an acre of landscaped grounds, which includes a herb garden and well established lawns, backing on to National Trust land. The inn is a free house, serving a good range of real ales – Marston's Pedigree, Interbrew Bass, Greene King Abbot Ale, Timothy Taylor Landlord – from hand pumps. The wine list also offers seven wines by the glass. Good regional ingredients are a feature of the menu. Take, for example, the classic ploughman's lunch comprising Melton Mowbray pork pie, Colston Bassett Stilton or Cheddar, home-cured ham, pickles and bread. Alternatives in the bar include game pie, or fresh gnocchi with oven roasted tomatoes, peppers, spinach and parmesan cream. Typical restaurant dishes are cod fillet with lobster ravioli, potato rösti and creamed leek sauce; and bacon-wrapped rump of lamb with potato fondant and Puy lentils. Dogs are allowed in the garden only.

Recommended in the area

Belvoir Castle; Belton House; The National Water Sports Centre at Holme Pierrepoint

Blenheim Palace, Woodstock

The Vines

Address: Burford Road, Bampton,
BLACK BOURTON, OX18 2PF
Tel: 01993 843559 **Fax:** 01993 840080
Email: info@vineshotel.com
Website: www.vinesblackbourton.co.uk
Map ref: 3 SP20
Directions: From A40 Witney, take A4095 to
Faringdon, then 1st right after Bampton to Black
Bourton **Open:** all week Mon-Fri eve only (Sat-Sun L
& D) **Closed:** Mon-Fri L ⓑ ⓘⓞⓘ L Sat-Sun 12-2
D Mon-Sat 6-9 Sun 7-9 **Facilities:** Parking Garden Wi-fi **Notes:** ⓦ FREE HOUSE ⓘ

Situated in a picturesque village setting, The Vines is a traditional stone-built inn with an elegant, contemporary feel and surrounded by delightful gardens. The restaurant and bar were designed by the BBC *Real Rooms* team. Food is offered from the carte menu, with dishes prepared from fresh local produce, especially fish. An alternative venue for a drink or a snack is the comfortable lounge with its leather sofas and cosy winter fire. On sunny days dine on the patio or play a game of Aunt Sally.

Recommended in the area

Cogges Manor Farm Museum; Cotswold Wildlife Park; Blenheim Palace

High Street at Burford

The Lamb Inn

★★★ 83% ◉◉ SMALL HOTEL
Address: Sheep Street, BURFORD, OX18 4LR
Tel: 01993 823155
Fax: 01993 822228
Email: info@lambinn-burford.co.uk
Website: www.cotswold-inns-hotels.co.uk/lamb
Map ref: 3 SP21
Directions: M40 junct 8, follow A40 & Burford signs,
1st turn, down hill into Sheep St
Open: all day all week ⓑ ⓘ L all wk 12-2.30 D all
wk 7-9.30 **Rooms:** 17 (4 GF) D £150-£175 **Facilities:** Garden Wi-fi
Notes: ⊕ FREE HOUSE ⓘⓘ ⓘ

This ancient inn dates back to 1420 and was originally built as weavers' cottages. In complete harmony
with its lovely setting in the Cotswolds, it really does deserve the description of 'charming old inn'.
From the wisteria-clad walls to the stone-flagged bar, from the delightful dining room to the beautifully
refurbished bedrooms, The Lamb has been sympathetically restored to offer all the comfort of today
while retaining the atmosphere of yesteryear. With its stone floor, log fire and fine selection of wines
and traditional English real ales, the welcoming bar draws in guests and locals alike and is a favourite
spot to exchange news and views. There is an extensive menu if you should wish to lunch or dine in
these relaxed surroundings. The finest fresh ingredients, many produced locally, are used to create
a cuisine that is contemporary English with strong traditional influences. A daily fish board is also
available. Alternatively enjoy a drink or lunch in the walled patio garden, a veritable sun-trap which
leads down to a beautiful traditional English cottage garden, a lovely area in which to relax, read or take
an afternoon nap.

Recommended in the area

Blenheim Palace; Cotswold Wildlife Park; Burford Garden Company

The Red Lion Inn

Address: The High Street, CHALGROVE, OX44 7SS
Tel: 01865 890625
Email: raymondsexton@btinternet.com
Website: www.redlionchalgrove.co.uk
Map ref: 3 SU69
Directions: B480 from Oxford ring road, through
Stadhampton, left then right at mini-rdbt.
At Chalgrove Airfield right into village **Open:** all week
11.30-3 6-mdnt (Sat 11.30-3 6-1am Sat 11.30am-
1am Sun 11.30am-mdnt in summer) 🛏 🍽 L Mon-

Sat 12-2, Sun 12-3 **D** Mon-Sat 6-9 **Facilities:** Garden **Notes:** ⊕ FREE HOUSE ⁛ 🐾

Rather unusually, the local parish church owns the 15th-century Red Lion. How appropriate then,
that the surname of the landlords and chefs, Suzanne and Raymond, is Sexton. Food is served in the
bar, restaurant and front or back garden from 'a menu that tries to please everyone'. Starters include
spicy lamb samosas with mixed leaf salad, with main courses such as braised shank of lamb with root
vegetables, and pan-fried fillet of halibut on risotto rice with chorizo and baby peas.
Recommended in the area
City of Oxford; Courthouse, Ridgeway Path; Long Crendon (NT)

The Sir Charles Napier

◉◉

Address: Spriggs Alley, CHINNOR, OX39 4BX
Tel: 01494 483011 **Fax:** 01494 485311
Website: www.sircharlesnapier.co.uk
Map ref: 3 SP70
Directions: M40 junct 6 to Chinnor. Turn right at
rdbt, up hill to Spriggs Alley
Open: noon-4 6-mdnt (Sun noon-6) **Closed:** 25-26
Dec, Mon, Sun eve 🛏 L Tue-Fri 12-2.30 D Tue-Fri
6.30-9 🍽 L Tue-Sat 12-2.30, Sun 12-3.30 D Tue-
Sat 6.30-10 **Facilities:** Parking Garden **Notes:** ⊕ FREE HOUSE ⁛ 🐾 ⚲ 12

The Sir Charles Napier is in the scenic Chiltern Hills surrounded by beech woods and fields. The
furnishings are eclectic, and wonderful sculptures are exhibited throughout the year. In summer, lunch
is served on the terrace beneath vines and wisteria, overlooking the herb gardens and lawns. The wine
list complements blackboard dishes and imaginative seasonal menus. Typical dishes are halibut with
pea purée, and sea bream with saffron and crayfish tails.
Recommended in the area
The Chiltern Hills; West Wycombe Park; Garsington Opera

Coach & Horses Inn

★★★ ⇔ INN

Address: Watlington Road,
CHISELHAMPTON, OX44 7UX
Tel: 01865 890255 Fax: 01865 891995
Email: enquiries@coachhorsesinn.co.uk
Website: www.coachhorsesinn.co.uk
Map ref: 3 SU59
Directions: From Oxford on B480 towards
Watlington, 5m Open: all day all week ⓑ L Mon-Sat
12-2 ⓘ L all wk 12-2 D Mon-Sat 7-9.30 Rooms: 9
en suite Facilities: Parking Garden Wi-fi Notes: ⊕ FREE HOUSE ⓣ 10

A charming, family-run 16th-century inn, just 200 yards from the River Thame. When it's chilly someone lights the huge log fire in the bar, while in the summer it's hard to beat the courtyard or lawn for a pleasant drink. You may eat outside, or in the oak-beamed, candlelit restaurant, from a seasonal menu featuring Angus steaks, game and fresh seafood, while at lunchtimes bar meals and snacks are available. The bedrooms are ranged around the courtyard, with most looking out over the countryside.
Recommended in the area
City of Oxford; Ridgeway Path; Hughenden Manor

The Trout at Tadpole Bridge

★★★★ ⇔ INN

Address: Buckland Marsh, FARINGDON, SN7 8RF
Tel: 01367 870382
Email: info@troutinn.co.uk
Website: www.troutinn.co.uk
Map ref: 3 SU29 Directions: From A420
(between Oxford & Swindon) take A417 into
Faringdon, onto A4095 signed Bampton, pub approx
2m Open: 11.30-3 6-11 Closed: 25-26 Dec, Sun eve
(Nov-Apr) ⓑ ⓘ L all wk 12-2 D 7-9 Rooms: 6 en
suite S £80-£100 D £120-£150 Facilities: Parking Garden Wi-fi Notes: ⊕ FREE HOUSE ⓣ♦ ⟟ ⓣ 12

Right by the Thames Path, with six bedrooms and berthing for six boats, the historic Trout is a destination in its own right, as so many drinkers, diners and overnight guests would undoubtedly testify. Standing proud among its many awards - AA Pub of the Year for England 2009/2010. The kitchen makes expert use of the best ingredients and from a recent menu come Cornish crab, avocado and home-cured gravadlax with toasted brioche, or free-range Great Farm guinea fowl cooked three ways.
Recommended in the area
Kelmscott Manor; Badbury Hill; Kingston Lisle Park

All Souls College from St Mary's Tower, Oxford

Miller of Mansfield

★★★★★ ◉ RESTAURANT WITH ROOMS

Address: High Street, GORING on Thames,
nr Reading, RG8 9AW
Tel: 01491 872829 **Fax:** 01491 873100
Email: reservations@millerofmansfield.com
Website: www.millerofmansfield.com
Map ref: 3 SU68
Directions: From Pangbourne take A329 to
Streatley. Right on B4009, 0.5m to Goring **Open:** all
day all week 8am-11pm ⬛ all wk 12-10 ᵀᴼ᷄ **L** all wk
12-4.30 **D** all wk 6.30-10 **Rooms:** 13 en suite **Facilities:** Parking Garden **Notes:** ⊞ FREE HOUSE ⁍⁍ ⚡

Standing in a quiet Thames-side village and overlooking beautiful countryside is this renovated inn. Its
unusual name is said to come from an old ballad about a miller who offered venison he had unlawfully
shot to Henry II, who in return knighted him. Enjoy impressive Modern British and European cooking
in the bar, restaurant or terrace garden. Produce is sourced locally, to both minimise food miles and
support the community. Sumptuous bedrooms are individually styled.
Recommended in the area
Basildon House (NT); The Ridgeway Path; Beale Park

The Five Horseshoes

Address: Maidensgrove,
HENLEY-ON-THAMES, RG9 6EX
Tel: 01491 641282
Fax: 01491 641086
Email: admin@thefivehorseshoes.co.uk
Website: www.thefivehorseshoes.co.uk
Map ref: 3 SU78
Directions: From Henley-on-Thames take A4130,
in 1m take B480 to right, signed Stonor. In Stonor
left, through woods, over common, pub on left

Open: all week noon-3.30 6-11 (Sat noon-11 Sun noon-6) ⬛ ᵀᴼ᷄ **L** Mon-Fri 12-2.30, Sat 12-3,
Sun 12-4 **D** Mon-Sat 6.30-9.30 **Facilities:** Parking Garden **Notes:** ⊞ BRAKSPEAR ⁍⁍ ⚡

The Five Horseshoes is in an Area of Outstanding Natural Beauty with amazing views over the Chilterns.
This 17th-century pub exudes old world character with its wooden beams and open fires; there are two
snug bar areas and a large restaurant. Dishes, created from locally sourced produce, include game
terrine with fig chutney, roasted crayfish, haunch of wild Oxfordshire venison or home-made pork pie.
Recommended in the area
River & Rowing Museum; Mapledurham House & Watermill; Warburg Nature Reserve

The Baskerville

★★★★ INN

Address: Station Road, LOWER SHIPLAKE,
Henley-on-Thames, RG9 3NY
Tel: 0118 940 3332
Email: enquiries@thebaskerville.com
Website: www.thebaskerville.com
Map ref: 3 SU77 **Directions:** Just off A4155, 1.5m from
Henley **Open:** all week 11.30-2.30 6-11, Sun 12-4.30 7-10.30
Closed: 1 Jan 🍴 🍽 **L** Mon-Fri 12-2, Sat 12-2.30,
Sun 12-3.30 **D** Mon-Thu 7-9.30, Fri-Sat 7-10
Rooms: 4 **S** £75 **D** £85 **Facilities:** Parking Garden Wi-fi
Notes: ⊕ ENTERPRISE INNS ♦♦ ⌘ ♟ 12

It's said that Arthur Conan Doyle was inspired to write *The Hound of the Baskervilles* by the menacing stone dogs' heads on the gates at nearby Crowsley Park, where real Baskervilles once lived. Be that as it may, there's nothing to disconcert visitors to this welcoming gastro-pub 200 metres from the River Thames. With a modern-rustic interior, it also has an attractive 100-seat garden where barbecues are held in summer. Seasonal, well-balanced menus feature British cuisine with European and Far-Eastern influences, a principle that declares its hand through dishes such as crispy baby squid with aromatic Asian salad and honey, lemon and chilli dressing; hazelnut-crumbed French goat's cheese with lemon and beetroot salad; salt beef with horseradish mash, watercress cream sauce, whisky- and honey-glazed carrots and curly kale; rich chicken liver and Cointreau parfait with toasted bread, kumquat chutney and dressed leaves; and a Shiplake butcher's beef, pork and chilli sausages with bubble and squeak cake. The Regatta Room, a private dining area for up to 12, is named for the Henley Regatta, a popular event that makes booking a table and staying overnight in the superb accommodation essential.

Recommended in the area

Cliveden (NT); Stonor Park; Henley-on-Thames

The Black Boy Inn

Address: MILTON, Banbury, OX15 4HH
Tel: 01295 722111
Fax: 01295 722978
Email: info@blackboyinn.com
Website: www.blackboyinn.com
Map ref: 3 SP43
Directions: From Banbury take A4260 to Adderbury. After Adderbury turn right signed Bloxham. Onto Milton Road to Milton. Pub on right
Open: all week 12-3 5.30-11.30 (Sat-Sun noon-11.30) 🍺 🍽 L Mon-Sat 12-2.30, Sun 12-3 D Mon-Sat 6.30-11 Facilities: Parking Garden
Notes: ⊕ FREE HOUSE ♨ ➳ ♇ 8

Although this 16th-century coaching inn has been completely refurbished, its stylish interior and solid pine furniture are entirely in keeping with such an old building. Located in picturesque Milton, the pub is thought to take its name from the dark-skinned Charles II, although other theories point to the slave trade. The long room has a real wood stove at one end and a comfortable dining room at the other; in between is the bar, with conservatory-style dining. Outside there is plenty of seating on the patio and in the garden, the latter providing a half-acre of space for children to run around. A rotating list of guest ales and a selection of wines by the glass ensure that drinkers can enjoy the informal atmosphere of this quintessentially English inn. Food is important here, with modern British dishes based on fresh seasonal ingredients at sensible prices. There are plenty of pub classics, including beer-battered cod and home-made chips with crushed peas, as well as up-market mains such as roasted fillet of sea trout with crab tagliatelle and fennel. Excellent desserts, vegetarian options and a wide range of fresh salads and tempting sandwiches are also on offer.

Recommended in the area

Broughton Castle; Blenheim Palace; Waterperry Gardens

The Anchor

Address: 2 Hayfield Road, Walton Manor,
OXFORD, OX2 6TT
Tel: 01865 510282
Email: theanchorinfo@gmail.com
Website: www.theanchoroxford.com
Map ref: 3 SP50
Directions: A34 (Oxford ring road N), exit Peartree rdbt, 1.5m down Woodstock Rd then right at Polstead Rd, follow road to bottom, pub on right **Open:** all day all week **Closed:** 25 & 26 Dec ⓑ ⓘ L all wk 12-2.30 D Mon-Sat 6-9.30 (Sun 6.30-8.30) **Facilities:** Parking Garden Wi-fi **Notes:** ⊕ WADWORTH ⚤ 🐕

Strikingly Art Deco, a true local in well-heeled North Oxford. Its relaxed atmosphere is perfect for making the most of the great seasonal food from the kitchen of Jamie King, whose team delivers steak and kidney pudding; smoked haddock fishcakes with ginger lime mayo; and duck confit with creamed haricot beans. Daily specials are a treat, especially the fresh fish, winter game and goose at Christmas. Real ales, log fires, quiz nights, board games, coffee mornings and a monthly book club all contribute to The Anchor's success.
Recommended in the area
Ashmoleon Museum; Blenheim Palace; Bicester Village

Broughton Castle, Banbury

The Crown Inn

Address: PISHILL, Henley-on-Thames, RG9 6HH
Tel: 01491 638364
Email: enquiries@thecrowninnpishill.co.uk
Website: www.thecrowninnpishill.co.uk
Map ref: 3 SU78
Directions: On B480 off A4130, 8m NW of Henley-on-Thames
Open: all week 11.30-3 6-11 (Sun noon-3 7-10)
Closed: 25-26 Dec ⓮ ⓙ **L** all wk 12-2.30
D all wk 7-9.30 **Facilities:** Parking Garden
Notes: ⊕ FREE HOUSE ⅰⅰ ⅰ

A pretty 15th-century brick and flint former coaching inn, The Crown has enjoyed a colourful history. It began life in medieval times, serving ale to members of the thriving monastic community, then in later years, served as a refuge for Catholic priests escaping Henry VIII's draconian rule. It contains possibly the largest priest hole in the country, complete with a sad story about one Father Dominique, who met his end there. Moving forward to the swinging 60s, the thatched barn housed a nightclub hosting the likes of George Harrison and Dusty Springfield. Nowadays, the barn is licensed for civil ceremonies as well as serving as a function room. In the pub itself, the bar is supplied by mostly local breweries, including Marlow, and the menu changes frequently and features local produce cooked fresh to order. Lunch and dinner are served every day and can be enjoyed inside the pub with its three log fires or in the picturesque garden overlooking the valley, depending on the season. Bed and breakfast accommodation is available. The name of the village is often a subject of conversation, some say it was to do with wagon horses relieving themselves once they had got to the top the hill or maybe simply because peas used to be grown around here!

Recommended in the area

Stonor Park; Greys Court, (NT); River and Rowing Museum

The Royal Oak

Address: High Street, RAMSDEN, OX7 3AU
Tel: 01993 868213
Fax: 01993 868864
Website: www.royaloakramsden.com
Map ref: 3 SP31
Directions: From Witney take B4022 towards
Charlbury, then right before Hailey, through
Poffley End
Open: all week 11.30-3 6.30-11 (Sun 12-3
7-10.30) **Closed:** 25 Dec ⌷ ⍟ **L** all wk 11.30-2
D all wk 7-10 **Facilities:** Parking Garden **Notes:** ⊕ FREE HOUSE ⌀ ⍗ 30

Once upon a time, stagecoaches between London and Hereford stopped at this 17th-century inn
standing opposite the church in the pretty Cotswold village of Ramsden. These days it is popular with
walkers exploring the lovely countryside, but whether you feel like walking or not, stop here for its
old beams, warm fires, stone walls and, of course, refreshment. As a free house it offers beers for
which real ale aficionados would willingly join the rambling fraternity, while the 200-bin wine list would
particularly appeal to those appreciating their Bordeaux, with many of them available by the glass.
The bar menu regularly features a pie of the week, and there are also favourites such as real Italian
meatballs; home-made beef burgers; and wild mushroom pasta with shiitake and porcini mushrooms.
The main menu features the very best of fresh, local, seasonal food, with regular fish deliveries. To start
your meal, expect moules marinière (with Hebridean mussels); chicken liver parfait with cognac and
raisins; and baked avocado, cheese and prawn gratin. Main courses include smoked haddock cooked
with whisky, cream and cheese; confit of duck leg with quince sauce and Puy lentils; and pan-fried
calf's liver with wild mushroom sauce.

Recommended in the area

Blenheim Palace; Minster Lovell Hall; Rollright Stones

The Mason's Arms

Address: Banbury Road, SWERFORD,
Chipping Norton, OX7 4AP
Tel: 01608 683212 **Fax:** 01608 683105
Email: admin@masons-arms.com
Website: www.masons-arms.com
Map ref: 3 SP33
Directions: Between Banbury & Chipping Norton on
A361 **Open:** all week 10-3 6-11 **Closed:** 25-26 Dec
L Mon-Sat 12-2 D Mon-Sat 7-9 L Mon-Sat
12-2, Sun 12-3.30 D all wk 7-9 **Facilities:** Parking Garden Wi-fi **Notes:** ⊕ FREE HOUSE ♦♦ ☂ 20

This charming free house offers a great combination of delicious food enjoyed in a fun atmosphere
with stylish interior. Over the years it has gained numerous awards, including an AA Rosette, and offers
enticing dishes made using fresh, locally sourced produce and rare breed meat. The kitchen has its own
pastry chef, and the home-made breads, puddings and chocolates are irresistible. The pub is easy to
find with a large car park and spacious garden with panoramic views overlooking the Cotswold Valley.
Recommended in the area
Burford Wildlife Park; Hook Norton Brewery and Pottery; Wiggington Waterfowl Sanctuary

The Crown Inn

Address: Sydenham Road, SYDENHAM, OX39 4NB
Tel: 01844 351634
Website: www.crownsydenham.co.uk
Map ref: 3 SP70
Directions: M40 junct 6 take B4009 towards
Chinnor. Left onto A40. At Postcombe turn
right to Sydenham
Open: 12-3 5.30-11 (Sat noon-11 Sun noon-3)
Closed: 1 wk Jan, 1 wk Aug, Sun eve, Mon
L Tue-Sun 12-2.30 D Tue-Sat 7-9.30
Facilities: Garden **Notes:** ⊕ THE SYDENHAM PUB CO ♦♦ 🐾

Good news travelled fast in 2008 when Max, the chef/landlord, and his wife Louise arrived in this
village just under the scarp slope of the Chilterns to take over its 16th-century pub. The real fires create
an atmosphere both warm and welcoming, and the seasonal menus, real ales and worldly wines rapidly
earned a fine reputation. Food from local suppliers is freshly prepared so the menu is short but sweet,
barely a dozen lines long. Booking is advisable. There is a large garden with Aunt Sally pub game.
Recommended in the area
Hell Fire Caves; Stonor Park; City of Oxford

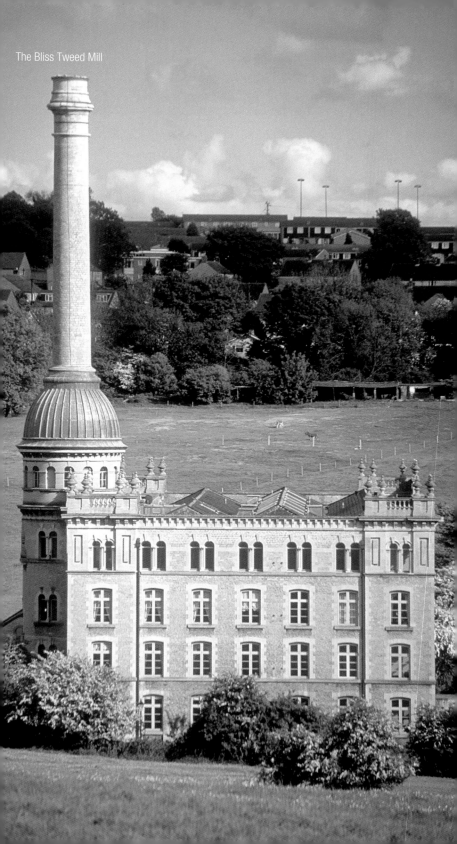
The Bliss Tweed Mill

SHROPSHIRE

The Iron Bridge, Ironbridge

The Crown Inn

★★★★ 🍽 INN

Address: Hopton Wafers,
CLEOBURY MORTIMER, DY14 0NB
Tel: 01299 270372 **Fax:** 01299 271127
Website: www.crownathopton.co.uk
Map ref: 2 SO67
Directions: On A4117 8m E of Ludlow, 2m W of
Cleobury Mortimer **Open:** all week 🍽 **L** Mon-Fri
12.30-2, Sat 12-2.30, Sun 12-8 **D** Mon-Fri 6-9, Sat
6-9.30, Sun 12-8 **Rooms:** 18 en suite **S** £59.50-
£69.50 **D** £95-£115 **Facilities:** Parking Garden **Notes:** ⊕ FREE HOUSE ♦♦ 🐾 ♛ 25

Surrounded by streams, farmland, wooded valleys and immaculately kept gardens with a duck pond, this 16th-century, one-time coaching inn appears to be constructed from Virginia creeper, so densely does its foliage cover the façade. It was once estate property and local tenants paid whatever they owed in the Rent Room, now one of the three restaurants, and offering traditional pine kitchen-style seating. The second area is Poachers, with exposed beams, bare stonework and a large inglenook fireplace, while number three is the Shropshire Restaurant extension, overlooking The Crown's rural surroundings. Locally born chef Kevin Clark, who achieved two AA Rosettes here in an earlier spell, has returned to work his magic again. A believer in using regional produce, he goes for such dishes as grilled asparagus wrapped in Parma ham with mixed cress, rocket and hollandaise sauce; medallions of monkfish with tiger prawns and couscous and dill cream; fillet of beef on beetroot risotto with port reduction; and Mediterranean vegetable and goat's cheese Wellington with roasted tomato sauce. Typically, specials are seared king scallops, asparagus and radish salad with lemon dressing, and chargrilled chicken and vegetable kebab with basil aioli.

Recommended in the area

Clee Hill; Severn Valley Railway; Ironbridge

SOMERSET

Exmoor National Park from Dunkery Beacon

The Marlborough Tavern

Address: 35 Marlborough Buildings, BATH, BA1 2LY

Tel: 01225 423731

Email: joe@marlborough-tavern.com

Website: www.marlborough-tavern.com

Map ref: 2 ST76

Directions: 200mtrs from W end of Royal Crescent, on corner of Marlborough Buildings. **Open:** all day all week noon-11 (Fri-Sat noon-12.30am)

Closed: 25 Dec ⬛ 🍽 L Mon-Sat 12.30-2.30, Sun 12.30-4 **D** Mon-Sat 6-9.30, Sun 6-9 **Facilities:** Garden Wi-fi **Notes:** ⊕ FREE HOUSE 🏃 🐕 ▾ 23

Located just a stone's throw from the Royal Crescent, the award-winning Marlborough Tavern has provided food and drink to visitors and residents of Bath since the 18th century. The owners offer great British dishes, but without the stuffiness, successfully achieved judging by the critical acclaim and AA Rosette. With produce obtained from local suppliers, try pan-fried Cornish grey mullet with black olive mash and spiced aubergine, or 8oz Hereford sirloin steak with slow-roasted tomato and peppercorn sauce.

Recommended in the area

Thermae Bath Spa; Pulteney Bridge; Longleat House and Safari Park

The Royal Crescent, Bath

The Hunters Rest

★★★★ INN

Address: King Lane, Clutton Hill,
CLUTTON, BS39 5QL
Tel: 01761 452303
Fax: 01761 453308
Email: info@huntersrest.co.uk
Website: www.huntersrest.co.uk
Map ref: 2 ST65
Directions: On A37 follow signs for Wells through
Pensford, at large rdbt left towards Bath, 100mtrs
right into country lane, pub 1m up hill **Open:** all week noon-3 6-11 (Fri-Sun noon-11)
🍴 🍽 L Mon-Thu 12-3, Fri-Sun 12-10 D Mon-Thu 6-10, Fri-Sun 12-10 **Rooms:** 5 en suite
S £65-£75 D £90-£125 **Facilities:** Parking Garden Wi-fi **Notes:** 🌐 FREE HOUSE 📶 🐾 ☕ 10

Originally a hunting lodge that was built for the Earl of Warwick in about 1750, the inn is situated amid beautiful countryside high on Clutton Hill overlooking the Cam Valley to the Mendips and the Chew Valley to Bristol. Historic character, including beams, exposed stonework and log fires, has been complemented by modern amenities, creating a cosy atmosphere inside. There's a landscaped garden outside, complete with a miniature railway to carry passengers around the grounds. The beers served here include Otter Ale, Sharp's Own, Hidden Quest and Butcombe, and there is a reasonably priced wine list with a good choice by the glass. Home-made dishes from the menu range through bakehouse rolls and giant oggies (pasties) with a variety of fillings, to grills and other popular pub fare, while the list of daily specials might include rack of lamb with rosemary and garlic gravy, or salmon fishcakes with dill mayonnaise. The inn offers accommodation in individually designed bedrooms. These include fourposter suites, antique furniture, direct dial telephones, LCD televisions and Wi-fi.

Recommended in the area

Bath; Cheddar Caves; Wells Cathedral

The Queens Arms

Address: CORTON DENHAM, DT9 4LR
Tel: 01963 220317
Email: relax@thequeensarms.com
Website: www.thequeensarms.com
Map ref: 2 ST62
Directions: From A30 (Sherborne) take B3145 signed Wincanton.
Approx 1.5m left at red sign to Corton Denham. 1.5m, left down
hill, right at bottom into village. Pub on left
Open: Mon-Sat 11-11 (Sun, BH 12-10.30)
⬛ ⭘ L all wk 12-3 D Mon-Sat 6-10, Sun 6-9.30
Facilities: Parking Garden Wi-fi
Notes: ⊕ FREE HOUSE ⋔ ⚲ ⚟ 30

Tucked away in the ancient village of Corton Denham, on the Somerset-Dorset border, The Queens
Arms, AA Pub of the Year 2009, offers real drink, real food and real comfort. Food is simple but
good, sourced mainly from the surrounding countryside, as well as from home-reared pork and
chickens. In the bar you might want to order a pint of local beer or cider, or a bottled beer from the
wide international selection, and maybe ask for a pork pie at the same time. There are also eight
local apple juices on offer with a well chosen wine and whisky list. Or, having booked a lunch table in
the bustling dining room, try the chowder made with smoked haddock, scallops and salmon, or Old
English sausages and mash with rich gravy and red onion marmalade. The dinner menu typically offers
Corton Denham lamb with black pudding crumble topping, potato knish and rosemary sauce; Brixham
crab-crusted brill with sauce vièrge; and herb pancakes with goat's cheese, balsamic mushrooms, local
squash and tomato basil sauce. Stay over in one of the individually-styled bedrooms.

Recommended in the area

Fleet Air Arm Museum; Montacute House (NT); Haynes International Motor Museum

The Luttrell Arms

★★★ 73% HOTEL

Address: High Street, DUNSTER, TA24 6SG
Tel: 01643 821555
Fax: 01643 821567
Email: info@luttrellarms.fsnet.co.uk
Map ref: 1 SS94
Directions: From A39 (Bridgewater to Minehead), left onto A396 to Dunster (2m from Minehead)
Open: all week 8am-11pm ☕ L all wk 11.30-3, all day summer D all wk 7-10 ⦿ L Sun 12-3
D all wk 7-10 **Rooms:** 28 S £80-£135 D £190-£200 **Facilities:** Garden
Notes: ⊕ FREE HOUSE ⊪ ⌁

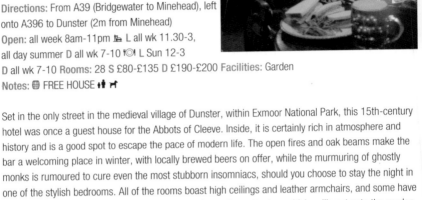

Set in the only street in the medieval village of Dunster, within Exmoor National Park, this 15th-century hotel was once a guest house for the Abbots of Cleeve. Inside, it is certainly rich in atmosphere and history and is a good spot to escape the pace of modern life. The open fires and oak beams make the bar a welcoming place in winter, with locally brewed beers on offer, while the murmuring of ghostly monks is rumoured to cure even the most stubborn insomniacs, should you choose to stay the night in one of the stylish bedrooms. All of the rooms boast high ceilings and leather armchairs, and some have four-posters. The hotel has two eating places to choose from: the bar, which spills out onto the garden in summer months and serves such warming delights as rib-sticking wild venison casserole, or the more formal restaurant. Diners can enjoy meals such as smoked haddock fishcakes, followed by wild pigeon and mushroom parcels with cider jus in the latter. Desserts include sticky ginger parkin with vanilla-steeped pineapple and ginger ice cream in the restaurant, and clotted cream rice pudding in the bar. Locally brewed beers and a good-value wine list complete the picture.

Recommended in the area

Dunster Castle (NT); Exmoor National Park; Dunster Station Steam Railway

The Helyar Arms

★★★★ ◈ INN

Address: Moor Lane, EAST COKER, BA22 9JR
Tel: 01935 862332 **Fax:** 01935 864129
Email: info@helyar-arms.co.uk
Website: www.helyar-arms.co.uk
Map ref: 2 ST51
Directions: 3m from Yeovil. Take A57 or A30, follow East Coker signs **Open:** all week ♿ ⊠ L all wk 12-2.30 D all wk 6.30-9.30 **Rooms:** 6 en suite **Facilities:** Parking Garden **Notes:** ⊕ PUNCH TAVERNS ♿ ⋔

Parts of this traditional village inn date back to 1468. Forget the TV and games machines; instead enjoy the rustic charm of a beamed bar, open log fire, horse brasses, copper pots and a traditional skittle alley. Virtually all the food is prepared to order by whoever's name is on the notice board by the bar. Stocks, sauces, ice creams and chutneys are all home made, and what the pub can't grow or produce itself is sourced mostly from Somerset and Dorset. Remember to leave room for one of the award-winning puddings. Character en suite rooms offer good amenities.

Recommended in the area

Glastonbury Tor; Barrington Court; Somerset Levels

Glastonbury Tor

The Globe

★ ★ ★ ◉ INN

Address: Fore Street, MILVERTON, TA4 1JX
Tel: 01823 400534
Email: info@theglobemilverton.co.uk
Website: www.theglobemilverton.co.uk
Map ref: 2 ST12
Directions: On B3187
Open: noon-3 6-11 (Fri-Sat noon-11.30) **Closed:**
Sun eve, Mon L 🍴 ⦿ L Tue-Sun 12-2
D Mon-Sat 6.30-9 **Rooms:** 2 en suite
Facilities: Parking Wi-fi **Notes:** ⊕ FREE HOUSE ♦♦ ♗ 9

Originally a coaching inn, The Globe is a village free house with a difference. A Grade II listed building, it has been refurbished in a clean-looking, contemporary style that creates both its distinctive character, which follows through to the two en suite bedrooms, and its warm, friendly atmosphere. In addition, husband-and-wife team Mark and Adele Tarry are building an excellent reputation for their quality home-cooked food and have been awarded an AA Rosette. As a result, the community has taken them to their hearts, and the walls of the restaurant and bar are adorned with the work of local artists. All of the food here is home made, including the bread, and the menus, which draw heavily on West Country sources, change frequently to offer attractions such as broccoli and gorgonzola soup; River Fowey mussels; traditional steak and kidney pie; grilled pollack with kale; slow-roasted Gloucester Old Spot belly pork; Mark's mum's faggots; and baked parsnip and onion tart with roasted root vegetables. The children's menu is also thoughtfully compiled, while a real taste of the west comes in the form of the cheese board. Local ales from Exmoor and Cotleigh sit alongside guest ales from brewers such as Otter and Quantock, with local cider and English wines also available.

Recommended in the area

Exmoor National Park; Hestercombe Gardens; Dunster Castle (NT)

George Inn

Address: High St, NORTON ST PHILIP,
nr Bath, BA2 7LH
Tel: 01373 834224
Email: georgeinn@wadworth.co.uk
Website: www.georgeinnnsp.co.uk
Map ref: 2 ST75 **Directions:** From Bath take
A36 to Warminster, after 6m take A366 on right to
Radstock, village 1m **Open:** all day all week

L Mon-Fri 12-2.30 **D** Mon-Thu 6-9, Fri 6-9.30
L Mon-Fri 12-2.30, Sat-Sun 12-9 **D** Mon-Thu
7-9, Fri 7-9.30, Sat-Sun 12-9 **Facilities:** Parking Garden **Notes:** ⊕ WADWORTH ♦♦ ♠ ♟ 32

Over 700 years old, this Grade I-listed building is one of the country's oldest continuously licensed inns. Just over a decade ago, the Wadworth brewery meticulously restored it, and during the process uncovered medieval wall paintings, now preserved. Other noteworthy features are the stone-slated roof, massive doorway, cobbled courtyard (where you can also dine), impressive timbered galleries and accommodation. There are two menus (bar and beamed restaurant) using produce sourced locally.
Recommended in the area
Bath and Roman Baths; Longleat; Cheddar Gorge

Dunster Castle

The Carpenters Arms

Address: STANTON WICK, Nr Pensford, BS39 4BX
Tel: 01761 490202
Fax: 01761 490763
Email: carpenters@buccaneer.co.uk
Website: www.the-carpenters-arms.co.uk
Map ref: 2 ST66
Directions: A37 to Chelwood rdbt, then A368.
Pub 8m S of Bath
Open: all day all week 11-11 (Sun 12-10.30)
Closed: 25-26 Dec ⓑ ⋮◎⋮ L Mon-Sat 12-2, Sun
12-9 **D** Mon-Thu 6-9.30, Fri-Sat 6-10, Sun 12-9
Facilities: Parking Garden
Notes: ⊕ FREE HOUSE ♦♦ ⓟ 10

Just 20 minutes from either Bath or Bristol, this charming stone-built pub is set in the tranquil hamlet of Stanton Wick, overlooking the Chew Valley. It began life as a row of miners' cottages and retains its cottagey style, with a spacious terrace, perfect for summer drinks. Behind the pretty flower bedecked façade, you'll find a low-beamed bar with a convivial atmosphere and no intrusive music. A choice of real beers is served, including Butcombe, Sharp's Doom Bar, and an extensive wine list combining New and Old World favourites. The menu changes regularly to offer the best seasonal produce, including fish from Cornwall, West Country beef and local game in season. Typical dishes include a starter of trio of smoked halibut, salmon and trout with light horseradish cream, and a main course of pork chop on mashed potato with braised savoy cabbage and an onion and thyme sauce. A function room is available for use by groups of 20–36.

Recommended in the area

Cheddar Gorge; Longleat; Wookey Hole Caves

Thor's Cave, Manifold Valley, Peak District National Park

The Yorkshireman

Address: Colton Road, COLTON, WS15 3HB
Tel: 01889 583977
Email: theyorkshireman@btconnect.com
Website: www.wine-dine.co.uk
Map ref: 3 SE54
Directions: 10m from Stafford; 10m from Lichfield
Open: all week noon-2.30 5.30-11 (Sat noon-11pm
Sun noon-6) 🍴 L Mon-Sat 12-2.30, Sun 12-6
D Mon-Fri 6-9.30, Sat 6-11 🍽 L Mon-Sat 12-2.30,
Sun 12-6 D Mon-Sat 6-9.30 **Facilities:** Parking
Garden Wi-fi **Notes:** 🌐 FREE HOUSE 👬 🐾 🍷 10

For train travellers arriving at Rugeley station, the Railway Tavern was the first port of call, now The Yorkshireman. The town once had a notorious serial-murdering doctor who poisoned many of his patients, thus unintentionally providing local Blythe's brewery with the name Palmer's Poison, one of its beers sold in the bar. Curled up in the bar is Dahl, the pub's greyhound. The kitchen sources as much as it can from the locality, availability being reflected in the modestly priced, daily changing menu.

Recommended in the area

Shugborough Hall (NT); Cannock Chase; Lichfield Cathedral

Sherbrook Valley, Cannock Chase

The Holly Bush Inn

Address: Salt, STAFFORD, ST18 0BX
Tel: 01889 508234
Fax: 01889 508058
Email: geoff@hollybushinn.co.uk
Website: www.hollybushinn.co.uk
Map ref: 7 SJ92
Directions: Telephone for directions
Open: all day all week 12-11 (Sun 12-10.30)
🍽 food served all day **Facilities:** Parking Garden
Notes: ⊕ FREE HOUSE ⸙ ♟ 12

In an area cut through by several major trunk roads, it's good to find such a peaceful spot, and then take time to discover the glorious Staffordshire countryside that lies hidden away from the highways. The Holly Bush Inn was licensed during the reign of Charles II (1660–85), although the building itself dates from around 1190, and heavy carved beams, open fires and cosy alcoves still characterise the comfortably old-fashioned interior. Like most other landlords, owner Geoff Holland aims to serve good quality real ales and wines. What helps to differentiate Geoff, though, is his insistence on providing non-processed, mostly organic, fully traceable food, and on minimising his hostelry's impact on the environment by setting up a worm farm. Traditional British dishes on the main menu include grilled pork chops with a honey and whole-grain mustard glaze; braised lamb and apples flavoured with nutmeg and allspice; and breaded wholetail scampi. Daily specials might be butternut squash and goats' cheese lasagne; fillet of beef Wellington; chargrilled red snapper with Jamaican spiced chutney; and baked perch with watercress sauce. Holly Bush mixed grill is a favourite plateful. At lunchtime tripledecker sandwiches, jacket potatoes and toasties are available. Beers include Adnams, Pedigree and guest ales.

Recommended in the area

Shugborough Hall (NT); Weston Park; Cannock Chase; Trentham Gardens; Alton Towers

The Crown Inn

Address: Den Lane, WRINEHILL, Crewe, CW3 9BT
Tel: 01270 820472
Fax: 01270 820547
Email: mark_condliffe@hotmail.com
Map ref: 6 SJ74
Directions: Village on A531, 1m S of Betley. 6m S of Crewe; 6m N of Newcastle-under-Lyme
Open: all week noon-3 6-11 (Sun noon-4 6-10.30)
Closed: 25-26 Dec ⚓ L Mon-Sat 12-2, Sun 12-3 D Mon-Fri 6.30-9.30, Sat 6-10, Sun 6-9
Facilities: Parking Garden **Notes:** ⊕ FREE HOUSE ⚥ ☋ 10

A former coaching inn within a village setting, The Crown stands six miles equidistant from Crewe and Newcastle-under-Lyme. The interior is largely open plan but retains its oak beams and large inglenook fireplace, and the renovated garden has an attractive patio area for dining. A family-run free house for some 30 years, the pub has a great reputation for its real ales. There is always a choice of six traditional cask ales, including Marstons Pedigree, Adnams Bitter and Timothy Taylor Landlord, and there are two regularly changing guest beers; wine is an integral part of the inn's drinks portfolio. Food also plays a significant part and the inn is renowned for its generous portions and consistent good quality. The monthly changing menus reflect the time of year and the fresh produce available locally. The team here is well established – Charles and Sue Davenhill run the business with their daughter and son-in-law, Anna and Mark Condliffe. Mother and daughter are both vegetarians, so the food on offer always includes meat-free choices and a vegan dish. Meat-eaters are spoilt for choice, with such dishes as piri-piri chicken; Cumberland grill; and plaice roulade with a hazelnut and gruyère crust. Desserts include sticky toffee pudding, ice cream sundaes and home-made jam sponge and custard.

Recommended in the area

The Potteries; Bridgemere Garden World; Trentham Gardens and Monkey Forest

SUFFOLK

River Stour, Dedham

The Queen's Head

Address: The Street, Bramfield,
HALESWORTH, IP19 9HT
Tel: 01986 784214
Email: qhbfield@aol.com
Website: www.queensheadbramfield.co.uk
Map ref: 4 TM37
Directions: 2m from A12 on A144
towards Halesworth
Open: all week 11.45-2.30 6.30-11 (Sun noon-3

7-10.30) **Closed:** 26 Dec 🔥 **L** all wk 12-2 **D** Mon-Fri
6.30-9.15, Sat 6.30-10, Sun 7-9 **Facilities:** Parking Garden **Notes:** ⊕ ADNAMS ♦♦ 🐕 🍷 8

A lovely old building with a pretty garden by the village church with its unusual round bell tower. Inside, picture exposed beams, enormous fireplaces, scrubbed pine tables and a vaulted bar serving Adnams beers. Over the years, Mark Corcoran has built a formidable reputation for high quality, home-made meals produced from local, often organic, produce. A typical meal might comprise carrot and ginger soup, local partridge braised in red wine with bacon, and warm Bakewell tart.

Recommended in the area

Suffolk Heritage Coast; Minsmere Nature Reserve; Snape Maltings

The Star Inn

Address: The Street, LIDGATE, Newmarket, CB8 9PP
Tel/Fax: 01638 500275
Email: tonyaxon@aol.com
Map ref: 4 TL75
Directions: From Newmarket clocktower in High St follow signs
towards Clare on B1063. Lidgate 7m
Open: noon-3 6-mdnt **Closed:** 25-26 Dec, 1 Jan, Mon
🔥 🍽 **L** Tue-Sun 12-3 **D** Tue-Sat 7-10
Facilities: Parking Garden **Notes:** ⊕ GREENE KING ♦♦

This pretty Elizabethan building is made up of two cottages with gardens front and rear; inside, two traditionally furnished bars with heavy oak beams, log fires and pine furniture lead into the dining room. Yet The Star's quintessentially English appearance holds a surprise, for here you'll find a renowned Spanish restaurant offering authentic Mediterranean cuisine. The inn provides an important meeting place for local residents; it's also popular with Newmarket trainers on race days.

Recommended in the area

Newmarket Racecourse; National Horseracing Museum and Tours

The Swan Inn

◎◎

Address: The Street, MONKS ELEIGH,
Ipswich, IP7 7AU
Tel: 01449 741391
Email: carol@monkseleigh.com
Website: www.monkseleigh.com
Map ref: 4 TL94
Directions: On B1115 between Sudbury & Hadleigh
Open: noon-2.30 7-11 **Closed:** 25-26 Dec, 2wks
in summer Sun eve & Mon ⓑ ⓘ L Tue-Sun 12-2
D Tue-Sat 7-9 **Facilities:** Parking Garden **Notes:** ⊕ FREE HOUSE ⦁⦁

Carol and Nigel have run this attractive thatched village pub situated in a quiet village since 1999, watching their customers warming themselves by the log fire, enjoying a snack or three-course meal, or maybe sitting outside, enjoying the views. They have received many awards and plaudits for their fresh, locally sourced seasonal food, including two AA Rosettes. The menu changes almost daily and is influenced by the fresh ingredients available from their local butcher, fish or vegetable supplier.
Recommended in the area
Wolves Wood (RSPB); Thomas Gainsborough's House; Museum of East Anglian Life

The Crown Inn

Address: Bridge Road, SNAPE,
Nr Saxmundham, IP17 1SL
Tel: 01728 688324
Email: snapecrown@tiscali.co.uk
Website: WWW.snape-crown.co.uk
Map ref: 4 TM35
Directions: A12 N to Lowestoft, right to
Aldeburgh, then right again in Snape at x-rds by
church, pub at bottom of hill
Open: all week ⓑ ⓘ L all wk 12-2.30

D all wk 6-9.30 **Facilities:** Parking Garden **Notes:** ⊕ ADNAMS ⦁⦁ ⌃ ⍒ 12

Within walking distance of Snape Maltings, this atmospheric pub is the perfect place for a pre- or post show meal. Inside, it is not too difficult to imagine its 15th-century incarnation as a haunt of smugglers. The old beams and brick floors are still in place, but now you will find a warm welcome from landlord/chef Garry Cook and his wife Teresa, top quality Adnams ales, and superb food. Garry offers modern British cuisine using own home reared meats, vegetables from their allotment, plus other local produce.
Recommended in the area
Suffolk Coast National Nature Reserve; RSPB Mismere and Orford Ness reserves; Framlingham Castle

The Crown Hotel

★★ 85% ® HOTEL
Address: The High Street, SOUTHWOLD, IP18 6DP
Tel: 01502 722275 **Fax:** 01502 727263
Email: crown.hotel@adnams.co.uk
Website: www.adnams.co.uk
Map ref: 4 TM57
Directions: A12 onto A1095 to Southwold. Into town
centre, pub on left **Open:** all week 8am-11pm (Sun
8am-10.30pm) Apr-Sep ᤈ L Sun-Fri 12-2, Sat 12-
2.30 **D** Sun-Fri 6-9, Sat 6-9.30 (5.30-9.30 summer)
Rooms: 14 **Facilities:** Parking Wi-fi **Notes:** ⊕ ADNAMS ⁑ ⚲ ⚱ 20

Fulfilling the roles of pub, wine bar, restaurant and small hotel, the multi-talented Crown is the flagship
for Southwold brewery, Adnams. An AA Rosette for Robert Mace and his team's high standard of
cooking is shown in dishes of East Coast sole with Anya potatoes and samphire; lamb kleftiko with
tzatziki; and polenta-crusted pan-fried goat's cheese with potato, artichoke and sun-blushed tomato.
Intriguingly twisting corridors and staircases lead to 14 delightful bedrooms.
Recommended in the area
Minsmere RSPB Reserve; Southwold Pier; Suffolk Heritage Coast

Beach huts at Southwold

The Randolph

Address: 41 Wangford Road, Reydon,
SOUTHWOLD, IP18 6PZ
Tel: 01502 723603
Fax: 01502 722194
Email: reception@therandolph.co.uk
Website: www.therandolph.co.uk
Map ref: 4 TM57
Directions: A1095 from A12 at Blythburgh 4m,
Southwold 9m from Darsham train station
Open: all day all week 🍴 🍽 L all wk 12-2
D all wk 6.30-9 **Facilities:** Parking Garden Wi-fi
Notes: 🍺 ADNAMS PLC 🛉 🐕

This grand late-Victorian pub/hotel was built in 1899 by Adnams, the ubiquitous local brewers, who named it after Lord Randolph Churchill, Sir Winston's father. Standing in the quiet residential area of Reydon, which is just a 15-minute walk from the centre of picturesque Southwold, it successfully combines its functions as pub, restaurant and hotel, thanks to its owners David and Donna Smith. The lounge bar, serving Adnams beers and a wide selection of food, is pleasantly bright and overlooks a sunny, enclosed garden. Every meal is produced from the very best ingredients which, wherever possible, come from local suppliers. A wide range of ever-changing menu choices is also available in the large dining area, where you might follow steamed Brancaster mussels in Aspall Cyder and leek sauce with chargrilled rib-eye steak with garlic and parsley butter; Suffolk chicken and chestnut, mushroom and bacon linguini; or deep-fried line-caught cod in beer batter. Then you could order a dessert such as white chocolate and raspberry crème brûlée and biscotti, or warm apple and blackberry crumble with crème anglaise. The Randolph provides the perfect base for exploring the Suffolk Heritage Coast.

Recommended in the area

Amber Museum; Aldeburgh Festival; Pleasurewood Hills Theme Park

The Anchor

Address: Main Street, WALBERSWICK,
Southwold, IP18 6UA

Tel: 01502 722112 Fax: 01502 724464

Email: info@anchoratwalberswick.com

Map ref: 4 TM47

Directions: From A12 turn at B1387. Follow signs
for Walberswick. Continue on Main St, pub on right

Open: all day all week 🍺 ⬤ L all wk 12-3 D all wk
6-9 Facilities: Parking Garden Wi-fi Notes: ⚦ 🐕 🍷 22

Sophie Dorber's long-standing connections with the Suffolk coast, include running the food franchise at Aldeburgh yacht club; in London, husband Mark ran what was twice voted the UK's top pub, The White Horse on Parson's Green SW6. Then one day in 2004, breakfasting with friends on a golden Walberswick beach, they decided to buy The Anchor's lease and create a family-friendly village local. And that's what they've done. They stock a good range of characterful real ales, twenty world-class bottled beers and 150 wines from some highly inspired winemakers, choosing to offer: "Only (what) we would actively seek to drink if the flood waters were to surround Walberswick and we became an island". Their approach to food is robust, following the seasons with produce from their own garden and villagers' allotments. Starter examples would be West Mersea oysters with red onion vinaigrette; main courses of mushroom and Stilton risotto; roast cod with brioche herb crust; and Suffolk rib-eye steak with horseradish and caper butters; and for dessert, Jamaican ginger bread with clotted cream ice cream. Curry nights are every second Friday. Plans are in hand to renovate the dining room, turn a corridor into a bar, and sow wild flowers to create a picnic meadow. There is a splendid rear terrace and garden.

Recommended in the area

Suffolk Heritage Coast; Snape Maltings; Minsmere RSPB

The Westleton Crown

★★★ 79% ®® HOTEL

Address: The Street, WESTLETON,
Nr Southwold, IP17 3AD
Tel: 01728 648777
Fax: 01728 648239
Email: info@westletoncrown.co.uk
Website: www.westletoncrown.co.uk
Map ref: 4 TM46
Directions: A12 N, turn right for Westleton just after
Yoxford. Hotel opposite on entering Westleton
Open: all day all week 7am-11pm (Sun 7.30am-10.30pm) ⓵ ⓵ L all wk 12-2.30
D all wk 7-9.30 **Rooms:** 34 (12 GF) **S** £80-£100 **D** £90-£215 **Facilities:** Parking Garden Wi-fi
Notes: ⓵ FREE HOUSE ⓵ ⓵ ⓵ 11

Nestled in a quiet village close to Suffolk's wild salt marshes, the coast and RSPB bird reserves, is this atmospheric and hospitable inn. Its origins go back to the 12th century, but the building itself dates from the 17th. The original buildings belonged to nearby Sibton Abbey, and the Crown has succeeded in combining the rustic charm of its heritage with the comforts of contemporary living. Inside you will find crackling log fires, real ales, good wines and an enticing menu. The team at the Crown are passionate about cooking. Impressive meals are made from fresh, locally-sourced ingredients, and can be taken in the bar, elegant dining room or stylish Garden Room. Start with baked goats' cheese with red onion crumble, or spicy pumpkin tart, before moving on to roast loin of venison with Griottine cherries and root vegetable creamed potatoes, or the Crown's own cod and chips. Leave some space for dessert, which may take the form of pear tarte Tatin with blackberry ice cream, home-made Arctic roll, or marmalade and orange steamed sponge pudding with English egg custard sauce.

Recommended in the area

Aldeburgh; Suffolk Heritage Coast; Southwold; Minsmere RSPB; Dunwich

SURREY

Footbridge over River Mole, Brockham

The Bat & Ball Freehouse

Address: 15 Bat & Ball Lane, Boundstone,
FARNHAM, GU10 4SA
Tel: 01252 792108
Email: info@thebatandball.co.uk
Website: www.thebatandball.co.uk
Map ref: 3 SY84
Directions: From A31 Farnham bypass follow signs
for Birdworld. Left at Bengal Lounge into School Hill.
At top over staggered x-rds into Sandrock Hill Rd.
After 0.25m left into Upper Bourne Lane, signed

Open: all day all week 11-11 (Sun noon-10.30) 🍴 L Mon-Sat 12-2.15, Sun 12-3 **D** Mon-Sat 7-9.30,
Sun 6-8.30 **Facilities:** Parking Garden **Notes:** ⊞ FREE HOUSE 💁 🐕 🍷 8

Tucked down a lane in a wooded valley south of Farnham, this 150-year-old inn is well worth seeking
out. Hops for the local breweries in Farnham and Alton were once grown in the valley, and originally the
hop pickers were paid in the building that eventually became the pub. An enterprising tenant began to
provide the pickers with ale, relieving them of some of their hard earned cash! Very much a community
pub, the interior features terracotta floors, oak beams, a roaring fire on colder days, and plenty of
cricketing memorabilia. The lovely garden has a terrace with vine-topped pergola and a children's play
fort. Expect six regularly changing cask-conditioned ales, a range of quaffable wines, and home-cooked
food at reasonable prices. Starters and light meals might include a platter of dips with olives, prosciutto
ham, sundried tomatoes and breads to share, or deep-fried whitebait with home-made tartare sauce.
Cassoulet of guinea fowl, bacon and Toulouse sausage, home-made corned beef hash topped with
poached eggs, and grilled sea bass fillet are typical of the flavoursome dishes on offer. There's live
music on the last Sunday of the month, and a beer, cider and music festival every June.

Recommended in the area

Birdworld; Frensham Ponds; Alice Holt Forest and Go Ape

Hare and Hounds

Address: Common Road, LINGFIELD, RH7 6BZ
Tel: 01342 832351
Email: info@hareandhoundspublichouse.co.uk
Website: www.hareandhoundspublichouse.co.uk
Map ref: 3 TQ34
Directions: From A22 follow signs for Lingfield
Racecourse into Common Rd **Open:** all day
Closed: 1-5 Jan, Sun eve ⓑ ⏍ **L** Mon-Sat 12-2.30
D Mon-Sat 7-9.30 **Facilities:** Parking Garden
Notes: ⊕ PUNCH TAVERNS ♦♦ ⌁

Situated close to Lingfield Park Racecourse, Tracy and Eric Payet took over this character pub in 2009 and have made a few discreet changes, but none that compromises the shabby-chic, somewhat bohemian feel created by mismatched furniture, cosy corners, open fireplace and scattered cushions. The rich and appetising menu offers traditional dishes with an exotic twist. Try honey-roast ham hock with free-range egg and pickled pineapple, or home-made potato gnocchi with butternut squash, chilli and aged Parmesan dressing, followed by Braeburn apple beignet with home-made cinnamon ice cream.

Recommended in the area

Lingfield Park Racecourse; Hever Castle; Tilgate Park

Bryce's at The Old School House

◉

Address: OCKLEY, Dorking, RH5 5TH
Tel: 01306 627430
Fax: 01306 628274
Email: fish@bryces.co.uk
Website: www.bryces.co.uk
Map ref: 3 TQ14
Directions: 8m S of Dorking on A29
Open: noon-3 6-11 **Closed:** 25-26 Dec, 1 Jan (Sun
pm Nov, Jan-Feb) ⓑ **L** all wk 12-2.30 **D** all wk

6-9.30 ⏍ **L** all wk 12-2.30 **D** 7-9.30 **Facilities:** Parking **Notes:** ⊕ FREE HOUSE ♦♦ ⌁ ⏛ 15

Formerly a boarding school, this Grade II listed building dates from 1750 and has been established for 18 years as Bryce's. The village is set amid lovely countryside offering some great downland walking. Its distance from the sea may come as a surprise, as Bill Bryce is passionate about fresh fish and offers seven starters and main courses of exclusively fish dishes in the restaurant, with non-fish daily specials and a vegetarian selection. The bar has its own tempting menu, and there are excellent house wines.

Recommended in the area

The Hannah Peschar Sculpture Garden; Leith Hill; Denbies Wine Estate, Dorking

Rye Harbour

The Coach and Horses

Address: DANEHILL, RH17 7JF
TelFax: 01825 740369
Map ref: 3 TQ42
Directions: From East Grinstead, S through Forest Row on A22 to junct with A275 (Lewes road), right on A275, 2m to Danehill, left onto School Lane, 0.5m, pub on left **Open:** all week 11.30-3 6-11 (Sat-Sun 12-11) **Closed:** 25 Dec ⚫ ⦿ L all wk 12-2, Sat-Sun 12-2.30 **D** Mon-Fri 7-9, Sat 7-9.30 **Facilities:** Parking Garden Wi-fi **Notes:** ⊕ FREE HOUSE ⭑ ⭑ ⚑ 8

Built in 1847 of local sandstone, The Coach and Horses is ideal for walkers and lovers of stunning scenery. Homely winter fires and neatly tended gardens add plenty of character, and half-panelled walls, highly polished wooden floorboards and vaulted beamed ceilings give the place a charming, timeless feel. Food plays a key role in the pub's success; locally sourced produce features heavily on the varied menu - lamb from the neighbouring farm, fish landed on the Sussex coast and delivered daily, plus vegetables, venison and game from nearby suppliers.

Recommended in the area

The Ashdown Forest; Sheffield Park Gardens (NT);The Bluebell Railway

Sussex countryside at Ditchling

The Bull

★★★★ ➾ INN

Address: 2 High Street, DITCHLING, BN6 8TA
Tel/fax: 01273 843147
Email: info@thebullditchling.com
Website: www.thebullditchling.com
Map ref: 3 TQ31
Directions: S on M23/A23 5m. N of Brighton follow
signs to Pyecombe/Hassocks then signs to Ditchling,
3m **Open:** all day all week 11-11 (Sun noon-10.30)
L Mon-Fri 12-2.30, Sat 12-9.30, Sun 12-9

D Mon-Fri 6-9.30, Sat 12-9.30, Sun 12-9 **Rooms:** 4 en suite **Facilities:** Parking Garden Wi-fi
Notes: ⊞ FREE HOUSE ♦♦ ⌁ ♙ 18

The Bull, a 16th-century former coaching inn, is the place to head for following a day on the South
Downs. It's been restored with passion (and a contemporary touch) by Dominic Worrall, yet still exudes
historic charm and character. In the bar you'll find feature fireplaces with glowing log fires, sagging
ceiling timbers, bare boards and a mixture of simple benches, carved settles and farmhouse chairs at
big scrubbed wooden tables. Quirky objets d'art, modern art and vases of lilies on the bar add a touch
of class. There are four individually decorated bedrooms, each named after their principle colour. Ruby,
for example, has bright red walls, white-painted wall timbers, Thai silk curtains, a plasma TV/DVD
player, digital radio, a sleigh bed with Egyptian cotton sheets and a claw-foot bath in the tiled bathroom.
Local is the watchword when it comes to food and drink, with top notch ales from Harvey's (Lewes)
and Welton's (Horsham) breweries on hand pump and a quaffable fizz from Ridge View Vineyard up the
road. Menus change daily and make good use of lamb from Foxhole Farm on the edge of the village,
seasonal game, including venison from the Balcombe Estate and south coast fish.
Recommended in the area
Booth Museum of Natural History; Royal Pavilion, Brighton; Borde Hill Garden

The Hatch Inn

Address: Coleman's Hatch, HARTFIELD, TN7 4EJ
TelFax: 01342 822363
Email: nickad@bigfoot.com
Website: www.hatchinn.co.uk
Map ref: 3 TQ43
Directions: A22, 14m, left at Forest Row rdbt, 3m to Colemans Hatch, right by church. Straight on at next junct, pub on right
Open: all week 11.30-3 5.30-11 (Sat-Sun all day) Closed: 25 Dec ⓑ ⒣ L all wk 12-2.15 D Mon-Thu 7-9.15, Fri-Sat 7-9.30
Facilities: Garden Notes: ⊕ FREE HOUSE ⅰⅰ ⚞ ⚲ 10

Reputedly dating back to 1430, The Hatch Inn was converted from three cottages thought to have housed workers at the local water-driven hammer mill, and it may also have been a smugglers' haunt. The pub is well placed for country walking, and features in a number of 'top ten pubs' lists, as well as serving as a filming location for television dramas and advertisements. There are two large beer gardens for alfresco summer dining, one of which enjoys views out over the forest, and is only minutes away from the restored Poohsticks Bridge, immortalised in A.A. Milne's *Winnie the Pooh* stories. Owner Nicholas Drillsma and his partner, Sandra Barton, have collected many accolades over the last 14 years. Quality ingredients and imaginative techniques make for exciting menus created by head chef Gregory Palmer and his team. Evening appetisers might include a red onion marmalade and goat's cheese tart Tatin with roast beetroot salad, Roquefort and walnuts, followed by roast rump of lamb with dauphinoise potatoes and rosemary and port reduction. All desserts are home made – highly recommended is the sticky toffee pudding, hot toffee sauce and locally made ice cream. No reservations are available at lunchtime and evening booking is essential.

Recommended in the area

Pooh Bridge; Ashdown Forest; Standen (NT); Royal Tunbridge Wells

The Middle House

Address: High Street, MAYFIELD, TN20 6AB
Tel: 01435 872146
Fax: 01435 873423
Email: kirsty@middle-house.com
Website: www.middlehousemayfield.co.uk
Map ref: 4 TQ52
Directions: E of A267, S of Tunbridge Wells
Open: all week ⅃ L Mon-Fri 12-2, Sat 12-2.30
D Mon-Sat 6.30-9.30, Sun all day
⧉ L Tue-Sun 12-2 D Tue-Sat 6.30-9
Facilities: Parking Garden **Notes:** ⊕ FREE HOUSE ⅰ♀ 9

Built in 1575 for Sir Thomas Gresham, Elizabeth I's Keeper of the Privy Purse and founder of the London Stock Exchange, The Middle House is one of the finest timber-framed buildings in Sussex, with a wonderfully ornate wooden façade. Inside, the house retains many of its original features, including a Grinling Gibbons' fireplace and a splendid oak-panelled restaurant. This is a family-run business specialising in a very wide variety of food using all local, fresh produce. On offer are over 40 dishes, including a large fish selection and vegetarian options on an ever-changing menu. Among the choices to be enjoyed in the cosy bar or the more formal restaurant are chicken breast filled with leeks and gruyère cheese wrapped in filo pastry with a parsley, cream and white wine sauce; seared tuna loin steak on a bed of pak choi with a sweet and sour sauce; pan-fried local venison steak served with game crisps and a rich bacon lardon, port and prune sauce. An extensive wine list offers wines and champagne by the glass, and the pub's bar offers real ales including Harveys, the local brew and several guest beers. A great high street pub whether you're nipping in for a pint or stopping a little longer to enjoy both the food and the atmosphere. Ample parking is available.

Recommended in the area

Bateman's (NT); Spa Valley Railway; Royal Tunbridge Wells

The Ypres Castle Inn

Address: Gun Garden, RYE, TN31 7HH
Tel: 01797 223248
Email: info@yprescastleinn.co.uk
Website: www.yprescastleinn.co.uk
Map ref: 4 TQ92
Directions: Behind church & adjacent to Ypres Tower
Open: all day all week 🍺 🍽 L all wk 12-3 D Mon-Sat 6-9
Facilities: Garden Wi-fi
Notes: ⊕ FREE HOUSE ⁕ ☗ 12

'The Wipers', as locals call it, was once the haunt of smugglers. Built in 1640 in weather-boarded style, and added to by the Victorians, it's the only pub in the citadel area of the old Cinque Port of Rye with a garden. The garden, with roses, shrubs and views of the 13th-century Ypres Tower, once defensive which then became a prison before becoming a museum, and of the River Rother with its working fishing fleet. Colourful art and furnishings help make the interior warm and friendly. The seasonally changing menu is largely sourced locally, providing a good range of lunchtime snacks, including ploughman's, and sandwiches, backed by half a dozen daily specials. The evening menu may propose moules marinière, cracked Dungeness crab, grilled Rye Bay plaice and turbot, and meaty options of grilled rack of Romney salt marsh lamb, organic Winchelsea beef and pork, and home-made prime beefburger. There are usually four cask-conditioned ales and an extensive wine list. On Friday nights the atmosphere hots up with live jazz, rock and blues. The pub has no accommodation facilities, but there are plenty of possibilities nearby, including Rye Windmill, one of the town's most famous landmarks.

Recommended in the area

Smallhythe Place; Romney, Hythe & Dymchurch Railway; Port Lympne Wild Animal Park

The Best Beech Inn

Address: Mayfield Lane, WADHURST, TN5 6JH
Tel: 01892 782046
Email: info@bestbeechinn.co.uk
Website: www.bestbeechinn.co.uk
Map ref: 4 TQ63
Directions: 7m from Tunbridge Wells. On A246 at lights turn left onto London Rd (A26), left at mini rdbt onto A267, left then right onto B2100. At Mark Cross signed Wadhurst, 3m on right **Open:** Mon-Fri 12-3, 6-11, Sat 12-11, Sun 12-6 🖻 🍽 **L** Mon-Fri 12-2.30, Sat all day, Sun 12-5 **D** Tue-Fri 6-9.30, Sat all day (Sun-Mon closed for dinner) **Facilities:** Parking Garden **Notes:** ⊕ SHEPHERD NEAME ♥♥ 🐾

Located firmly in the Weald, that ravishing countryside between the North and South Downs, The Best Beech has new owners in brothers Brian and David White. Off the beaten track and surrounded by wonderful beech woods, this unusually-named pub has a varied history that can be traced back to the 17th century. In its time the building has been used as a butcher's shop and as an early petrol station, while an old Community Village Circle symbol on a chimney signifies that once it had become an inn it welcomed cyclists. It still does, of course. A recent sympathetic refurbishment has created a new bar, with comfortable chairs, exposed brickwork and open fireplace, yet preserved the essentially Victorian character of its heyday. In one of the two beautifully designed restaurant rooms, dine from a Modern British menu with European influences, courtesy of chef Anthony Wilmshurst and the farmers and suppliers of Kent, Sussex, and London's Billingsgate. Typical dishes are roast duckling with port, apricot and thyme sauce; braised lamb shank with herb crust and mint jelly; roast belly pork with confit of apple and fennel; and salmon fillet with champ-style new potatoes. Accommodation and private dining are available.

Recommended in the area

Bewl Bridge Reservoir; Batemans (NT); Royal Tunbridge Wells

The Lamb Inn

Address: WARTLING, Herstmonceux, BN27 1RY
Tel: 01323 832116
Website: www.lambinnwartling.co.uk
Map ref: 4 TQ60
Directions: A259 from Polegate to Pevensey rdbt.
Take 1st left to Wartling & Herstmonceux Castle.
Pub 3m on right
Open: all week Tue-Sat 11-3 6-11 (Sun 12-3)
Closed: Sun eve, Mon 🍺 🍽 L Tue-Sun 12-2.15 D Tue-Sat 7-9
Facilities: Parking Garden **Notes:** ⊕ FREE HOUSE 🚶 🐾 ♟ 8

Established in 1526, the family-run Lamb Inn is on the Pevensey
Levels, a wetlands habitat dominated by nature. Since 2002 it's
been owned by occasional part-time Royal butler Robert (he's out front with his team) and
Alison (she's in the kitchen with hers) and Freddie, their golden retriever. Although they recently
refurbished throughout they've kept the traditional feel, which means, among other things, no pool tables
or fruit machines. The comfortable lounge is perfect for a pint of one of the guest ales or a
glass of wine, and for studying the menu. Dine in the restaurant, with lovely fires in winter, or outside
in the enclosed patio garden. Meats are usually from local farms, while catches from the ports of Rye,
Hastings and Newhaven underpin the extensive fresh fish menu. Try starters such as scallops with bacon,
white wine and Parmesan crumbs; baked egg with wild mushrooms and Gruyère cheese; or salad of
roasted beetroot, bacon and Stilton with pesto. Follow with Gloucester Old Spot pork chops with black
pudding and apple mash; steak and kidney pie; loin of cod and scallops with pea purée; puff pastry fish
pie; or vegetarian risotto. Finish with home-made mocha and hazelnut crème brûlée, or chocolate praline
bread and butter pudding. Burgers, toasted sandwiches and ploughman's are also available.

Recommended in the area

Battle Abbey; Herstmonceux Castle; Beachy Head

Weald and Downland Open Air Museum

George & Dragon

Address: BURPHAM, Arundel, BN18 9RR
Tel: 01903 883131
Email: sara.cheney@btinternet.com
Website: wwwgdinn.co.uk
Map ref: 3 TQ00
Directions: Off A27 1m E of Arundel, signed Burpham, 2.5m pub on left
Open: all week Mon-Sun 12-3 6-11
L Mon-Fri 12-2, Sat-Sun 12-3 D Mon-Sun 6.30-9 **Facilities:** Parking Garden **Notes:** FREE HOUSE

In a tranquil village at the end of a long no-through road, this lovely old pub has the church and cricket pitch as its close neighbours. The interior is full of old-world character, with beams and worn flagstone floors providing a setting for the modern prints on the walls. Smaller rooms have been opened out to create space, but there are still some nooks and crannies for that quiet meal or drink. Real ales come from nearby Arundel Breweries, with guests from surrounding counties. The owners acknowledge that during the last 30 years the pub has developed from a village local serving mostly beer, into not so much a gastro-pub, but a 'traditional pub that serves excellent food'. It offers a seasonal, largely locally-sourced menu of British rustic cooking, but with clear international influences as seen in honey-roasted Scottish salmon on citrus couscous, pan-roasted vegetables and soy sauce dressing. From nearer home might come wild mushroom, garlic, leek and thyme crumble topped with Sussex Cheddar. Diners don't risk breaking the bank with the compact wine list. The area is well endowed with walks, especially over the South Downs and along the River Arun (dogs are welcome in the bar area).
Recommended in the area
Arundel Castle; Amberley Working Museum; Goodwood

The Fox Goes Free

Address: CHARLTON, nr Goodwood, PO18 OHU
Tel: 01243 811461 **Fax:** 01243 811712
Email: enquiries@thefoxgoesfree.com
Website: www.thefoxgoesfree.com
Map ref: 3 SU81
Directions: A286, 6m from Chichester towards
Midhurst. 1m from Goodwood racecourse
Open: all day all week 11-11 (Sun noon-11)
Closed: 25 Dec eve ⓑ **L** Mon-Fri 12-2.30,
Sat-Sun 12-10 **D** Mon-Fri 6.30-10, Sat-Sun 12-10
ⓘⓞⓘ **L** all wk 12-2.30 **D** all wk 6.30-10 **Facilities:** Parking Garden **Notes:** ⊞ FREE HOUSE ⓲ 🍴 🍷 8

King William III loved this beautiful old brick and flint building, often bringing his royal cronies down
from London to enjoy the hunting. Today the surrounding countryside, part of the Goodwood Estate,
remains unspoilt, while the pub itself is full of period charm, with low-beamed ceilings, brick floors,
two huge fireplaces and a bread oven. The friendly, welcoming bar offers a good selection of local
real ales, including one named after the pub, and well-chosen wines. Delicious, locally sourced West
Sussex produce is offered in a choice of seven different seating areas, so that in winter you may enjoy
the warmth from open fires, and on summer days the charming, apple-tree-filled garden, aka "the
best room in the house", the South Downs in view all around. Bar favourites include home-made steak
and kidney pie, and beer-battered cod and chips, while the main, daily changing menu offers crispy
leg of Gressingham duck confit with savoy cabbage, bacon and plum sauce; belly of pork with Chinese
five-spice and stir-fried vegetables; whole Brixham lemon sole with garlic and herb butter; and roasted
pepper stuffed with couscous, olives and caramelised onions with red pepper coulis. Five en suite
bedrooms are available.

Recommended in the area

Weald & Downland Open Air Museum; Goodwood House; West Dean Gardens

Royal Oak Inn

★★★★★ ◉ 🛏 INN

Address: Pook Lane, East Lavant, CHICHESTER, PO18 0AX
Tel: 01243 527434
Email: info@royaloakeastlavant.co.uk
Website: www.royaloakeastlavant.co.uk
Map ref: 3 SU80
Directions: A286 from Chichester signed Midhurst, 2m then right at mini-rdbt, pub over bridge on left
Open: all day all week 7am-11.30pm Closed: 25 Dec
🍴 food served all day 🍽 L all wk 12-2.30 D all wk 6-9
Rooms: 8 en suite (2 GF) S £80-£130 D £95-£230
Facilities: Parking Garden Notes: ⊕ FREE HOUSE 👬 🍷 16

In a quiet village two miles north of Chichester stands this archetypal country pub and restaurant, offering stylish en suite rooms and two self-catering cottages. The interior is characterised by beams, bare brick walls, fireplaces and an intimate bar area with highly slumpworthy sofas and armchairs. The restaurant itself is furnished with pine tables and tall, modern leather chairs, and serves French, Mediterranean and New English cuisine backed by daily blackboard specials, all crying out to be accompanied by one of the many world-sourced wines. Extensively used local ingredients include crab and scallops from the English Channel. Try a starter of tian of smoked salmon, fresh salmon and salmon roe, or West Sussex pork and rabbit terrine with fig chutney, warm toast and salad leaves. Main courses might include duck, duck and duck (breast, ballantine and Charlotte), pan-fried skate with confit of pork belly, or smoked garlic polenta cake, chargrilled haloumi and harissa-spiced aubergine provençale. Among the inviting desserts are spiced plum and oat crumble with home-made custard, and glazed lemon tart with a hedgerow compote and mascarpone.

Recommended in the area

Chichester Cathedral; Goodwood House; South Downs Way

The Fish House

★★★★★ ◎◎ RESTAURANT WITH ROOMS

Address: High Street, CHILGROVE,
Nr Chichester, PO18 9HX
Tel: 01243 519444
Email: info@thefishhouse.co.uk
Website: www.thefishhouse.co.uk
Map ref: 3 SU81
Directions: On B2141 between Chichester &
Petersfield **Open:** all day all week ₤ ⎥O⎢ L all wk 12-
2.30 D all wk 6-10 **Rooms:** 15 en suite (11 GF)
S £80-£110 D £120-£160 **Facilities:** Parking Garden Wi-fi **Notes:** ⊕ FREE HOUSE ⅰ↑ ⌐ ☗ 24

Low ceilings, beams, an Irish marble-topped bar and decorative brickwork combine with leather sofas in this 300-year-old building. Why the name? Well, there is the atmospheric Fish Bar with its show-stopping oyster counter and there are the fish tanks, through which you can see chef Alan Gleeson and his team craft the finest seafood and other ingredients into classics and international dishes, all locally and organically sourced. Bar staff are used to serving oysters with Guinness, but they stock local ales and ciders too; the bar also has its own menu and daily specials. John Holt paintings adorn the walls of the two AA Rosette restaurant, and contrasting linen and drapes set off the oak and limestone floor. From the carte come wild brill with salsify, local ceps and red wine jus; Selsey lobster Thermidor; South Coast John Dory with Jerusalem artichoke risotto; and red-leg partridge with roast squash. Sunday roasts are served until 4pm. The 200-bin wine list includes more than 20 by the glass; you can ask to see the cellars. Overnight accommodation consists of 15 rooms, all uniquely themed and furnished to the very highest of standards, each equipped with 42-inch plasma televisions, espresso machines, mini-bars and luxurious bathrooms.

Recommended in the area

Weald and Downland Museum; Fishbourne Roman Palace; Chichester Festival Theatre

The Foresters Arms

Address: The Street, GRAFFHAM, GU28 0QA
Tel: 01798 867202
Email: info@forestersgraffham.co.uk
Website: www.forestersgraffham.co.uk
Map ref: 3 SU91 **Directions:** Telephone for directions
Open: 12-3 6-late (all day in summer) 🍺 🍴 L all wk 12-2.30
D Mon-Sat 6-9.15 (Sun 6-8) **Facilities:** Parking Garden
Notes: ⊕ FREE HOUSE 🍴 🐾 ♟ 9

This 17th-century country pub is situated in the heart of the South Downs National Park, and well placed for racing at Goodwood and polo at Cowdray Park. In the bar you'll find old beams and a large smoke-blackened fireplace, as well as good real ale choices and a carefully selected wine list. With ingredients sourced as close to home as possible, freshly prepared dishes on the concise Mediterranean-influenced British menu include seared calves' liver and pancetta; filo with spiced provençale ratatouille and goat's cheese velouté; Selsey crab fishcakes; and Harvey's ale-battered smoked haddock. There is a large, secluded garden and accommodation is available.

Recommended in the area

South Downs Way; Amberley Museum & Heritage Centre; Petworth House (NT)

The Anglesey Arms at Halnaker

Address: HALNAKER, Chichester, PO18 0NQ
Tel: 01243 773474 **Fax:** 01243 530034
Email: angleseyarms@aol.com
Website: www.angleseyarms.co.uk
Map ref: 3 SU90
Directions: From centre of Chichester 4m E on A285 (Petworth road) **Open:** all week 11-3 5.30-11 (Sat-Sun 11-11) 🍺 🍴 L Mon-Sun 12-2.30, Sun 12-4
D Mon-Sat 6.30-9.30 **Facilities:** Parking Garden
Wi-fi **Notes:** ⊕ PUNCH TAVERNS 🍴 🐾 ♟ 14

Standing in two acres of landscaped grounds on the Goodwood Estate, this charmingly old-fashioned Georgian inn offers a warm welcome whether you pop in for a quick drink or a meal in the dining room. Bowman Swift One and Young's Bitter are amongst the hand-pulled ales, plus there is an extensive wine list. Hand-cut sandwiches, ploughman's and local sausages are popular, or choose from the main menu. The kitchen team makes skilful use of organic meats especially steaks hung for at least 21 days, plus local fish. The area is noted for shooting, so game and venison are available in season.

Recommended in the area

Goodwood events; Boxgrove; Chichester

Chichester Cathedral

The Hollist Arms

Address: The Street, LODSWORTH,
Petworth, GU28 9BZ
Tel: 01798 861310
Email: george@thehollistarms.co.uk
Website: www.thehollistarms.co.uk
Map ref: 3 SU92
Directions: 0.5m between Midhurst & Petworth, 1m
N of A272, adjacent to Country Park **Open:** 11am-
11pm 🍺 🍽 **L** 12-2.30, **D** 6-9 **Facilities:** Parking
Garden Wi-fi **Notes:** ⊕ FREE HOUSE 👫 🐕 🍷 9

Named after Hasler Hollist, who was landlord in 1838, the pub is actually much older than that, dating
from the 15th century. It's a proper pub, a description that pub aficionados will understand. There's
a defined bar area and a 50-cover seating area with two large leather sofas in front of a roaring fire,
while other small rooms, again with fires, add to the comfortable atmosphere. Food is traditional
pub, all cooked fresh to order with big portions at reasonable prices. The absence of music and fruit
machines means the pub itself and its customers have to provide the ambiance. They do.

Recommended in the area

Cowdray Park; Uppark (NT); Hollycombe Steam Collection

Petworth House and Park

The Grove Inn

Address: Grove Lane, PETWORTH, GU28 0HY
Tel: 01798 343659
Email: steveandvaleria@tiscali.co.uk
Website: www.groveinnpetworth.co.uk
Map ref: 3 SU92
Directions: On outskirts of town, just off A283 between Pullborough & Petworth. 0.5m from Petworth Park
Open: Tue-Sat 12-3 6-11 (Sun 12-3) **Closed:** Sun eve & Mon (ex BH) ⬛ †◎ L Tue-Sun 12-2.30 D Tue-Sat 6-9.15 **Facilities:** Parking Garden **Notes:** 🛢 FREE HOUSE

The Grove Inn is a 17th-century free house in the heart of the South Downs. It sits on the outskirts of historic Petworth, a town much visited for its many and varied antique shops. Inside, the inn provides a cosy bar with oak-beamed ceilings and a large stone inglenook fireplace, as well as the Conservatory Restaurant, where diners can look out over the garden and enjoy good views of the South Downs. There is also a patio area with a pergola. Dishes are chosen from a seasonal menu, which is completely rewritten every six to eight weeks, with some daily changes for good measure. Typical starters include smoked salmon, chive and cream cheese roulade; home-made parsnip soup; and duck liver and mushroom terrine. Among the main courses are natural smoked haddock topped with Welsh rarebit; well-matured chargrilled fillet steak with truffle mash and cracked black peppercorn sauce; and wild mushroom risotto with parmesan and truffle oil. To follow there could be banana pancake with honey rum toffee sauce or lemon posset, as well as a choice of cheeseboards. Three whites, three reds and a rosé are available by the glass, with many more available on the main wine list.

Recommended in the area

Cowdray Park; Lurgashall Winery; Petworth House and Park

Royal Oak Inn

Address: The Street, POYNINGS, BN45 7AQ
Tel: 01273 857389
Fax: 01273 857202
Email: ropoynings@aol.com
Website: www.royaloakpoynings.biz
Map ref: 3 TQ21
Directions: N on A23 just outside Brighton, take A281 signed Henfield & Poynings, then follow signs into Poynings
Open: all day all week 11-11 (Sun noon-10.30)

🍴 🍽 food served all day **Facilities:** Parking Garden Wi-fi **Notes:** ⬡ FREE HOUSE 👫 🐾 🍷 14

Here since the 1880s, the award-winning Royal Oak clearly remains a popular village pub. Indeed, should you chance by and look in through the windows, particularly at night when the lights are on, you might expect to be seduced by its contemporary décor, comfy sofas, solid oak floors and old beams hung with hop bines. You will find a bar serving Lewes-brewed Harveys real ales and globally sourced wines from Enotria, one of the UK's leading wine importers. In the restaurant you can choose from a constantly evolving regular menu that may list confit leg and pan-roasted breast of Sussex pheasant with game faggot, buttered cavalo nero, shallot and sherry vinegar jus; spiced lamb kofta with a rich tomato sauce, carrot and coriander couscous and tzatziki; fish pie with free-range egg, Cheddar-glazed creamed potato and dressed mixed leaves; and asparagus and red pepper risotto with parmesan shavings, and balsamic syrup. Then again, some of the dishes are good old pub favourites like hand-made Henfield sausages with creamed potato, rich gravy and red onion jam. The chalkboard specials menu changes daily, and there are also tapas-size portions from the grazing menu, sandwiches and ciabattas. A barbecue menu is popular during the summer.

Recommended in the area

Devil's Dyke; Newtimber Place; Brighton Pavilion

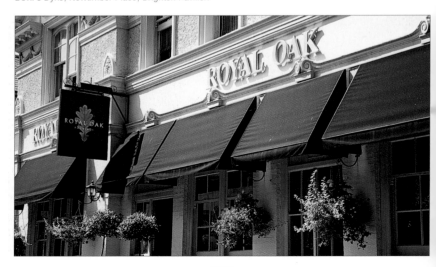

The Countryman Inn

Address: Countryman Lane, SHIPLEY, RH13 8PZ
Tel: 01403 741383
Fax: 01403 741115
Email: countrymaninn@btinternet.com
Website: www.countrymanshipley.co.uk
Map ref: 3 TQ12
Directions: From A272 at Coolham into Smithers Hill Ln.
1m to junct with Countryman Ln
Open: all week 10-4 6-11 🍴 L all wk 11.30-3.30
D all wk 6-10 **Facilities:** Parking Garden
Notes: ⊕ FREE HOUSE 🐕 ♀ 18

A rural hostelry in the traditional style, The Countryman is set in open countryside close to the small village of Shipley, surrounded by 3,500 acres of farmland owned by the Knepp Castle Estate. The area is in the process of being turned back to a more natural state, with the introduction of fallow deer, free-roaming Tamworth pigs, Exmoor ponies and English Longhorn cattle. Many wild birds have also been encouraged to return to the area, as the new growth of wild grasses and plant life provide a welcoming habitat. You can even do a bit of bird watching from the inn's garden in fine weather. During the winter you'll find warming log fires, Harvey's and organic Horsham ales in the cosy bar, together with over 30 wines from around the world, and freshly ground coffee. Free-range meat and vegetables from local farms make their appearance on the restaurant menu alongside fresh fish from Shoreham and Newhaven and local game in season. Menus change frequently, and as well as the carte there is also a range of ploughman's lunches, bar snacks and daily specials. Shipley's historic eight-sided smock mill (so-called because of its likeness to a traditional farm labourer's smock) is worth a visit.

Recommended in the area

Leonardslee Lakes & Gardens; Parham House & Gardens; Amberley Working Museum

WARWICKSHIRE

The Garrick Inn, Stratford-upon-Avon

The Bell

Address: ALDERMINSTER,
Stratford-upon-Avon, CV37 8NY
Tel: 01789 450414 **Fax:** 01789 450998
Email: info@thebellald.co.uk
Website: www.thebellald.co.uk
Map ref: 3 SP24
Directions: On A3400 3.5m S of
Stratford-upon-Avon **Open:** 11.30-2.30 6-11 (Fri-Sat
11.30-11 Sun noon-4.30) **Closed:** Sun eve
🛏 ⊙I L Mon-Fri 12-2, Sat 12-2.30, Sun 12-3

D Mon-Thu 7-9, Fri-Sat 6-9 **Facilities:** Parking Garden **Notes:** 🛢 FREE HOUSE ♦♦ 🐾 ♥ 14

The interior of this award-winning, 18th-century coaching inn successfully brings together the traditional and the modern. The warm and welcoming traditional bar has flagstone floors, low beams, open fires and candlelit tables, while the more contemporary, spacious conservatory restaurant overlooks the courtyard. Friendly staff and a relaxed atmosphere make it a popular venue for any occasion. Great fresh food is prepared from seasonal produce sourced from local suppliers.

Recommended in the area

Stratford-upon-Avon; Anne Hathaway's Cottage; Hidcote Manor (NT)

The Granville @ Barford

Address: 52 Wellesbourne Road,
BARFORD, CV35 8DS
Tel: 01926 624236 **Fax:** 01926 624806
Email: info@granvillebarford.co.uk
Website: www.granvillebarford.co.uk
Map ref: 3 SP24
Directions: 1m from M40 junct 15. Take A429
signed Stow. Located at furthest end of Barford
village **Open:** noon-3 5.30-11 (Fri-Sat noon-11.30
Sun noon-11) 🛏 L Mon-Thu 12-2.30 D Mon-Fri 6-9

⊙I L Mon-Thu 12-2.30, Fri-Sat 12-10 Sun 12-5 D Mon-Fri 6-9, Fri-Sat 12-10 Sun 12-5
Facilities: Parking Garden Wi-fi **Notes:** 🛢 ENTERPRISE INNS PLC ♦♦ 🐾 ♥ 17

This friendly and stylish village dining pub in the heart of Shakespeare country is owned and run by Val Kersey. Relax on the leather sofas in the lounge with a pint or glass of wine. Everything on your plate here is home made from local produce, except for the local, rustic bread. Try smoked salmon, dill and cucumber crème fraîche doorstop sandwich, or perhaps butternut squash and herb risotto with Parmesan crisps.

Recommended in the area

Warwick castle; Stoneleigh Abbey, Kenilworth; Baddesly Clinton Hall

The Howard Arms

Address: Lower Green, ILMINGTON,
nr Shipston on Stour, CV36 4LT
Tel: 01608 682226 **Fax:** 01608 682874
Email: info@howardarms.com
Website: www.howardarms.com
Map ref: 3 SP24
Directions: Off A429 or A3400, 9m from Stratford-upon-Avon **Open:** all day all week **Closed:** 25 Dec
eve, 26 Dec eve 🚲 ❐❙ L Mon-Sat 12-2.30, Sun
12-4 **D** Mon-Sun 6.30-9.30 **Facilities:** Parking
Garden Wi-fi **Notes:** ⊕ FREE HOUSE ♦♦ ⌁ ♥ 32

On the picturesque village green of Ilmington, in the crook of the Cotswold Hills, lies The Howard Arms, a stunning, 400-year-old Cotswold stone inn. The stylish pub and dining room offer an appealing mix of old furniture, polished flagstones and a log fire that burns for most of the year. The imaginative menu changes two or three times a week; check out the blackboard above the inglenook fireplace. In warmer weather, relax in the garden, enjoying one of the award-winning beers or a glass of wine from the carefully selected list.
Recommended in the area
Batsford Arboretum; Shakespeare's Birthplace; Anne Hathaway's Cottage

The Red Lion

★★★★ ⊛ INN
Address: Main Street, Long Compton,
SHIPSTON ON STOUR, CV36 5JS
Tel: 01608 684221 **Fax:** 01608 684968
Email: info@redlion-longcompton.co.uk
Website: www.redlion-longcompton.co.uk
Map ref: 3 SP24 **Directions:** On A3400 between
Shipston on Stour & Chipping Norton
Open: all week Mon-Thu 10-2.30 6-11 (Fri-Sun all
day) 🚲 ❐❙ L Mon-Thu 12-2.30, Fri-Sun 12-9.30

D Mon-Thu 6-9, Fri-Sun 12-9.30 **Rooms:** 5 en suite **S** £55 **D** £80-£99 **Facilities:** Parking Garden
Wi-fi **Notes:** ⊕ FREE HOUSE ♦♦ ⌁ ♥ 11

Originally built as a coaching inn in 1748, this traditional Cotswold pub retains its old world atmosphere with oak beams, log fires, high-backed settles and inglenook fireplaces. Award-winning food is served in the character bar, smart restaurant area or in the garden or on the patio, offering traditional and modern British dishes made from local produce. There are five individually-styled bedrooms available.
Recommended in the area
Shakespeare's Birthplace; Warwick Castle; Cotswold Wildlife Park

Warwick Castle beside the River Avon

Gas Street Basin, Birmingham

The Malt Shovel at Barston

Address: Barston Lane, BARSTON, Solihull, B92 0JP
Tel/fax: 01675 443223
Website: www.themaltshovelatbarston.com
Map ref: 3 SP27
Directions: M42 junct 5, take turn towards Knowle.
1st left on Jacobean Ln, right at T-junct (Hampton
Ln). Sharp left into Barston Ln. Restaurant 0.5m
Open: all day all week ♿ **L** Mon-Sat 12-2.30, Sun
12-4 **D** Mon-Sat 6-9.30 🍽 **L** Sun 12-4 **D** Mon-Sat
7-9.30 **Facilities:** Parking Garden **Notes:** ⊕ FREE HOUSE

Converted from an early 20th-century mill where malt was ground, this delightful country pub and restaurant features log fires, stripped wooden floors, heavy fabrics and a beautiful garden. Cask-conditioned ales are served in the bar, where you can lunch on faggots, chilli chicken, or a fresh fish special. In a converted barn is the stylish restaurant, offering a seasonally-changing menu of dishes such as baby pork ribs with home-made marinade, or corn-fed duck breast, celeriac and potato rösti.
Recommended in the area
National Exhibition Centre (NEC); Birmingham city centre; Solihull countryside

Walsall Arboretum

ISLE OF WIGHT

Shanklin Chine

The Seaview Hotel & Restaurant

Address: High Street, SEAVIEW, PO34 5EX
Tel: 01983 612711
Fax: 01983 613729
Email: reception@seaviewhotel.co.uk
Website: www.seaviewhotel.co.uk
Map ref: 3 SZ69
Directions: B3330 (Ryde to Seaview road), left via Puckpool along seafront road, hotel on left
Open: all week ⌂ L all wk 12-2.30 D all wk 6.30-9.30 ⌂ L all wk 12-2 (summer), Sat-Sun 12-2 (winter) D all wk 6.30-9.30
Rooms: 28 (4 GF) **S** £99-£220 **D** £125-£255 **Notes:** ⊕ FREE HOUSE ⫯ ⇥

In a sailing-mad Victorian village, this smart, sea-facing hotel is crammed with nautical associations. There are ships' wheels, oars, model ships, and lots of polished wood and brass. The Front Bar & Lounge resembles a naval wardroom and is home to a collection of naval artefacts, while the Pump Bar at the back is like a traditional pub, with a fish-focused menu. You may also eat in the small Victorian dining room, or the Sunshine restaurant and conservatory, both of which share a modern European (with a hint of British) menu that offers the very best of the season, caught or grown around the island – fish straight from the sea; pork and beef from its lush grazing land; venison from the hotel's own farm; and tomatoes, garlic and herbs from its garden. The menu might include spider crab risotto with fennel sauce as a starter; Wight lamb shepherd's pie, carrot purée and beef sauce; or lightly curried cod, spiced lentils, buttered spring greens and herb crème fraîche sauce as a main course; and pineapple parfait, black pepper ice cream, with sweet red pepper and chilli syrup for dessert.

Recommended in the area

Seaview Wildlife Encounter (Flamingo Park); Osborne House; Isle of Wight Steam Railway

The New Inn

Address: Mill Lane, SHALFLEET, PO30 4NS
Tel/Fax: 01983 531314
Email: info@thenew-inn.co.uk
Website: www.thenew-inn.co.uk
Map ref: 3 SZ48 **Directions:** 6m from Newport to Yarmouth on A3054 **Open:** all day all week ⛽ ⌖ L all wk 12-2.30 D all wk 6-9.30 **Facilities:** Parking Garden Wi-fi
Notes: ⊞ ENTERPRISE INNS ⁑ ⚡ ⚘ 11

Built in 1743 to replace its fire-razed predecessor, this well-regarded dining pub is at the head of the Newtown estuary, putting it in pole position for nautical types. Inglenooks, flagstones and low beams provide bags of character, while its waterside location gives it enviable access to the best fish and seafood, such as specials of cracked crab, fillets of pollock and grilled mackerel. On the same board are slow-roasted pork belly and pan-fried chicken breast, while the standard menu offers steaks, prawn specialities, baguettes and salads. Island-brewed beers are on tap and more than 60 wines are always available.

Recommended in the area

The Needles; Blackgang Chine; Isle of Wight Steam Railway

The Needles

The Crown Inn

Address: Walkers Lane, SHORWELL,
nr Newport, PO30 3JZ
Tel/Fax: 01983 740293
Email: pamela@notjust.org.uk
Website: www.crowninnshorwell.co.uk
Map ref: 3 SZ48
Directions: Turn left at top of Carisbrooke
High Street, Shorwell approx 6m
Open: all day all week 🐾 🍴 all day 12-9
Facilities: Parking Garden Wi-fi
Notes: ⊕ ENTERPRISE INNS ♦♦ 🐾 ☗ 12

Outdoor types recently voted The Crown their favourite destination pub. While it must help that it is only five miles from the centre of the island, they clearly love its authentic country atmosphere, winter log fire and summer rear garden with an arum lily-decorated trout stream. Also exerting a strong pull, no doubt, are the six real ales, including an island brew. The building is part 17th century, and different floor levels attest to many alterations, but while the most recent rebuild has seen a large increase in floor area, the pub is still full of character. Certainly nothing has upset the resident female ghost who shows her disapproval of card playing by scattering cards on the bar floor overnight. Food consists of home-made favourites based on locally sourced lamb, beef, fish and seasonal game. Make sure you check out the award-winning specials board that usually lists ten choices, such as sea bass, salmon and roasted duck breast; or there are classic pub dishes like sausage and mash; wild mushroom risotto; Spanish chicken; and smoked salmon and prawn tagliatelle. Other fish dishes include dusted lemon and pepper plaice, and luxury fisherman's pie. A Wendy house, slide and swings keep youngsters amused.

Recommended in the area

Blackgang Chine; Needles Old Battery (NT); Isle of Wight Steam Railway

Stonehenge

Red Lion Inn

Address: AXFORD, Marlborough, SN8 2HA
Tel: 01672 520271
Email: info@redlionaxford.com
Website: www.redlionaxford.com
Map ref: 3 SU27
Directions: M4 junct 15, A246 Marlborough centre.
Follow Ramsbury signs. Inn 3m **Open:** 12-3 6-11
Closed: 1st 2wks Jan, Sun eve, Mon ▥ ⦿ **L** Tue-
Sun 12-2 **D** Tue-Sat 6-9 **Facilities:** Parking Garden
Notes: ⊕ FREE HOUSE ⁛

For over 400 years, this eye-catching inn has welcomed travellers passing along the Kennet valley. From the flower-bedecked terrace, divine views percolate to the river and surrounding countryside of the North Downs Area of Outstanding Natural Beauty. Tables and chairs, cunningly constructed from half-barrels, squashy sofas and inglenook fireplace complete the atmosphere in the convivial bar. Elsewhere, brick and flint feature walls are the backdrop for the lounges and Garden Restaurant. Enjoy a glass of vintage wine or Axford Ale while perusing a modern European menu strong on game and fish.

Recommended in the area

Marlborough; Avebury; Savernake forest

Marlborough

The Three Crowns

Address: BRINKWORTH, Chippenham, SN15 5AF
Tel: 01666 510366
Website: www.threecrowns.co.uk
Map ref: 3 SU08
Directions: From Swindon take A3102 to Wootton Bassett, then B4042, 5m to Brinkworth
Open: all day all week 10am-mdnt
Closed: 25-26 Dec ▙ ⍥ L Mon-Sat 12-2, Sun 12-9 D Mon-Sat 6-9.30, Sun 12-9
Facilities: Parking Garden Wi-fi
Notes: ⊕ ENTERPRISE INNS ➤ ♟ 27

The current licensees, Anthony and Allyson Windle, have been here over 20 years and are now well into researching this quiet little pub's history. They know that it opened with its current name in 1801, but suspect that in the 18th century it traded under a different name. In 1927 Kelly's directory lists it as a hotel, serving teas and light refreshments; today it is one of the area's most popular eating venues. Menus are written on large blackboards, which make it easy to keep up with the daily, market-driven changes. Everything is home made using top quality ingredients, main dishes being typified by aged West Country beef, lamb and mint pie, supreme of halibut and vegetarian tagliatelle, all cooked to order and served with a generous selection of fresh vegetables. Lighter lunches range from Caesar salad to slow-roast belly pork and beef chilli. The bar stocks a wide range of well-kept cask ales, keg beers and lagers, and Anthony and his wine merchant have carefully chosen (and tasted, over a period, naturally!) an 80-bin wine list. In winter there is an open log fire, while in summer the doors are flung open to the peaceful patio and garden.

Recommended in the area

Westonbirt Arboretum; Cotswold Water Park; Lydiard Park

The Dove Inn

★★★ ⍟ INN

Address: CORTON, Warminster, BA12 0SZ
Tel: 01985 850109 **Fax:** 01985 851041
Email: info@thedove.co.uk
Website: www.thedove.co.uk
Map ref: 2 ST94
Directions: A36 (Salisbury towards Warminster), in 14m turn left signed Corton & Boyton. Cross rail line, right at T-junct. Corton approx 1.5m, turn right into village **Open:** all week noon-3 6-11.30
♨ ⍟ **L** all wk 12-3 **D** all wk 7-9.30 **Rooms:** 5 en suite (4 GF)
Facilities: Parking Garden Wi-fi **Notes:** ⊕ FREE HOUSE ⸙ 🐾

Little changed by the passage of time, The Dove is a 19th-century free house in a village in the Wylye valley. Inside is a flagstone and oak-floored bar with a log-framed wood-burning stove, where locals enjoy a beer or two - several real ales are always on offer - and a bit of banter. The bar extends into a comfortable, relaxing restaurant and conservatory where diners can enjoy a sumptuous meal or light snack freshly prepared by the talented young chef and his creative team. There are grazing menus featuring cheese fondue, cured meats and smoked salmon; and starters of sautéed Sicilian-style courgette caponata with Somerset brie and toasted brioche; and steamed Shetland mussels with chorizo and Stowford Press cider sauce. Mains might include grilled whole spatchcock baby chicken; wild mushroom and truffle with fresh potato gnocchi; Sharps Doom Bar-battered haddock fillet; and local wild rabbit, pancetta, wild mushroom and cider pie. Finally, there are the desserts - sticky date pudding with caramel sauce and double cream, and macadamia nut crème brûlée. Whatever you choose, the reason for the AA Rosette will be apparent. Outside in the courtyard, cottage-style bedrooms overlook a pretty, apple tree-shaded beer garden.

Recommended in the area

Longleat House and Safari Park; Westbury White Horse; Stonehenge

The Fox and Hounds

Address: The Green, EAST KNOYLE,
Salisbury, SP3 6BN
Tel: 01747 830573
Fax: 01747 830865
Email: pub@foxandhounds-eastknoyle.co.uk
Website: www.foxandhounds-eastknoyle.co.uk
Map ref: 2 ST83
Directions: 1.5m off A303 at the A350 turn off,
follow brown signs
Open: all week 11.30-3 5.30-11 ⓑ ⓘⓞⓘ L all wk
12-2.30 D all wk 6-9 **Facilities:** Parking Garden Wi-fi
Notes: ⊕ FREE HOUSE ⚬ᵗ ⚘ ⚑ 15

Surrounded by excellent walking and with stunning views of the Blackmore Vale, The Fox and Hounds is a picturesque 15th-century thatched free house that was built originally as three cottages. Here, guests can enjoy an imaginative menu and a range of traditional ales and ciders from West Country brewers as well as many wines by the glass. The village, which is situated on a greensand ridge, was once home to the family of Jane Seymour, Henry VIII's third wife, as well as Christopher Wren, whose father was the local vicar. Inside the pub, all is comfortable and cosy, with flagstone flooring, natural stone walls and sofas positioned next to wood-burning fires in winter. Diners can enjoy a meal in the light, airy conservatory or in the patio area. A varied menu, based on local produce, contains a range of snacks and main meals. These might include ploughman's or pizzas (from the clay oven), as well as lamb chump on mash, venison, 21-day-old fillet or sirloin steak with a choice of sauces, Thai green curry or Moroccan vegetable tagine. For those with room to spare, Pavlova with passion fruit coulis and warm chocolate fudge cake are among the desserts.

Recommended in the area

Stonehenge ; Stourhead House and Gardens (NT); Longleat

The Angel Coaching Inn

Address: High Street, HEYTESBURY, BA12 0ED
Tel: 01985 840330
Fax: 01985 840931
Email: admin@angelheytesbury.co.uk
Website: www.angelheytesbury.co.uk
Map ref: 2 ST94
Directions: From A303 take A36 towards Bath, 8m, Heytesbury on left
Open: all week ⬛ ⦿ L all wk 12-2.30
D all wk 6.30-9.30 **Facilities:** Parking Garden Wi-fi
Notes: ⊕ GREENE KING ⬤ ⟊ ⦇ 8

A 16th-century inn surrounded by countryside best appreciated on foot, so why not embark on one of the walks that start and end here. The Angel's interior is a blend of its original features and the contemporary; the beamed bar, for instance, has scrubbed pine tables, warmly decorated walls and an attractive fireplace with a wood-burning stove. It's often packed with locals, dogs by their sides, discussing everything from the local shoots to the price of beer. Exposed brickwork and antique dressers add a rustic feel to the more formal dining areas. A talented team in the kitchen produce an ever-changing menu to reflect the excellent West Country larder. As much as possible, produce is locally sourced – local steaks are a firm favourite. From an imaginative menu, a choice for dinner may be duck egg with caramelised apple and black pudding Scotch egg, followed by rack of Wiltshire lamb with Lyonnaise potatoes, runner beans and port sauce, with trio of chocolate – brownie, mousse and ice cream – to finish. Alternatively, for a quick bite just pop in for a plate of home-cooked ham with chunky hand-cut chips and salad.

Recommended in the area

Stonehenge; Old Sarum; Longleat

The Lamb at Hindon

★★★★ ⊛ INN

Address: High Street, HINDON, Salisbury, SP3 6DP
Tel: 01747 820573
Fax: 01747 820605
Email: info@lambathindon.co.uk
Website: www.lambathindon.co.uk
Map ref: 2 ST93
Directions: From A303 follow signs to Hindon.
At Fonthill Bishop right onto B3089 to Hindon.
Pub on left **Open:** all day all week 7.30am-mdnt

🛏 ⊠ L all wk 12-2.30 D all wk 6.30-9.30 **Rooms:** 19 en suite (2 GF) **S** £50-£115 **D** £60-£175
Facilities: Parking Garden Wi-fi **Notes:** ⊕ BOISDALE ♦♦ ⌐ ♟ 10

The Lamb is set in the centre of a charming village just 20 minutes from Salisbury. It began trading
as a public house as long ago as the 12th century and by 1870 it supplied 300 horses to pull coaches
on the London–West Country route. The inn is part of the Boisdale group, with two other establishments
in London (Belgravia and Bishopsgate), and this is reflected in the distinctive interior design and in the
quality of the food and wine. The building still has plenty of historic character, with beams, inglenook
fireplaces, and wood and flagstone floors, all set off by fine antique furniture, old paintings and open
fires. Food is served from breakfast to dinner in the dining room or the intimate Whisky and Cigar Bar.
Dishes are prepared from carefully sourced ingredients, including fresh fish and game in season.
A dinner menu might feature main courses such as Macsween haggis; Gloucester Old Spot sausages
with Beaune mustard mash and gravy; and the 'famous Boisdale' burger; plus a fish of the day and pie
of the day. The Meeting Room, in a sunken area just off the main dining room, is available for private
dining or meetings. Each bedroom is richly decorated and has LCD screens.

Recommended in the area

Longleat; Stonehenge; Stourhead House & Gardens

Compasses Inn

★★★★ ◉ INN

Address: LOWER CHICKSGROVE,
Nr Tisbury, SP3 6NB
Tel: 01722 714318
Email: thecompasses@aol.com
Website: www.thecompassesinn.com
Map ref: 2 ST92
Directions: On A30 (1.5m W of Fovant) take 3rd
right to Lower Chicksgrove. In 1.5m turn left into
Lagpond Lane, pub 1m on left **Open:** all week noon-

3 6-11 (Sun noon-3 7-10.30) **Closed:** 25-26 Dec ⮜ ⭗ **L** all wk 12-2 **D** all wk 6.30-9 **Rooms:** 5 en
suite **S** £50-£85 **D** £70-£130 **Facilities:** Parking Garden Wi-fi **Notes:** ⊕ FREE HOUSE ⭗ ⭗ ⭗ 8

This 14th-century thatched inn comes brimful of character and atmosphere. Its original beams derive
from decommissioned galleons, while stone walls, uneven flagstones and high settle booths add further
charm. The cooking's modern though, making intelligent use of carefully sourced produce, with regularly
changing menus chalked on blackboards. Four attractive bedrooms and a cottage are available.
Recommended in the area
Longleat; Stonehenge; Farmer Giles Farmstead

Salisbury Cathedral

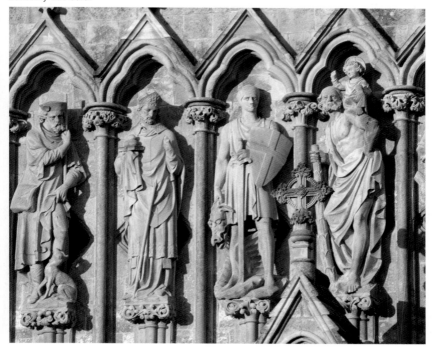

The George & Dragon

★★★★ ◉◉ RESTAURANT WITH ROOMS

Address: High Street, ROWDE, SN10 2PN
Tel: 01380 723053
Email: thegandd@tiscali.co.uk
Website: www.thegeorgeanddragonrowde.co.uk
Map ref: 2 ST96
Directions: 1m from Devizes, take A342 towards Chippenham **Open:** Mon-Sun L **Closed:** Sun eve
🍴 🍽 L Mon-Sat 12-3, Sun 12-4 D Mon-Fri 7-10, Sat 6.30-10 **Rooms:** 3 (2 en suite) (1 pri fac)

wkdays £55-£85 wkends £80-£105 **Facilities:** Parking Garden **Notes:** ⊕ FREE HOUSE 🍴 🐾 🍷 10

Successfully combining the charm of a 16th-century inn with the relaxed atmosphere of a modern gastro-pub, The George and Dragon is located on Rowde High Street, a stone's throw from the Kennet and Avon Canal and the dramatic Caen Hill flight of locks. In summer the garden is a delight, with its lawned area and cottage-style flower borders, and there's seating for an alfresco meal or a quiet drink. During winter there are welcoming log fires in the panelled bars and dining room, and an interesting original feature is a carved Tudor rose on one of the old beams in the restaurant. Seafood delivered directly from Cornwall is the speciality of the house, so diners can take their pick from the latest catch. The choice is huge, and may comprise sea bass, lobster, lemon sole, John Dory, mackerel, scallops, turbot and mussels. Blackboards above the bar list the fish dishes of the day, while the carte offers a range of local meat and game options. The emphasis of the award-winning food is on home-made delicacies, and this extends from the bread served at the start of the meal, to the delicious desserts and ice creams, and the chocolate fudge served with coffee. Draught beers include Butcombe Bitter, Milk Street Brewery ales and Bath Ales Gem. There are three bedrooms available, each full of character.

Recommended in the area

Bowood House and Gardens; Lacock Abbey, Fox Talbot Museum & Village; Avebury

The Somerset Arms

★★★★ INN

Address: High Street, SEMINGTON, BA14 6JR
Tel: 01380 870067
Website: www.somersetarmssemington.co.uk
Map ref: 2 ST86
Directions: From Devizes towards Trowbridge on A361 (approx 8m) turn right at rdbt after rdbt junct with A350. Pub in village **Open:** all day all week 🍽 L all wk 12-3 D all wk 6.30-9 🍴 L all wk 12-3 D Sun-Thu 6.30-9, Fri-Sat 6.30-9.30 **Rooms:** 3 en suite **S** fr £65 **D** fr £75 **Facilities:** Parking Garden Wi-fi **Notes:** ⊕ FREE HOUSE 🛈 🐕 ♟ 16

A fine old coaching inn, the 17th century Somerset Arms was stylishly refurbished in 2009, its newly acquired muted green and cream interior now bringing out the best in its long-acquired character. Named after the Duke of Somerset, once a big noise round here, it is run by James, Darren and a strong team who together create an infectious atmosphere. The chefs use local ingredients as much as possible, all their meats, vegetables and dairy produce coming from local farms, their fish delivered fresh. A seasonally changing carte might well feature duck breast on sweet and sour pickled vegetables with egg noodles; pan-fried fillet of salmon with dill mash and saffron mussel sauce; rump of lamb with sautéed potatoes and wild mushroom Madeira jus; and vegetable cottage pie with roasted vine tomatoes. But although recognised as one of the best restaurants in the area, it hasn't forgotten its roots as a free house, and real ale lovers wouldn't fault its policy of supporting only breweries located within 50 miles of Semington, such as Bath Ales, Box Steam, Hopback, Stonehenge and Milk Street. Beer and cider festivals are regularly held here. Three boutique-style en suite B&B rooms are decorated with elegant wallpapers and fabrics.

Recommended in the area

City of Bath; West Kennet Long Barrow; Lacock Abbey (NT)

The Bridge Inn

Address: 26 Church Street, WEST LAVINGTON,
Devizes, SN10 4LD
Tel: 01380 813213
Email: portier@btopenworld.com
Website: www.the-bridge-inn.co.uk
Map ref: 3 SU05
Directions: Approx 7m S of Devizes on A360
towards Salisbury. On edge of village, beyond church
Open: noon-3 6.30-11 **Closed:** 2wks Feb, Sun
eve & Mon ⓑ ⓘ⊙ⓘ L Tue-Sun 12-2 **D** Tue-Sat 7-9
Facilities: Parking Garden **Notes:** ⊕ ENTERPRISE INNS ⓣ 12

Located on the outskirts of a village on the edge of Salisbury Plain, the well known Bridge is a pub and restaurant with a beamed bar and log fire, and local paintings adorning the walls. Real ales come from Wadworths with Plain Ales regularly available. Owned by Cyrille and Paula Portier since February 2004, this food-led establishment produces English food with a French twist, with light lunches, a regular carte and a specials board. In the large garden there is a boules pitch.

Recommended in the area

Longleat; Stonehenge; Lacock Abbey; Fox Talbot Museum & Village

Lacock Abbey

The Pear Tree Inn

★★★★★ ◎◎ RESTAURANT WITH ROOMS

Address: Top Lane, WHITLEY, Melksham, SN12 8QX
Tel: 01225 709131
Fax: 01225 702276
Email: peartreeinn@maypolehotels.com
Website: www.maypolehotels.com
Map ref: 2 ST86
Directions: A365 from Melksham towards Bath, at Shaw right onto B3353 into Whitley, 1st left in lane, pub at end
Open: all day all week breakfast-11pm
🍴 †◎† **L** all wk 12-2.30 **D** all wk 6.30-9.30 **Rooms:** 8 en suite (4 GF) **S** fr £70 **D** fr £90 **Facilities:** Parking Garden Wi-fi
Notes: ⊕ MAYPOLE GROUP PLC 🍴 🐾 ⚑ 8+

Here you'll find a delightful, stone-built country pub and restaurant that also offers cosy accommodation in beautifully designed bedrooms. Flagstone floors and two log fires help to give it a comfortable, lived-in feel, with pitchforks, old scythes and other agricultural antiques reminding one of its past as a farm. Indeed, the surrounding acres of wooded farmland prepare you for the possible imminent arrival of Farmer Giles for his pint of Sharp's Doom Bar, or one of the regularly changing guest beers. The food, prepared from locally supplied produce, has been much praised and awarded two AA Rosettes. The menu, served throughout the pub, including in the terracotta and mustard barn-conversion restaurant, offers an updated approach to traditional British food. A typical three-course meal comprising Middle White pork and apricot pâté with home-made piccalilli followed by braised and rolled lamb shoulder, pea mousse, courgette and mint chutney, and sticky peach pudding. There is a healthy menu for children. Outside, in addition to the lovely cottage garden, there is also a patio area.

Recommended in the area

Lacock Abbey; Avebury; Silbury Hill

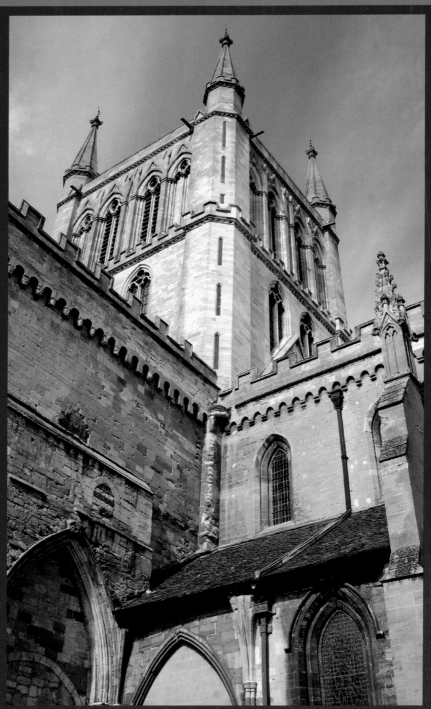

Pershore Abbey

The Fleece Inn

Address: The Cross, BRETFORTON,
Evesham, WR11 7JE
Tel: 01386 831173
Email: nigel@thefleeceinn.co.uk
Website: www.thefleeceinn.co.uk
Map ref: 3 SP04
Directions: From Evesham follow signs for B4035
towards Chipping Campden. Through Badsey into
Bretforton. Right at village hall, past church **Open:**
Mon-Tue 11-3 6-11 Wed-Sun 11-11 ⓑ L Mon-Sat
12-2.30, Sun 12-4 **D** Mon-Sat 6.30-9, Sun 6.30-8.30 **Facilities:** Garden **Notes:** ⊞ FREE HOUSE ⁙ ⏍ 12

The Fleece was built as a longhouse 600 years ago and its last private owner, Lola Taplin, – who died
in the snug in 1977, bequeathing it to the National Trust, – was a direct descendant of the man who
built it. Restorations after a fire in 2004 ensured that The Fleece looks as good as ever. Home-made
dishes include local sausage of the day with mash, pork belly marinated in plum cider brewed on the
premises and a fresh fish dish of the day. Look out for Morris dancers, folk singing and asparagus!
Recommended in the area
Chipping Campden; Hidcote Manor (NT); Cotswold Way; Abbey Park, Evesham

14th-century Almonry, Evesham

251

Captain Cook's Monument, Cleveland Way, Easby Moor

The Black Bull Inn

Address: 6 St James Square, BOROUGHBRIDGE,
Nr York, YO51 9AR
Tel: 01423 322413 **Fax:** 01423 323915
Website: www.blackbullboroughbridge.co.uk
Map ref: 8 SE36
Directions: From A1(M) junct 48 take B6265 E for
1m **Open:** all day all week 11-11 (Fri-Sat 11am-mdnt,
Sun noon-11) ♿ ⚑ **L** all wk 12-2 **D** all wk 6-9
Facilities: Parking **Notes:** ⊕ FREE HOUSE ♦ ⌖ ♟ 11

Built in 1258, The Black Bull was one of the main watering holes for coaches travelling what is now the A1, and Dick Turpin allegedly stayed here. Back then it had stables and a blacksmith's shop attached; and these days, it still retains plenty of original features, including old beams, low ceilings and roaring open fires, not to mention the supposed ghost of a monk. Traditional pub fare is the order of the day here, with extensive menus covering all the options. Starters such as chicken liver pâté with Cumberland sauce; king prawn tails and queen scallops; and Scottish smoked salmon are sure to whet the appetite. The main courses that follow might include rump of English lamb with rosemary and olive mashed potato; chicken breast wrapped in Parma ham with pan-fried wild mushroom; and a selection of very substantial steak dishes. Several fish options are also available, including the likes of salmon, halibut, sea bass, tuna and Dover sole. Desserts include banoffee meringue roulade with toffee sauce; dark chocolate truffle torte; apple pie with custard; and mixed ice creams encased in brandy snap with fruit purées. Sizeable bar snacks range from pork and chive sausage with onion gravy, and deep-fried prawns, to Thai beef strips with egg noodles and stir fry vegetables. Among the array of sandwiches are hot roast pork and apple sauce; and cold smoked salmon with dill mayonnaise. Yorkshire beers are available, and there is a selection of 17 malts.

Recommended in the area

Newby Hall and Gardens; Mother Shipton's Cave; Ripon city and cathedral

Malt Shovel Inn

Address: BREARTON, Harrogate, HG3 3BX
Tel: 01423 862929
Email: bleikers@themaltshovelbrearton.co.uk
Website: www.themaltshovelbrearton.co.uk
Map ref: 8 SE36
Directions: From A61 (Ripon/Harrogate) onto B6165 towards Knaresborough. Left & follow Brearton signs. In 1m right into village
Open: Wed-Sun L **Closed:** Mon, Tue, Sun eve
🏠 🍴 L Wed-Sat 12-2, Sun 12-3 **D** Wed-Sat 6-9
Facilities: Parking Garden **Notes:** ⊕ FREE HOUSE ♦♦ ♟ 21

At the heart of the picturesque village of Brearton lies the Malt Shovel, a fine family-run 16th-century inn. Although the pub is surrounded by rolling farmland, it is just 15 minutes from Harrogate and within easy reach of both Knaresborough and Ripon. One of the oldest buildings in an ancient village, it was taken over by the Bleiker family in 2006 and has been transformed into an atmospheric venue for eating and drinking, with open fires in winter, flagstoned floors and pianos in the bar and conservatory. Swiss-born Jürg's innovative cooking specialises in fresh fish – there's an on-site smoking kiln – classic sauces and well-sourced local produce, and diners can choose from the lunchtime and early evening bistro menu or opt to eat à la carte. The family bring their wealth of experience in food, hospitality and entertainment to create an ambience that combines elegance and theatricality – Anna and D'Arcy Bleiker are international opera soloists, and it's not unheard of for the odd aria to be served up at dinner. However it's their commitment to great food, fine wine (over twenty are served by the glass), impeccable cask ales and the warmest of welcomes that bring customers back again and again.

Recommended in the area

Ripley Castle; Fountains Abbey (NT); Yorkshire Dales

The Bull

Address: BROUGHTON, nr Skipton, BD23 3AE
Tel: 01756 792065
Email: enquiries@thebullatbroughton.com
Website: www.thebullatbroughton.com
Map ref: 7 SD95
Directions: 3m from Skipton on A59 **Open:** all day all week Mon-Sat noon-11pm, Sun noon-10.30pm **Closed:** 25 Dec
L Mon-Sat noon-2, Sun noon-8.30 **D** Mon-Fri 6-9, Sat 5.30-9, Sun noon-8.30 **Facilities:** Parking Garden
Notes: FREE HOUSE

Long one of the county's landmark pubs, The Bull takes its name from the surrounding 3,000-acre Broughton Hall estate's famous herd of Shorthorns. Summer offers alfresco dining on the patios overlooking this parkland, which is often used for location filming; winter means eating and drinking warmed by blazing log fires. Real ales include Timothy Taylor Landlord and the unusual Saltaire Raspberry Blonde. The restaurant is acclaimed chef Nigel Haworth's first venture into Yorkshire (he honed his skills in Lancashire!). Star of BBC2's *Great British Menu*. He loves working with the region's farmers, growers and fine food suppliers to create dishes strong on local tradition, thus it should be no surprise to find a menu offering Yorkshire game pudding, forager's mash potato, roasted root vegetables and game sauce; The Bull North Sea fish pie; and Taste Tradition rare breed 10oz sirloin steak. An option among the hot and cold sandwich fillings is 'real' chips cooked in dripping – your waistline has been warned! Desserts include warm Skipton pudding with Lane Ends Farm organic cream; traditional English pancakes; and home-made organic ice creams and milkshakes.
Recommended in the area
Yorkshire Dales National Park; Malham Cove; Haworth

The Fox & Hounds

Address: CARTHORPE, Bedale, DL8 2LG
Tel: 01845 567433
Website: www.foxandhoundscarthorpe.co.uk
Map ref: 7 SE38
Directions: Off A1, signed on both N'bound &
S'bound carriageways
Open: Tue-Sun 12-3 7-11 **Closed:** 25-26 Dec eve
& 1st wk Jan, Mon 🍽 **L** Tue-Sat 12-2 **D** Tue-Sat
7-9.30 **Facilities:** Parking **Notes:** ⊕ FREE HOUSE ♦♦

Near the Great North Road, but in rural surrounds, The Fox and Hounds has been serving travellers for the past 200 years, and for the last 27 of them the same family have been making a thoroughly good job of continuing the tradition. The restaurant, once the village smithy, serves up imaginative dishes, and the midweek set-price menu is particularly good value, with dishes such as pan-fried lambs' liver with bacon and onion gravy or, from the specials board, grilled whole Dover sole with parsley butter. Home-made desserts might include chocolate fondue and almond raspberry tart with vanilla ice cream.
Recommended in the area
Ariel Extreme; Snape Arboretum; Black Sheep Brewery Visitor Centre

Great Ayton to Cleveland Hills

The Durham Ox

Address: Westway, CRAYKE, York, YO61 4TE
Tel: 01347 821506 **Fax:** 01347 823326
Email: enquiries@thedurhamox.com
Website: www.thedurhamox.com
Map ref: 8 SE57
Directions: Off A19 from York to Thirsk, then to Easingwold. From market place to Crayke, turn left up hill, pub on right
Open: all week 12-2.30 6-11 **Closed:** 25 Dec
🛌 🍽 L Mon-Sat 12-2.30, Sun 12-3 D Mon-Sat 6-9.30, Sun 6-8.30 **Rooms:** 5 en suite (2 GF) **S** £80-£150 **D** £100-£150
Facilities: Parking Garden Wi-fi **Notes:** ⊕ FREE HOUSE 🐕 ♟ 10

Three hundred years old, and family-owned for the last ten, The Durham Ox is an award-winning traditional pub with flagstone floors, exposed beams, oak panelling and roaring fires. Situated in historic Crayke, with breathtaking views over the Vale of York on three sides, and a charming view up the hill (reputedly the one the Grand Old Duke of York's men marched up and down) to the church. A print of the eponymous ox – and a hefty beast it was too – hangs in the bottom bar. The Ox prides itself on serving good pub food, using the best locally sourced ingredients when possible for seasonal menus, complemented by blackboard specials. Dishes likely to be found are Ox prawn cocktail with home-made bread; spicy vegetable fritters, chick pea and ginger hummous, yoghurt and cucumber dip; Mount Grace rib-eye steak with béarnaise sauce; or venison and root vegetable casserole, Mount St John horseradish dumplings and red wine sauce. On Sundays, traditional rib of beef and Yorkshire puddings, fresh fish and other dishes are complemented by delicious desserts. Snacks include eggs Benedict, or Florentine, with bacon; chargrilled Ox burger; and a variety of open sandwiches. Four converted farm cottages provide overnight accommodation.
Recommended in the area
Castle Howard; Scampston; Byland Abbey

The Blue Lion

Address: EAST WITTON, Nr Leyburn, DL8 4SN
Tel: 01969 624273 **Fax:** 01969 624189
Email: enquiries@thebluelion.co.uk
Website: www.thebluelion.co.uk
Map ref: 7 SE18
Directions: From Ripon take A6108 towards Leyburn
Open: all day all week 11-11 **Closed:** 25 Dec
🍺 L all wk 12-2.15 D all wk 7-9.30 ⭐ L Sun 12-
2.15 D all wk 7-9.30 **Facilities:** Parking Garden Wi-fi
Notes: 🌐 FREE HOUSE 👫 🐕 🍷 12

A sympathetically renovated country inn, built towards the end of the 18th century for coach travellers and cattle drovers journeying through Wensleydale. The bar, with an open fire and flagstone floor, is a beer drinker's heaven, while the freshly prepared food in the highly praised candlelit restaurant uses mainly Yorkshire ingredients. A meal might start with salad of black pudding, smoked bacon, shallots and poached egg, followed by chargrilled fillet of beef with shiraz sauce, lardons and mushrooms, and pineapple Tatin with home-made pineapple sorbet. Bar meals are listed on a blackboard.

Recommended in the area

Yorkshire Dales National Park; Jervaulx Abbey; Hardraw Force Waterfall

Hardraw Force, Yorkshire Dales National Park

The Plough Inn

Address: Main Street, FADMOOR, York, YO62 7HY
Tel: 01751 431515
Fax: 01751 432492
Email: enquiries@theploughfadmoor.co.uk
Website: www.theploughfadmoor.co.uk
Map ref: 8 SE68
Directions: 1m N of Kirkbymoorside on A170 (Thirsk to Scarborough road)
Open: noon-2.30 6.30-11 (Sun noon-5) **Closed:** 25 Dec, 1 Jan, Mon-Tue (ex BH), Sun eve 🍺 🍽
L Wed-Sat 12-2, Sun 12-3.30 **D** Wed-Sat 6.30-9 **Facilities:** Parking Garden **Notes:** ⊕ FREE HOUSE ♦♦

Ramblers sampling the delights of the North Yorkshire Moors National Park will be pleased to find this stylishly well-appointed country pub and restaurant in the pretty village of Fadmoor. The setting overlooking the village green could not be more idyllic, and the inn boasts dramatic views over the Vale of Pickering and the Wolds. Inside it is cosy, snug and welcoming, with log fires, beams and brasses in the bar: the ideal spot to enjoy a pint of Black Sheep Best. The food is an undoubted attraction, with meals available in the bar or in the attractively furnished rustic-style restaurant. A good value, two-course meal is available at lunchtime and early evening. Options include smoked salmon and asparagus terrine, followed by medallions of pork tenderloin with blue Stilton and white wine sauce, or home-made steak and ale pie. The à la carte menu features such dishes as deep-fried duck and mango spring rolls; seafood paella with Italian sausage; and pan-seared king scallops with a fricassée of spring onion, garlic and bacon as starters, followed by, for example, basil and parmesan crusted cod; slow roasted boneless half Gressingham duckling with orange and brandy sauce; or fillet of beef Wellington topped with liver pâté and Madeira sauce. There is a dedicated menu for vegetarians.

Recommended in the area

North Yorkshire Moors National Park; Rievaulx Terrace and Temples

The Bridge Inn

Address: GRINTON, Richmond, DL11 6HH
Tel: 01748 884224
Email: atkinbridge@btinternet.com
Website: www.bridgeinngrinton.co.uk
Map ref: 7 SE09
Directions: Exit A1 at Scotch Corner onto A6108 towards Richmond. Through Richmond. Left onto B6270 towards Grinton & Reeth
Open: all day all week ⓑ ⑪ food served all day
Facilities: Parking Garden Wi-fi
Notes: ⊕ JENNINGS BROTHERS PLC ⚑

With a host of activities such as walking, fishing, horse riding and mountain biking all on the doorstep, and a range of en suite rooms available to stay in, The Bridge Inn makes a good base for those in search of country pursuits. Situated on the banks of the River Swale in the heart of the Yorkshire Dales National Park, this fine former coaching inn dates from the 13th century. Now with its beamed ceilings and open fires tastefully restored, the inn is fast becoming known for its great food and ales. Customers are invited to sample Jennings award-winning cask ales, or try something a little different from a micro-brewery; there is also an extensive wine cellar. Menus are based on seasonal local produce under the experienced eye of resident chef John Scott, and flavoured with herbs from the pub's own garden. Light snacks such as hot or cold baguettes and jacket potatoes are served in the bar, while in the à la carte restaurant, typical main courses range from lamb shank in red wine and rosemary to spiced parsnip pie with herby pastry. For those with room to spare, the dessert menu includes a daily choice of old-fashioned traditional puddings.

Recommended in the area

Yorkshire Dales; Reeth; St Andrew's Church

The General Tarleton Inn

★★★★★ ◎◎ RESTAURANT WITH ROOMS

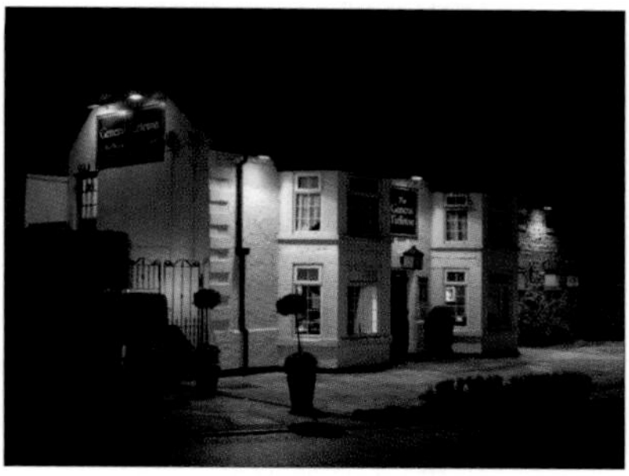

Address: Boroughbridge Road, Ferrensby, KNARESBOROUGH, HG5 0PZ
Tel: 01423 340284 **Fax:** 01423 340288
Email: gti@generaltarleton.co.uk
Website: www.generaltarleton.co.uk
Map ref: 8 SE35
Directions: A1(M) junct 48 at Boroughbridge, take A6055 to Knaresborough. Inn 4m on right
Open: all week 12-3 6-11 **L** all wk 12-2 **D** all wk 6-9.15 **L** Sun 12-1.45 **D** Mon-Sat 6-9.15 **Rooms:** 14 en suite (7 GF) **S** £75-£116 **D** £129-£150
Facilities: Parking Garden Wi-fi **Notes:** FREE HOUSE 11

A tastefully redesigned old coaching inn owned and run by John and Claire Topham. Sir Banastre Tarleton, after whom it was named, allegedly fired on surrendering troops during the American War of Independence and became known as "Bloody Ban"; he later became a Liverpool MP. The inn's low-beamed ceilings, rustic walls, log fires, cosy corners and modern black-and-white still lifes create welcoming surroundings. With two AA Rosettes, knowledgeable, friendly and professional staff serve honest British food using seasonal and local produce in an intimate and inviting atmosphere. The General Tarleton's reputation for fresh seafood partly depends on daily calls from fishing boat skippers; within hours perhaps mussel chowder or John's signature dish of seafood parcels in lobster sauce available in the bar brasserie or restaurant. In the latter you might well find Nidderdale oak-roast hot smoked salmon with Bloody Mary dressing; slow-braised Yorkshire beef and Black Sheep ale suet pudding; and trio of rhubarb - brûlée, crumble and compôte. Home-made dishes on the children's menu have been road-tested by the Topham offspring. Dine outdoors in the garden or covered courtyard in summer.

Recommended in the area

Fountains Abbey; Ripley Castle; Yorkshire Dales National Park

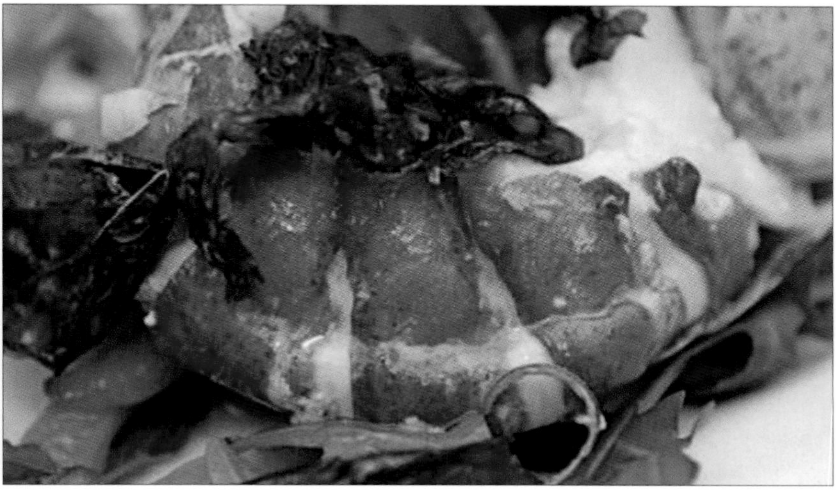

Sandpiper Inn

Address: Market Place, LEYBURN, DL8 5AT
Tel: 01969 622206
Fax: 01969 625367
Email: hsandpiper99@aol.com
Website: www.sandpiperinn.co.uk
Map ref: 7 SE19
Directions: From A1 take A684 to Leyburn
Open: 11.30-3 6.30-11 (Sun noon-2.30 7-10.30)
Closed: Mon & occasionally Tue ᴸ L all wk 12-2.30
🍽 L all wk 12-2.30 D all wk 6.30-9.30 Facilities:
Garden Notes: ⊕ FREE HOUSE ♦♦ ♖

Although the Sandpiper Inn has been a pub for only 30 years, the building is the oldest in Leyburn, dating back to around 1640. It has a beautiful terrace, a bar, snug and dining room, and the menu offers a varied mix of traditional (fish in real ale batter and chips, steaks) and more unusual dishes, which might include apple-smoked black pudding on a garlic mash with a port wine jus; warm goats' cheese on rocket and beetroot salad; and crispy duck leg with fried potatoes and oriental dressing.
Recommended in the area
Wensleydale Railway; Forbidden Corner

The Sportsmans Arms Hotel

Address: Wath-in-Nidderdale, PATELEY BRIDGE,
         Harrogate, HG3 5PP
Tel: 01423 711306
Fax: 01423 712524
Map ref: 7 SE16
Directions: A59/B6451, hotel 2m N of Pateley
Bridge Open: all week noon-2.30 6.30-11
Closed: 25 Dec ᴸ L all wk 12-2 D all wk 7-9
🍽 L Sun 12-2 D Mon-Sat 7-9 Facilities: Parking
Garden Wi-fi Notes: ⊕ FREE HOUSE ♟ 12

This very special pub is in one of the loveliest areas of the Yorkshire Dales. A custom-built kitchen, run by chef/patron Ray Carter for nearly 25 years (now assisted by his son), is the heart of the operation. True to the best pub traditions, real ales and wines accompany dishes served in an informal bar, while daily restaurant menus tempt all comers. Delights include loin of pork with mustard and mushroom sauce, and roast Scottish salmon with spring onions and stem ginger. Round off the meal in style with double chocolate roulade or the ever-popular Sportsmans summer pudding.
Recommended in the area
Fountains Abbey and Studley Royal; Stump Cross Caverns; Brimham Rocks

Fox & Hounds Country Inn

★★ 82% ◉ HOTEL

Address: Sinnington, PICKERING, YO62 6SQ
Tel: 01751 431577 **Fax:** 01751 432791
Email: fox.houndsinn@btconnect.com
Website: www.thefoxandhoundsinn.co.uk
Map ref: 7 SE78
Directions: 3m W of town, off A170 between
Pickering & Helmsley **Open:** all week 12-2 6-11
(Sun 12-2 6-10.30) **Closed:** 25-26 Dec
🖟 ⁑◎⁑ L all wk 12-2 D all wk 6.30-9 **Rooms:** 10
(4 GF) S £69-£89 D £90-£140 **Facilities:** Parking Garden **Notes:** ⊕ FREE HOUSE ⁑⁑ ⁑

Set in a pretty village with a river running by, and a large green with a small pack-horse bridge, this 18th-century inn offers good drinking, imaginative modern cooking, and well-designed rooms. In the bar, oak beams, wood panelling and an open fire make ideal surroundings for a pint of Black Sheep Special or a glass of wine. The menus range from sandwiches and light lunches to dishes like pan-fried calves' liver with spring onion mashed potato. The rooms are equipped with TV and drinks trays.
Recommended in the area
North Yorkshire Moors Railway; Rievaulx Abbey; Nunnington Hall

The Buck Inn

★★★ INN

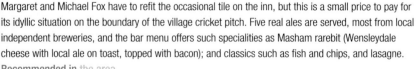

Address: THORNTON WATLASS, Ripon, HG4 4AH
Tel: 01677 422461
Fax: 01677 422447
Email: innwatlass1@btconnect.com
Website: www.buckwatlass.co.uk
Map ref: 7 SE28
Directions: From A1 at Leeming Bar take A684 to
Bedale, then B6268 towards Masham. Village 2m on
right, by cricket green
Open: all week 11-mdnt **Closed:** 25 Dec eve 🖟 ⁑◎⁑ L Mon-Sat 12-2, Sun 12-3 D all wk 6.30-9.30
Rooms: 7 (5 en suite) **Facilities:** Parking Garden **Notes:** ⊕ FREE HOUSE ⁑⁑ ⁑

Margaret and Michael Fox have to refit the occasional tile on the inn, but this is a small price to pay for its idyllic situation on the boundary of the village cricket pitch. Five real ales are served, most from local independent breweries, and the bar menu offers such specialities as Masham rarebit (Wensleydale cheese with local ale on toast, topped with bacon); and classics such as fish and chips, and lasagne.
Recommended in the area
Lightwater Valley Theme Park; Theakson Brewery Visitor Centre; Yorkshire Dales National Park

Robin Hood's Bay

Wombwell Arms

Address: WASS, York, YO61 4BE
Tel: 01347 868280
Email: wombwellarms@btconnect.com
Website: www.wombwellarms.co.uk
Map ref: 6 SE57
Directions: From A1 take A168 to A19 junct. Take York exit, then left after 2.5m, left at Coxwold to Ampleforth. Wass 2m **Open:** all week noon-3 6-11 (Sat noon-11 Sun noon-4, 6-10.30) 🍽 **L** Mon-Thu 12-2, Fri-Sat 12-2.30, Sun 12-3 **D** Mon-Thu 6.30-9, Fri-Sat 6.30-9.30, Sun 6.30-8.30 **Facilities:** Parking Garden Wi-fi **Notes:** 🍺 FREE HOUSE 👬 🐕 🍷 9

The pub was built as a granary around 1620, probably using stone from nearby Byland Abbey, before becoming an alehouse not long after. Original features include a large inglenook fireplace, oak beams, and flagstones that continue to stand up well to the diverse footwear of locals, walkers, cyclists and parents of pupils from nearby Ampleforth College, as well as the paws and claws of their canine companions. Three cask ales, including Timothy Taylor Landlord and Theakston Old Peculier, nine wines by the glass, and twelve malt whiskies are always available in the bars. Named as one of the best places to eat in the countryside, freshly prepared meals, made using locally sourced produce wherever possible, are available in Poachers Bar and in both restaurants. Starters include pigeon bruschetta with mushrooms, and trio of smoked fish and twice baked cheese soufflé. For a main course you might plump for chicken in creamy leek and Stilton sauce; South African bobotie; or king prawn paella with scallops, chicken and chorizo sausage. There's also the classic haddock in real ale batter with home-made chips and mushy peas; Masham pork and apple sausages with mash and gravy; or the pub's signature steak, Guinness and mushroom pie.

Recommended in the area

North Yorkshire Moors National Park; Byland Abbey; Mouseman Museum, Kilburn

'Needle's Eye' folly, Wentworth Woodhouse

The Fat Cat

Address: 23 Alma Street, SHEFFIELD, S3 8SA
Tel: 0114 249 4801
Fax: 0114 249 4803
Email: info@thefatcat.co.uk
Website: www.thefatcat.co.uk
Map ref: 8 SK38
Directions: Telephone for directions **Open:** all week noon-11 (Fri-Sat noon-mdnt) **Closed:** 25 Dec ♨ **L** Mon-Fri 12-3, Sat 12-8, Sun 12-3 **D** Mon-Fri 6-8
Facilities: Parking Garden **Notes:** ⊕ FREE HOUSE ♦♦ ⼧

A smart Grade II listed, back street city pub, The Fat Cat dates from 1852 and is reputed to be haunted. Ale afficionados will delight in the constantly changing list of guest beers, especially from micro-breweries. Traditional scrumpy and unusual bottled beers are also sold, while the Kelham Island Brewery, owned by the pub, accounts for at least four of the ten traditional draught real ales. There are open fires inside, and an attractive walled garden outside. Home-cooked food – steak pie, Mexican chicken casserole or spinach and red bean casserole – includes vegetarian and vegan options.
Recommended in the area
Kelham Island Museum; Winter Gardens; Millennium Galleries

Damflask reservoir from Bradfield Dale

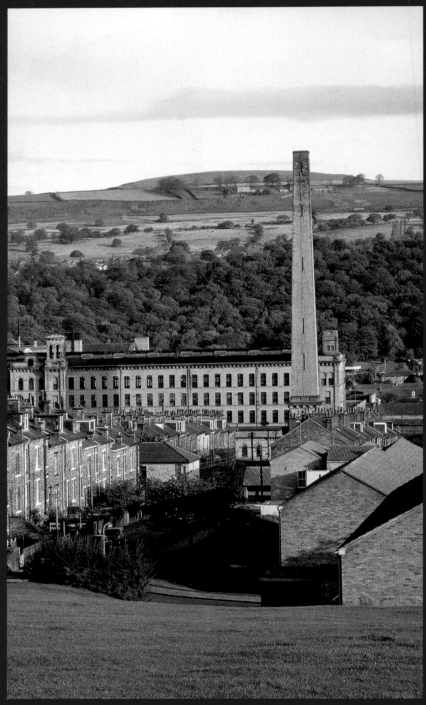

Saltaire Village

Shibden Mill Inn

★★★★ ⊛ INN

Address: Shibden Mill Fold, HALIFAX, HX3 7UL
Tel: 01422 365840 **Fax:** 01422 362971
Email: enquiries@shibdenmillinn.com
Website: www.shibdenmillinn.com
Map ref: 7 SE02
Directions: From A58 turn into Kell Ln. After 0.5m
left into Blake Hill **Open:** all week noon-2.30 5.30-11
(Sat-Sun noon-11) **Closed:** 25-26 Dec eve & 1 Jan
eve ⓗ L Mon-Sat 12-2, Sun all day **D** Mon-Sat
6-9.30 ⓘ L Sun 12-7.30 **D** Fri-Sat 6-9.30 **Rooms:** 11 (1GF) **S** £76-£122 **D** £89-£140
Facilities: Parking Garden Wi-fi **Notes:** ⊕ FREE HOUSE ⓯ ⓯ ⓯ 12

Overlooking Red Beck, in a fold of the Shibden Valley, this former corn mill has stood here since the
1600s. Steeped in history, it has been sympathetically renovated by owners, Simon and Caitlin Heaton,
and general manager, Glen Pearson, and enjoys a reputation for warm hospitality and impressive
gastro dining. The log fire-warmed, oak-beamed bar serves a range of real ales, including two
guests, and offers a menu (also available in the candlelit restaurant) listing roast pheasant breast with
confit potato, nettle and spinach purée, and truffle oil; crispy slow-cooked Dexter blade of beef with
horseradish risotto, buttered greens and blue cheese fritter; and grilled turbot with crushed potatoes,
steamed clams and bourguignon sauce. Less sophisticated dining is possible from the 'comfort and
favourites menu' on which you'll find Hanna's Happy Trotters free-range bacon chop with fried duck
egg, pineapple chutney and fries; piri piri chicken Caesar salad; and Shibden Tapas, comprising chorizo
and lamb breast stew, croquettes, Calderdale cheese, Yorkshire ham, and tomato and cucumber salsa.
Accommodation combines 17th century charm with modern day comforts.

Recommended in the area

National Museum of Photography, Film & Television; Dean Clough Arts Centre; Eureka Museum

SCOTLAND

River Dee and Mar Lodge Estate near Braemar

The Jigger Inn

Address: The Old Course Hotel,
ST ANDREWS, Fife, KY16 9SP
Tel: 01334 474371
Fax: 01334 477668
Email: reservations@oldcoursehotel.co.uk
Website: www.oldcoursehotel.co.uk
Map ref: 10 NO51
Directions: From M90 take junction 8 on to A91, follow signs to St. Andrews. Leave A 91 on exit at approach to town **Open:** all day all week 11-11 (Sun noon-11) **Closed:** 25 Dec ▙ ◉ all wk 12-9.30 **Facilities:** Parking Garden
Notes: ⊕ FREE HOUSE ♥ 8

This whitewashed, former stationmaster's lodge on a long-dismantled railway line stands now as the unique 19th hole in the grounds of the most famous golf course – The Old Course. St Andrew's is renowned, of course, throughout the world as the Home of Golf. Therefore, don't be surprised by the abundant golfing memorabilia, and golfers comparing their scorecards as they warm themselves in front of a crackling, open-hearth fire cradling a pint of Jigger Ale – a brew in the style of a classic Scottish Ale that is as unique as the Jigger Inn itself and available for consumption only within the pub's ancient walls. This traditional Scottish pub is always busy and offers warm hospitality at its very best. Tiger Woods, Justin Timberlake and Prince William have all been spotted here. All-day availability is one advantage of the short, simple menu that lists soups and salads such as Cullen skink and Caesar salad, or triple-decker sandwiches and wraps. For something more substantial, there is St Andrew's beer-battered fish with chunky chips, Speyside rib-eye steak, Jigger cheese and bacon burger, or garden vegetable pie and chips.

Recommended in the area

St Andrews Cathedral; West Sands Beach; Fife Folk Museum

Cawdor Tavern

Address: The Lane, CAWDOR, Nairn,
Highland, IV12 5XP

Tel: 01667 404777 **Fax:** 01667 493678

Email: enquiries@cawdortavern.co.uk

Website: www.cawdortavern.co.uk

Map ref: 12 NH85

Directions: A96 (Inverness-Aberdeen) take B9006
Cawdor Castle signs. In village centre **Open:** 11-3
5-11 (Sat 11am-mdnt Sun 12.30-11) all day Summer
Closed: 25 Dec, 1 Jan, 2wks mid Jan ⓑ ⓄI **L** Mon-
Sat 12-2, Sun 12.30-3 **D** all wk 5.30-9 **Facilities:** Parking Garden **Notes:** ⊕ FREE HOUSE ⓲ ⌂ ♟ 9

The Tavern is at the heart of a beautiful conservation village, close to the famous castle, and was
formerly a joinery workshop for the Cawdor Estate. The handsome oak panelling in the lounge bar
came from the castle and was a gift from the former laird. Roaring log fires keep the place cosy on long
winter nights, while in the summer guests can sit on the patio. The menu options include prime meats,
fresh local seafood, game and vegetarian dishes, complemented by a hand-picked wine list.

Recommended in the area

Cawdor Castle; Fort George; Culloden Battlefield

Cawdor Castle

The Plockton Hotel

★★★ 75% SMALL HOTEL

Address: Harbour Street,
PLOCKTON, Highland, IV52 8TN
Tel: 01599 544274
Fax: 01599 544475
Email: info@plocktonhotel.co.uk
Website: www.plocktonhotel.co.uk
Map ref: 11 NG83
Directions: On A87 to Kyle of Lochalsh take turn at

Balmacara. Plockton 7m N **Open:** all day all week
11am-mdnt (Sun 12.30pm-11pm) **Closed:** 25 Dec, 1 Jan ⓑ ⓘ **L** all wk 12-2.15 **D** all wk 6-10
Rooms: 15 (1 GF) **S** £55-£85 **D** £80-£120 **Facilities:** Garden Wi-fi **Notes:** ⊕ FREE HOUSE ⁑ ↾

The award-winning Plockton Hotel sits right next to the gently lapping waters of Loch Carron, a sheltered sea loch warmed by the Gulf Stream and fringed with palm trees. It is the only waterfront hostelry in this lovely National Trust village, the location for the cult film *The Wicker Man*. The breathtaking view, across the bay to the Applecross Hills, is enjoyed by many of the hotel's comfortable en suite bedrooms. Converted from a ship's chandlery in 1913, this establishment has been run by the Pearson family and their staff for more than 20 years. Menus are based on the very best of Highland produce, with seafood a major strength: expect to find locally caught langoustines, shellfish from Skye, fresh fish landed at Gairloch and Kinlochbervie, and smoked fish from Aultbea. Products from the smokehouse feature in one of the hotel's specialities – cream of smoked fish soup. Other starters may include Talisker whisky pâté and fresh Plockton prawns. Top quality Highland beef appears in flamed peppered whisky steaks from the charcoal grill. Other main courses include casserole of Highland venison, Argyle chicken, and wild boar burger with salad and fries. A fine range of malts is offered.

Recommended in the area

Isle of Skye; Eilean Donan Castle; Applecross Peninsula

Plockton Inn & Seafood Restaurant

Address: Innes Street, PLOCKTON,
Highland, IV52 8TW
Tel: 01599 544222
Fax: 01599 544487
Email: info@plocktoninn.co.uk
Website: www.plocktoninn.co.uk
Map ref: 11 NG83
Directions: On A87 to Kyle of Lochalsh take turn at
Balmacara. Plockton 7m N
Open: all day all week 🍴 **L** all wk 12-2.30 **D** all wk
6-9 🍽 **D** all wk 6-9 **Facilities:** Parking Garden Wi-fi **Notes:** ⊕ FREE HOUSE ♦♦ 🐾

Situated in one of Scotland's most beautiful fishing villages, near the harbour, this inn is a great base
to explore the Isle of Skye and the Torridon Mountains. The Inn has regular music nights in the bar,
making for a lively atmosphere. A good choice of real ales is offered, plus more than 50 malt whiskies.
There are two eating areas inside, the Dining Room and Lounge Bar, plus an area laid with decking
outside. Fresh West Coast fish and shellfish are a speciality, plus West Highland beef, game and lamb.
Recommended in the area
Eilean Donan Castle; Lochalsh Woodlands (NTS); Strome Castle (NTS)

Shieldaig Bar & Coastal Kitchen

★ ◉◉ SMALL HOTEL
Address: SHIELDAIG, Highland, IV54 8XN
Tel: 01520 755251 **Fax:** 01520 755321
Website: www.tighaneilean.co.uk
Map ref: 11 NG85
Directions: Off A896, in village centre
Open: all week 🍴 🍽 **L** all wk 12-2.30, Summer
12-9 **D** all wk 6-8.30 **Rooms:** 11 **Facilities:** Parking
Garden Wi-fi **Notes:** ⊕ FREE HOUSE ♦♦ 🐾 ♟ 8

Shieldaig's friendly local bar and Coastal Kitchen has a magnificent position on the sea front in the
centre of this picturesque fishing village, nestled beneath the Torridon Mountains. Enjoy the local craic
and foaming pints of Isle of Skye Brewery beers downstairs or book a table upstairs in the award-
winning Coastal Kitchen. Eat inside, on the balcony or on the outside deck and enjoy the views and
passing sea eagles; indeed, this is a wildlife-spotting hot spot. The impressive kitchen specialises in
fresh local seafood brought by the local fishermen from the jetty to the kitchen door each day, plus
pizzas and steaks cooked in the wood-fired oven.
Recommended in the area
Torridon Countryside Centre; Diabaig village; Glen Torridon

Pitlochry, The Queen's View, Loch Tummel

Anglers Inn

★★★ INN

Address: Main Road, GUILDTOWN, Perth, PH2 6BS
Tel: 01821 640329
Email: info@theanglersinn.co.uk
Website: www.theanglersinn.co.uk
Map ref: 10 NO13
Directions: 6m N of Perth on A93 **Open:** 11-3 5.30-mdnt **Closed:** Mon ₤ ᵀ⊙ᴵ **L** all wk 12-2 **D** all wk 6-9
Rooms: 6 en suite **Facilities:** Parking Garden Wi-fi
Notes: ⊕ FREE HOUSE ⁑ ⊀ ⍭ 10

Gawaine and Christina Maxwell bought the Anglers Inn in June 2010. It has six en suite rooms, a public bar and a restaurant which, even after a contemporary makeover, has lost none of its traditional feel. The kitchen's headed by chef Jonathan Greer, formally of Gleneagles and Ballathie House Hotel, where he first met the Maxwell family. The menu is seasonal with a range of local ingredients which create modern food with a French influence. Expect dishes such as risotto of autumn truffle and duck egg 64°C, followed by bressole of squab pigeon forestière, pomme rösti and beetroot espuma, plus a table d'hôte menu.
Recommended in the area
Scone Palace; Caithness Glass; Perth Racecourse

Moulin Hotel

★★★ 73% HOTEL

Address: 11-13 Kirkmichael Road, Moulin,
PITLOCHRY, Perth & Kinross, PH16 5EW
Tel: 01796 472196
Fax: 01796 474098
Email: enquiries@moulinhotel.co.uk
Website: www.moulinhotel.co.uk
Map ref: 10 NN95
Directions: From Pitlochry take A924 for half a mile. Moulin 0.75m **Open:** all day all week 11-11 (Fri-Sat 11am-11.45pm Sun noon-11) ₤ all wk 12-9.30 ᵀ⊙ᴵ **D** all wk 6-9 **Rooms:** 15 en suite **S** £45-£75 **D** £65-£90 **Facilities:** Parking Garden Wi-fi **Notes:** ⊕ FREE HOUSE ⁑ ⊀ ⍭ 25

Built in 1695 and situated on an old drovers' road near to Pitlochry, this inn is popular as a walking and touring base, and offers comfortable accommodation. Locals and visitors enjoy the home-brewed beers and menus that reflect the inn's location. Try haggis, neeps and tatties, or venison Braveheart. The courtyard garden is a delight in summer while winter log fires warm the interior's nooks and crannies.
Recommended in the area
Edradour Distillery; Scottish Hydro Electric Visitor Centre, Dam & Fish Pass; Blair Castle, Blair Atholl

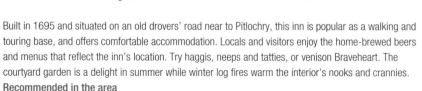

The Black Bull

★★★★ INN

Address: Market Place, LAUDER,
Scottish Borders, TD2 6SR
Tel: 01578 722208 **Fax:** 01578 722419
Email: enquiries@blackbull-lauder.com
Website: www.blackbull-lauder.com
Map ref: 10 NT54
Directions: In centre of Lauder on A68 **Open:** all day
all week 🕰 🍴 **L** Mon-Thu 12-2.30, Fri-Sun 12-9
D Mon-Thu 5-9, Fri-Sun 12-9 **Rooms:** 8 en suite
S £60-£70 **D** £85-£95 **Facilities:** Parking Wi-fi **Notes:** ⊕ PERTHSHIRE TAVERNS LTD 🛉 🐾 🍷 27

A former coaching inn, The Black Bull stands three storeys high and dates from 1750. The building has been restored to create a cosy haven in the heart of the Borders, just 20 minutes' drive from Edinburgh. The interior is full of character; the dining room used to be a chapel and the church spire remains. Food is also served in the Harness Room Bar or lounge. The same seasonal menu is served throughout, specialising in country fare prepared from locally grown produce. The beautiful bedrooms are decorated in period style.

Recommended in the area

Thirlstone Castle; Mellerstain House; Melrose Abbey

Carving on Melrose Abbey

Coll Hotel

Address: ARINAGOUR, Isle of Coll, PA78 6SZ
Tel: 01879 230334 **Fax:** 01879 230317
Email: info@collhotel.com
Website: www.collhotel.com
Map ref: 9 NH25
Directions: Ferry from Oban. Hotel at head of
Arinagour Bay, 1m from Pier (collections by
arrangement) **Open:** all day all week ⓑ ⓘ **L** all wk
12-2 **D** all wk 6-9 **Facilities:** Parking Garden Wi-fi
Notes: ⊕ FREE HOUSE ⦿

The award-winning Coll Hotel is the only Hebridean inn on the small island, and commands stunning views over the sea to Jura and Mull. It is a popular and cosy rendezvous for the islands 200 locals and many visitors, where pints of Loch Fyne ale are supped, malt whiskies are sipped, and the day's developments are digested. Food is served in the Gannet restaurant, bar or garden. Fresh produce is landed and delivered from around the island every day and features on the specials board. Here, seafood is a major component – Coll crab, langoustines, scallops, lobster and Connel mussels.

Recommended in the area

RSPB nature reserve; Na Sgeulachan standing stones; Crannog, Mill Lochs

WALES

Conwy Castle and Telford's Suspension Bridge

Caesars Arms

Address: Cardiff Road, CREIGIAU,
Cardiff, CF15 9NN
Tel: 029 2089 0486 **Fax:** 029 2089 2176
Email: caesarsarms@btconnect.com
Website: www.caesarsarms.co.uk
Map ref: 2 ST08
Directions: M4 junct 34, A4119 towards Llantrisant/
Rhondda. Approx 0.5m right at lights signed
Groesfaen. Through Groesfaen, past Dynevor Arms
pub. Next left, signed Creigiau. 1m, left at T-junct,
pass Creigiau Golf Course. Pub in 1m on left **Open:** noon-2.30 6-10 (Sun noon-4) **Closed:** 25 Dec,
1 Jan, Sun eve ♨ **L** Mon-Sat 12-2.30 ⒩ **L** Mon-Sat 12-2.30, Sun 12-4 **D** Mon-Sat 6-10
Facilities: Parking Garden **Notes:** ⊕ FREE HOUSE 🛉 🐕

Just ten miles outside Cardiff, Caesars Arms sits tucked away down winding lanes offering fine views
of the surrounding countryside from its heated patio and terrace. The restaurant has a vast selection of
fresh fish, seafood, meat and game taking pride of place. The emphasis here is on locally sourced food,
displayed on shaven ice. Starters might include imaginative choices such as Bajan fishcakes, or cherry-
smoked duck breast with organic beetroot. Main courses take in hake, halibut, Dover sole and lobster, as
well as a show-stopping Pembrokeshire sea bass baked in rock salt, which is cracked open and filleted
at your table. But it's not all about fish – other choices include steak from slow-reared, dry-aged pedigree
Welsh Blacks plus lamb and venison from the Brecon Beacons and free-range chickens from the Vale of
Glamorgan. Home-grown organic herbs, salads and vegetables are all used as much as possible, and the
inn has its own smokery. Another attraction is the farm shop, which provides a range of home-produced
honey, free-range eggs, Welsh cheeses, home-baked bread and chef's ready-prepared meals.
Recommended in the area
Castell Coch; Llandaff Cathedral; St Fagans: National History Museum

White Hart Thatched Inn & Brewery

Address: LLANDDAROG, Nr Carmarthen, SA32 8NT
Tel: 01267 275395
Email: bestpubinwales@aol.com
Website: www.thebestpubinwales.co.uk
Map ref: 2 SN51
Directions: 6m E of Carmarthen towards Swansea, just off A48 on B4310, signed Llanddarog
Open: 11.30-3 6.30-11 (Sun noon-3 7-10.30)
Closed: Jan, Wed 🍴 ⍟ **L** 11.30-3 **D** 6.30-11
Facilities: Parking Garden **Notes:** ⊕ FREE HOUSE ⁙

Built in 1371, with thatched roof, large open fireplace, old oak beams and heavily carved furniture oak settles, this family-run business has a restaurant in an old converted barn. Home cooked meals are prepared in the award-winning open-plan kitchen, using local produce, the inn's own pork and fresh eggs from their chickens. Roast dinners and a variety of traditional meals are served every lunchtime and evening. Handcrafted ales, lagers and stouts are brewed on site. On warm days, enjoy your meal or drink in the beautiful patio garden at the front or in the rear garden with children's play area and small home farm.

Recommended in the area

Folly Farm; National Botanic Gardens of Wales; Aberglasney House

The Norman keep of Cardiff Castle

Ty Gwyn Inn

★ ★ ★ ⇔ INN

Address: BETWYS-Y-COED, Conwy, LL24 0SG
Tel: 01690 710383 & 710787
Fax: 01690 710383
Email: mratcl1050@aol.com
Website: www.tygwynhotel.co.uk
Map ref: 5 SH75
Directions: At junct of A5 & A470, 100yds S of Waterloo Bridge
Open: all week noon-2 6.30-11 **Closed:** 1wk Jan

🔥 ⚟ **L** all wk 12-2 **D** all wk 6.30-9 **Rooms:** 13 (10 en suite) (1 GF)
Facilities: Parking **Notes:** ⊞ FREE HOUSE ♦♦

Judging from the many comments on the website, everybody who has drunk, eaten or stayed at this atmospheric old coaching inn, a few miles inside Snowdonia National Park, has thoroughly enjoyed their experience. In 1815 Thomas Telford built the impressive cast iron bridge opposite. Owned and run for the past 28 years by the Ratcliffes, Martin (chef since day one) and his wife Nicola are now in charge. Within, it's all beamed ceilings and white walls, and crammed with antiques, pictures and china. Locally well-regarded international cuisine is typified by starters of spicy Thai salad, sesame, soya and sweet chilli; and natural smoked cod and Mediterranean prawn gratin, with oven-baked rich creamy cheese and mustard sauce. The theme continues with fresh fillet of line-caught wild sea bass, king prawns, saffron and garlic; roast rack of venison loin, wild mushroom risotto and port reduction; and rosemary-scented roast rack of Snowdon lamb with roast onion and peppercorn marmalade. There is also a specials board. Sound out the next themed dinner evening. As well as some rooms having four-poster beds, two of the refurbished bedrooms now have relaxing spa tubs.

Recommended in the area

Conwy Castle; Llechwedd Slate Caverns; Mt Snowdon

The Groes Inn

★★★★★ ⊛ INN

Address: CONWY, Conwy, LL32 8TN
Tel: 01492 650545 **Fax:** 01492 650855
Email: reception@groesinn.com
Website: www.groesinn.com
Map ref: 5 SH77
Directions: Exit A55 to Conwy, left at mini rdbt
by Conwy Castle onto B5106, 2.5m inn on right
Open: all week 12-3 6.30-11 ♨ †◉┤ L all wk 12-2
D all wk 6.30-9 **Rooms:** 14 en suite (6 GF)
S £85-£160 **D** £105-£180 **Facilities:** Parking Garden Wi-fi **Notes:** ⊕ FREE HOUSE ♦† ⊮

Dating back to the 15th century, The Groes successfully blends the old world charm of beams and open fires with the contemporary style of its luxury bedrooms. Together with an award-winning restaurant and excellent service, the inn even has its own brew, Groes Ale. Fresh local ingredients are at the heart of the impressive traditional British and Welsh dishes. Set in beautiful countryside just minutes from Conwy and the North Wales coastline, it is a world away from the hustle and bustle of everyday life.

Recommended in the area

Snowdonia; Bodnant Gardens; Conwy Castle

Mynydd y Dref towards Penmaenbach

The Queens Head

Address: Glanwydden, LLANDUDNO JUNCTION, Conwy, LL31 9JP
Tel: 01492 546570
Fax: 01492 546487
Email: enquiries@queensheadglanwydden.co.uk
Website: www.queensheadglanwydden.co.uk
Map ref: 5 SH77
Directions: From A55 take A470 towards Llandudno. At 3rd rdbt right towards Penrhyn Bay, then 2nd right into Glanwydden, pub on left
Open: all week 11.30-3 6-10.30 (Sat-Sun 11.30-10.30) 🖴 🍽 **L** Mon-Fri 12-2, Sat-Sun 12-9 **D** Mon-Fri 6-9, Sat-Sun 12-9 **Facilities:** Parking Garden **Notes:** ⊕ FREE HOUSE 🍴 🍷 10

The village of Glanwydden is just five minutes' drive from the Victorian seaside resort of Llandudno, its shops and grand, curving beach. In the other direction lie the countryside and the mountains, making this 18th-century country pub and restaurant, once the wheelwright's cottage, well placed for both. Awarded AA's Pub of the Year for Wales 2009-2010 last year, Robert and Sally Cureton have created this smart pub with appealing menus, good selection of wine and beers, and a team of attentive staff. In winter the bar's log fire will be blazing, while in summer you can take your drinks out on to the pretty terrace. At any time of the year your fellow evening imbibers might, following their pre-theatre dinner, be heading for the town's Venue Cymru. Typically, a meal could be smoked salmon and trout mousse, then chargrilled Welsh rump steak, and raspberry and amaretto trifle to finish. Lighter dishes include salmon and coriander fishcakes, and fresh asparagus risotto, while more hearty are Jamaican chicken curry, and sautéed lamb's liver and crispy bacon. There's more of the same, as well as roasts, on Sundays, while the wine list offers plenty of choice too.

Recommended in the area

Conwy Castle; Great Orme Heritage Coast; Bodelwyddan

The Wynnstay Arms

★★★★ INN

Address: Well Street, RUTHIN, Denbighshire, LL15 1AN
Tel: 01824 703147 **Fax:** 01824 705428
Email: reservations@wynnstayarms.com
Website: www.wynnstayarms.com
Map ref: 5 SJ15
Directions: In town centre **Open:** all day all week
L all wk 12-2 **D** Mon-Sat 5.30-9.30, Sun 12-7 L Sun
D Tue-Sat **Rooms:** 7 en suite **S** £45-£60 **D** £65-£105
Facilities: Parking Wi-fi **Notes:** ⊕ FREE HOUSE

This 460-year-old, black and white timber-framed inn once
hosted meetings of the Jacobites. Food is most important in this
comfortable and contemporary town centre gastro-pub. The single menu, available in both Bar W, the
place for a casual drink and a meal, and in the more formal Fusions Brasserie, offers a good choice.
Typical are Welsh steaks with various sauces; pan-roasted pork tenderloin with bacon mash; chicken
curry; Italian meatballs; and pan-roasted sea bass. There are seven well-appointed en suite bedrooms.
Recommended in the area
Chester Roman City; Snowdonia National Park; Offa's Dyke Path

Ruins of Castle Dinas Bran, Llangollen

Penhelig Arms Hotel & Restaurant

Address: Terrace Road, ABERDYFI,
Gwynedd, LL35 0LT
Tel: 01654 767215 **Fax:** 01654 767690
Email: info@penheligarms.com
Website: www.penheligarms.com
Map ref: 2 SN69
Directions: On A493 W of Machynlleth **Open:** all day
all week **Closed:** 25-26 Dec ▣ **L** all wk 12-2 **D** all wk
6-9 ▣ **L** all wk 12-2 **D** all wk 7-9 **Facilities:** Parking
Wi-fi **Notes:** ⊕ S A BRAIN & CO LTD ⋔ ⊀ ☻ 20

The Penhelig Arms has been in business since 1870 and offers spectacular views over the tidal Dyfi estuary. Indeed, in the summer months the Penhelig's own seating area opposite is the place to enjoy the fine views. Great food is served in the bar or waterfront restaurant, and the brasserie-style menu is strong on fresh fish - crab and lobster arriving straight from the quay - backed up by Welsh beef and lamb. In winter a real log fire welcomes all to the wood-panelled Fisherman's Bar where an exceptional choice of real ales and fine wines is available.

Recommended in the area

Centre for Alternative Technology; Tal-y-Llyn Railway; Celtica

Snowdon Mountain Railway, Snowdonia National Park

Clytha Arms

Address: Clytha, ABERGAVENNY,
Monmouthshire, NP7 9BW
Tel: 01873 840206
Email: theclythaarms@tiscali.co.uk
Website: www.clytha-arms.com
Map ref: 2 SO21
Directions: From A449/A40 junction (E of
Abergavenny) follow signs for 'Old Road
Abergavenny/Clytha' **Open:** noon-3 6-mdnt (Fri-Sun
noon-mdnt) **Closed:** 25 Dec, Mon L ♨ ¶◎¶ L Tue-
Sun 12.30-2.30 **D** Mon-Sat 7-9.30 **Facilities:** Parking Garden Wi-fi **Notes:** ⊕ FREE HOUSE ♦♦ ⊅ ♟ 12

Andrew and Beverley Canning have been running this free house for 17 years. Once a dower house, it
is surrounded by lawns and interesting gardens, and is not far from the River Usk. Happily informal in
character, it offers six different real ales a week (that's 300-plus a year), a good choice of wines by the
glass, and snacks and tapas. In the restaurant, try leek and laver rissoles with beetroot chutney, fillet of
Hereford beef with pink peppercorns, or faggots and peas with Rhymney gravy.
Recommended in the area
Brecon Beacons National Park; Blaenafon World Heritage Site; Castell Dinas

The Greyhound Inn-Hotel

Address: LLANTRISANT, Nr Usk, Monmouthshire, NP15 1LE
Tel: 01291 672505 & 673447 **Fax:** 01291 673255
Email: enquiry@greyhound-inn.com
Website: www.greyhound-inn.com
Map ref: 2 ST39 **Directions:** From M4 junct 24, A449 towards
Monmouth, exit 1st junct for Usk. From M50 junct 4, A40/A449
towards Newport, exit signed Usk. In Usk, 1st left into Twyn Sq,
follow Llantrisant signs for 2.5m (under A449 bridge), Inn on right
Open: all day 11-11 **Closed:** 25 & 31 Dec, 1 Jan, Sun eve ⓛ
ⓘⓞⓘ **L** all wk 12-2.15 **D** Mon-Sat 6-10 **Rooms:** 10 en suite (5 GF)
Facilities: Parking Garden Wi-fi **Notes:** ⊕ FREE HOUSE ⧫ ⧖ ⧨ 10

A sensitively restored 17th-century Welsh longhouse with two
acres of award-winning gardens. The Greyhound Inn-Hotel combines the charm and atmosphere of a
traditional family-owned inn offering delicious home-cooked meals with very comfortable accommodation.
In winter enjoy several roaring log fires or in summer dine alfresco in the beautiful gardens. Lovers of
real ale will find an interesting range complimented by an impressive wine selection. Nick Davies, The
Greyhound owner for 30 years, heads a kitchen team that prepares deliciously cooked food for customers
in the candlelit dining room or any of the three other eating areas. They source locally the ingredients for
well-established favourites — steak and ale pie, lamb shank in red wine, liver and bacon, Welsh sirloin
steak, freshly grilled local trout, freshly battered cod, venison in season and vegetarian dishes. More
unusual dishes occupy the daily specials board so you will be spoilt for choice! Ten en suite bedrooms
are housed in the converted barn with all modern day facilities, perfect for an overnight stay, weekend
or longer breaks. You will receive a very warm welcome whether you want to spend the evening drinking
and chatting in the 'Locals' bar, an informal meal or snack in the lounges or eat in the dining room.

Recommended in the area

Tintern Abbey; Raglan Castle: Big Pit, Blaenavon

The Lion Inn

Address: TRELLECH, Monmouth,
Monmouthshire, NP25 4PA
Tel: 01600 860322 **Fax:** 01600 860060
Email: debs@globalnet.co.uk
Website: www.lioninn.co.uk
Map ref: 2 SO50
Directions: From A40 S of Monmouth take B4293,
follow signs for Trellech. From M8 junct 2, straight
across rdbt, 2nd left at 2nd rdbt, B4293 to Trellech
Open: 12-3 6-11 (Fri-Sat noon-mdnt, Sun 12-4.30,
Mon eve 7-11pm, Thu eve 6-mdnt) **Closed:** Sun eve ⓘ L Mon-Fri 12-2, Sat-Sun 12-2.30 **D** Mon
7-9.30, Tue-Sat 6-9.30 **Facilities:** Parking Garden **Notes:** ⊕ FREE HOUSE ♦♦ ᴘ

This popular and well-established free house is opposite St Nicholas's Church. Guests are greeted by
welcoming real fires in the winter months, while in the summer drinks and meals can be served in the
garden, which overlooks fields and features a stream and large aviary. The former brew house has won
many accolades for its food and hospitality over the years, and its reputation is growing. Visitors aiming
to explore the nearby walking trails and notable historic buildings, or visit Trellech's own archaeological
dig, will find it a useful staging post. The extensive pub menu caters for all tastes, from bar snacks
and basket meals to blackboard specials, including fresh fish dishes. There is also an adventurous
menu featuring wild and hedgerow ingredients, such as nettles and wild mushrooms. Real ales include
Bath Ales, Wye Valley Butty Bach, Rhymney Best, Cottage Brewery and many more regularly changing
brews. Anyone who wants to extend their visit to The Lion can stay overnight in the pub's one-bedroom
cottage, which is suitable for up to three guests. It features an en suite bathroom and kitchenette. Dogs
are allowed at the pub, and water and biscuits are provided for them.

Recommended in the area

Tintern Abbey; Chepstow Castle; Wye Valley Forest Park

St Brides Bay, Pembrokeshire Coast National Park

The Swan Inn

Address: Point Road, LITTLE HAVEN,
Haverfordwest, Pembrokeshire, SA62 3UL
Tel/Fax: 01437 781880
Email: enquiries@theswanlittlehaven.co.uk
Website: www.theswanlittlehaven.co.uk
Map ref: 1 SM81
Directions: From Haverfordwest take B4341 (Broad
Haven road). In Broad Haven follow signs for seafront
& Little Haven, 0.75m
Open: all day all week 11-mdnt ⬛ ❀ **L** all wk 12-2
D all wk 6-9 **Facilities:** Garden Wi-fi **Notes:** ⊕ FREE HOUSE ♦♦ ⌐

This historic seaside inn has been impeccably renovated but retains its rustic charm thanks to the beams, blazing log fires, old settles and exposed stone walls. It was built by a fisherman and is literally just a stone's throw from the beach, offering great Pembrokeshire views from some tables. Cooking, with the emphasis on seasonal, local produce, is modern British in style, and is very accomplished, though informal. Diners can eat in the elegant contemporary upstairs dining room, or in the intimate restaurant below. Seafood is the star here, be it pan-fried scallops with chorizo, whole roasted sea bass with caper butter and samphire, or beer-battered fish and chips. St Brides Bay crab and home smoked mackerel feature with other seaside favourites such as a pint of prawns and moules marinière. For the carnivores there may be Welsh fillet steak, local lamb or venison, as well as home baked bread and Welsh cheese. The busy bar serves a range of bar snacks and well-kept real ales, and there are many wines available by the glass, all to be enjoyed in one of the leather armchairs.
The Swan Inn is AA Pub of the Year for Wales 2010-2011.

Recommended in the area

Pembrokeshire Coast National Park; Skomer Island

The Stackpole Inn

Address: STACKPOLE, nr Pembroke, Pembrokeshire, SA71 5DF
Tel: 01646 672324 **Fax:** 01646 672716
Email: info@stackpoleinn.co.uk
Website: www.stackpoleinn.co.uk
Map ref: 1 SR99
Directions: From Pembroke take B4319 & follow signs for
Stackpole, approx 4m **Open:** 12-3 6-11 **Closed:** Sun eve (winter)
🍺 🍴 **L** Mon-Sat 12-2, Sun 12-2.30 **D** all wk 6-9 **Facilities:**
Parking Garden Wi-fi **Notes:** ⊕ FREE HOUSE ♦♦ 🐾 ☂ 12

Location, location, location. The meaning of the phrase becomes
crystal clear in the context of this 17th-century inn, standing in
beautiful gardens within the Pembrokeshire Coast National Park.
Nearby are stunning cliffs, bays and beaches, and the huge natural arch known as the Green Bridge
of Wales. It's a freehouse, and there's always a guest from elsewhere to accompany three Welsh ales.
The bar surface is made from slate, while the wood for the ceiling beams came from ash trees grown
on the estate. Warmth is provided by a wood-burning stove set within the stone fireplace. Produce
from the local countryside and coastal waters plays a major part in the home-cooked repertoire. At
lunchtime, for instance, Thai style fish cakes on sticky vegetable rice with soy reduction; steamed
Bantry Bay mussels in garlic and Parmesan cream; and a vegetarian dish of the day. Evening starters
include Perl Las (organic Welsh blue cheese), bitter leaf salad, pickled walnuts and grapes poached
in Sauternes; and chicken liver, toasted hazelnut and roast garlic parfait. Typical mains are slow-roast
shoulder of Welsh lamb on fennel confit with light rosemary jus; and baked field mushroom, spinach
and red lentil gâteau with rich wild mushroom gravy. Mackerel, fresh lobster and sea bass tend to
feature as specials. Wines come from around the world, including Wales.

Recommended in the area

Pembrokeshire Coastal Path; Caldey Island; Gower Peninsula

The White Swan Inn

Address: Llanfrynach, BRECON, Powys, LD3 7BZ
Tel: 01874 665276
Fax: 01874 665362
Email: lee.harward@hotmail.co.uk
Website: www.the-white-swan.com
Map ref: 2 SO02
Directions: 3m E of Brecon off A40, take B4558,
follow Llanfrynach signs **Open:** 11.30-3 6.30-11.30
Closed: 25-26 Dec, 1st 2wks Jan, Mon & Tue (ex
summer, Dec & BH) ⅃ ⎵ **L** Wed-Sat 12-2, Sun
12-2.30 **D** Wed-Sun 7-9 **Facilities:** Parking Garden **Notes:** ⊕ FREE HOUSE ⅋⅋ ♟ 8

A 17th-century coaching inn, completely restored, The White Swan is set in the village of Llanfrynach,
by the foothills of the Brecon Beacons, an outstandingly beautiful area. The bar has oak flooring, old
beams and leather sofas by an open fire, providing the perfect setting for traditional local ales. There
is also a spacious restaurant with a coal burner, flagstone floors and beams; in summer you can sit
outside. A seasonal menu of innovative dishes is based on produce sourced from local farms.
Recommended in the area
Brecon Beacons National Park; South Wales Borderers Museum; Hay-on-Wye book shops

Talybont Reservoir, Brecon Beacons National Park

Nantyffin Cider Mill Inn

Address: Brecon Road, CRICKHOWELL, NP8 1SG
Tel: 01873 810775
Email: info@cidermill.co.uk
Website: www.cidermill.co.uk
Map ref: 2 SO21
Directions: At junct of A40 & A479,
1.5m W of Crickhowell
Open: noon-3 6-11 **Closed:** Mon (ex BH), Sun eve
Oct-Mar 🍴 ⚬I **L** Sun 12-2.30 **D** Fri-Sat 6.30-9.30
Facilities: Parking Garden
Notes: ⊕ FREE HOUSE ♦♦ 🐕 ♟ 10

Originally a drovers' inn, this family-run, 16th-century inn lies at the foot of the Black Mountains. Until the mid-1960s, it was well known for its cider; the old mill wheel and original press, still in working order, are in the oak beamed Mill Room Restaurant, once used as an apple store. There's room to eat in the bars, all full of character, serving local real ales and more than a few draught and bottled ciders, including a mulled offering in the winter. Recognised as a great food destination, the inn successfully combines the traditional values of the great British pub with Mediterranean influences. Menus are full of choice wild game from nearby estates, Welsh beef and lamb, hearty casseroles, pot roasts, puddings and pies. Other possibilities include home-cured meat and smoked fish platters, lamb cawl (soup), rib-eye steak and free-range duck. The daily specials board is always structured around the best line-caught fish and shellfish in season, but is also likely to include starters such as game broth, and warm salad of Madgett's Farm chicken livers with smoked bacon and black pudding. Among the desserts might be apricot bread and butter pudding, sticky toffee pudding and a slate of Welsh cheeses.

Recommended in the area

Brecon Beacons National Park; Big Pit, Blaenavon; Brecon Mountain Railway

The Castle Coaching Inn

Address: TRECASTLE, nr Brecon, Powys, LD3 8UH
Tel: 01874 636354
Fax: 01874 636457
Email: enquiries@castle-coaching-inn.co.uk
Website: www.castle-coaching-inn.co.uk
Map ref: 2 SN82
Directions: On A40 W of Brecon **Open:** all week
noon-3 6-11 (Sun 7-10.30) ⓑ Ⓞ **L** Sat-Sun 12-2
D Mon-Sat 6.30-9, Sun 7-9 **Facilities:** Parking
Garden Wi-fi **Notes:** ⊕ FREE HOUSE ⁑ ⚐

Once a Georgian coaching inn on the old London to Carmarthen coaching route, The Castle sits right on the northern edge of the Brecon Beacons/Black Mountain area, with myriad streams flowing down to join the River Usk nearby. The inn has been carefully restored in recent years, and retains lovely old fireplaces, a remarkable bow-fronted bar window and has a peaceful terrace and garden. A good selection of real ales is on offer, including Fuller's London Pride, Breconshire Brewery Red Dragon and Timothy Taylor Landlord. Food can be eaten in the bar or more formally in the restaurant, and bar lunches feature tempting, freshly-cut sandwiches (maybe roast beef, turkey or Stilton), a ploughman's with cheese or perhaps duck and port pâté, and hot crusty baguettes with fillings such as steak with melted Stilton or bacon with mushrooms and melted mature Cheddar. Of the more substantial offerings, specialities include mature Welsh 12oz sirloin steak served with mushrooms and onion rings; home-made lasagne with parmesan cheese; and supreme of chicken with a Marsala and mascarpone sauce. The tempting desserts are worth saving room for, and might include strawberry crush cake, hot jaffa puddle pudding, and Dutch chunky apple flan. Or perhaps sample the fine selection of Welsh farmhouse cheeses. There is a separate children's menu.

Recommended in the area

Dan-yr-Ogof The National Showcaves Centre; Brecon Beacons National Park; Usk Reservoir

Usk Reservoir at sunset, Brecon Beacons National Park

KEY TO ATLAS PAGES

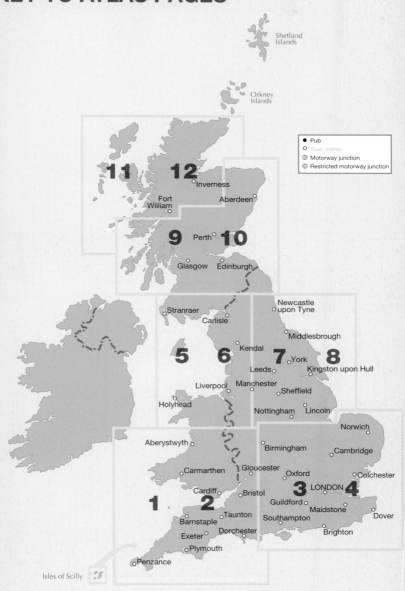

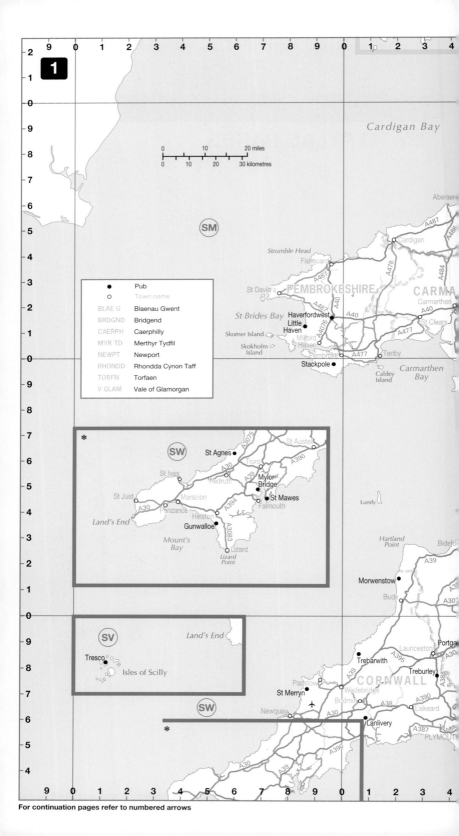

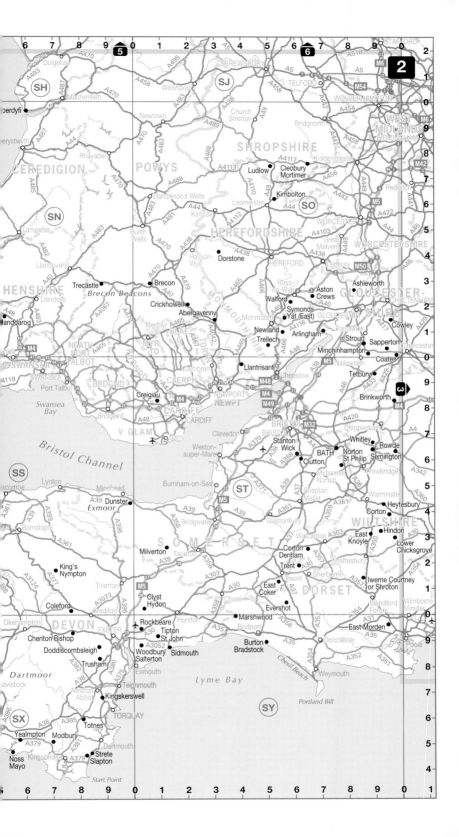

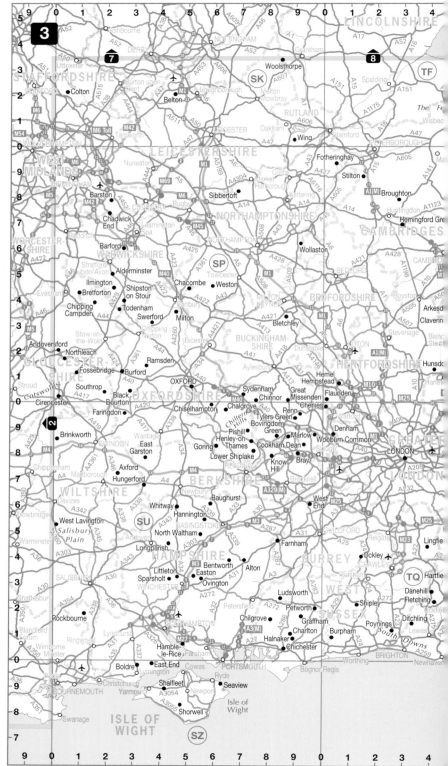

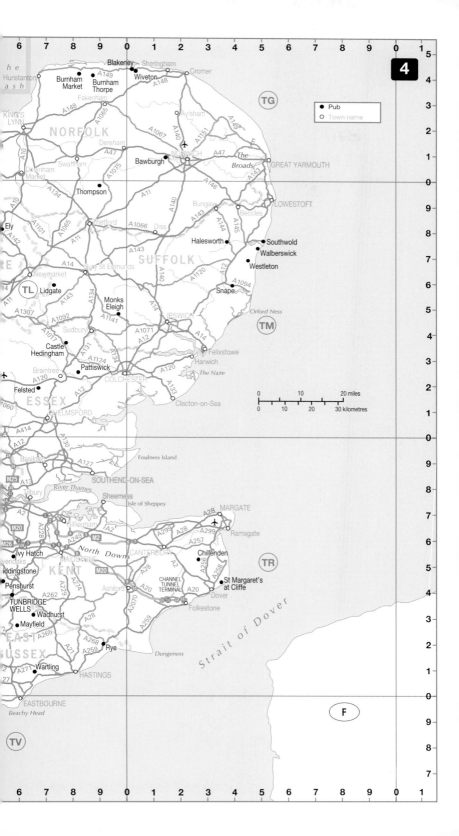

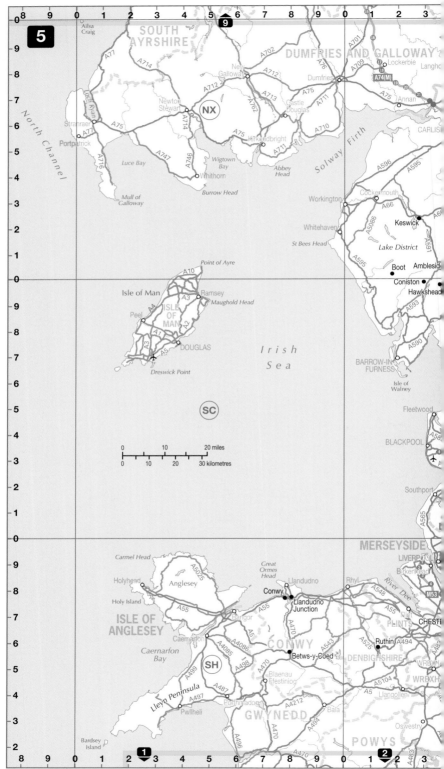

North Channel

SOUTH AYRSHIRE

Ailsa Craig

DUMFRIES AND GALLOWAY

A77
A714
A702
A701
Lockerbie
Langho

New Galloway
A712
Dumfries
A74(M)
Annan

Newton Stewart
NX
A713
A762
Castle Douglas
A711
A75
A75

Loch Ryan
Stranraer
A75
A714
A746
A75
Kirkcudbright
A711
A710
Solway Firth
CARLISL

Portpatrick
A716
A747
Wigtown Bay
Abbey Head

Luce Bay
Whithorn
A596
A595

Cockermouth
A66
A66

Mull of Galloway
Burrow Head
Workington
A5086
Keswick

Whitehaven
A591
Lake District

St Bees Head
A595
Boot
Amblesid

Point of Ayre
A10
Coniston
Hawkshead

Isle of Man
Ramsey
A3
Maughold Head

Peel
ISLE OF MAN
A2

A1
A18
A590

A3
DOUGLAS
Irish Sea
BARROW-IN-FURNESS

A5
Dreswick Point
Isle of Walney

SC
Fleetwood

0   10   20 miles
0   10   20   30 kilometres
BLACKPOOL
A58

Southport

A565

MERSEYSIDE
LIVERPOOL

Carmel Head
Great Ormes Head
Llandudno
Rhyl
River Dee
Birkenhead
M53

Holyhead
A5025
Anglesey
Conwy
A548
A55
Flint
CHEST

Holy Island
A55
Llandudno Junction
A55
PLINTS

ISLE OF ANGLESEY
Bangor
A5
A470
A543
Ruthin
A494

Caernarfon
A4085
A4086
CONWY
A525
DENBIGHSHIRE
WREXH

Caernarfon Bay
SH
A498
Betws-y-Coed
WREXH

A487
A470
Blaenau Ffestiniog
A5104
Llangollen

Lleyn Peninsula
A497
Porthmadog
A4212
Bala
Oswestr

Pwllheli
GWYNEDD
A494
A5

Bardsey Island
A496
A470
POWYS
A483

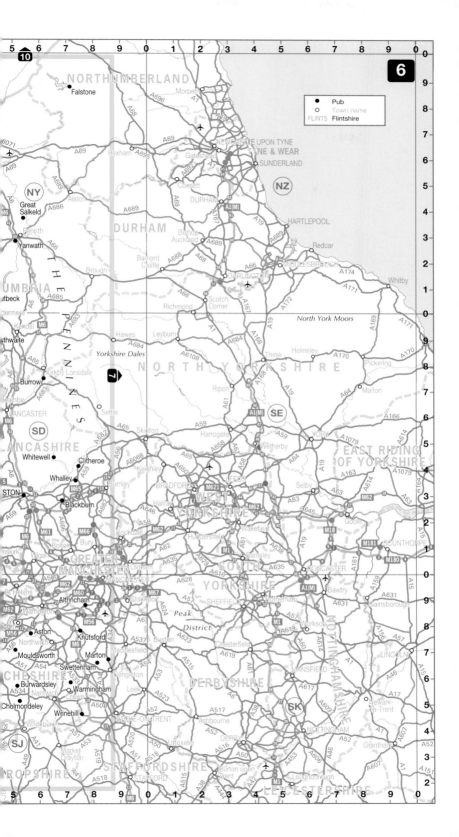

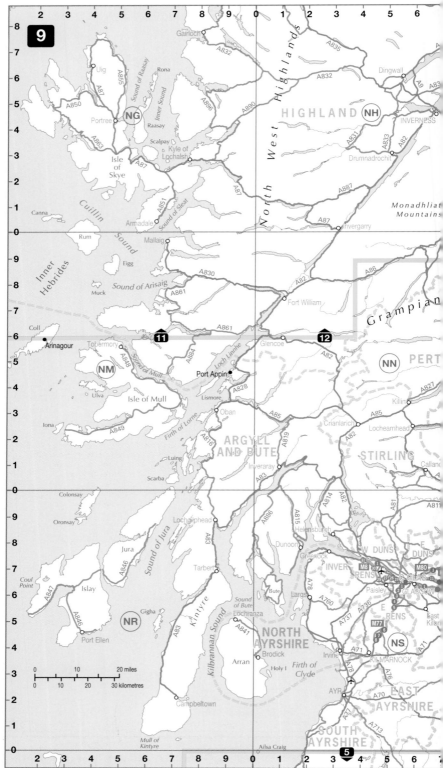

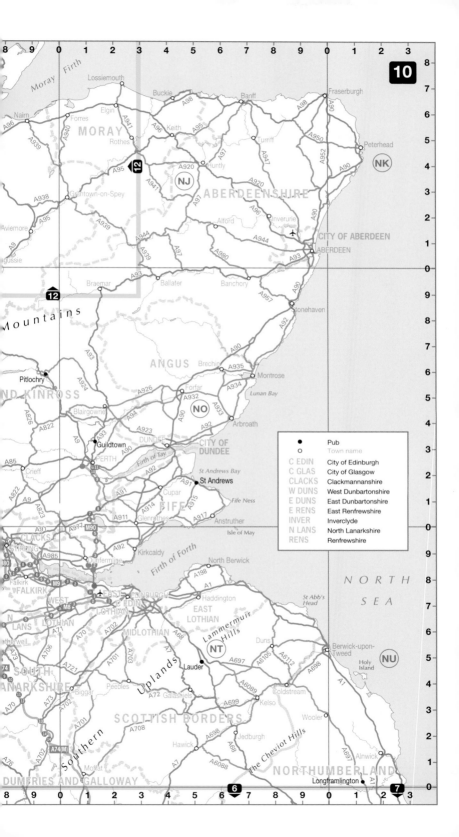

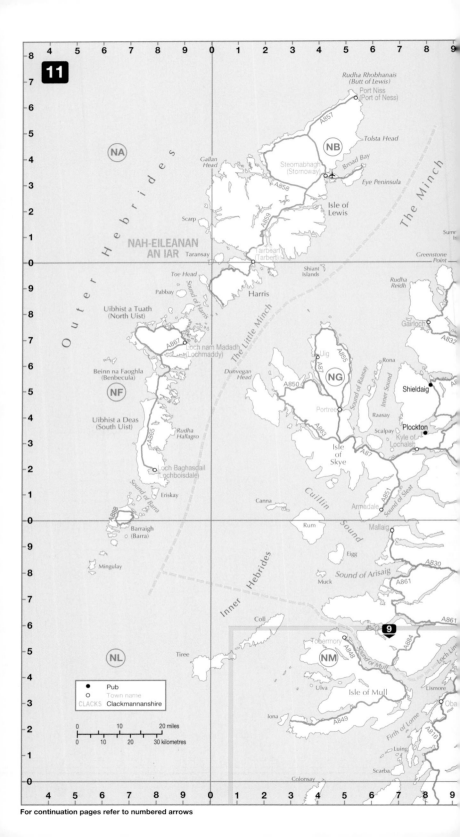

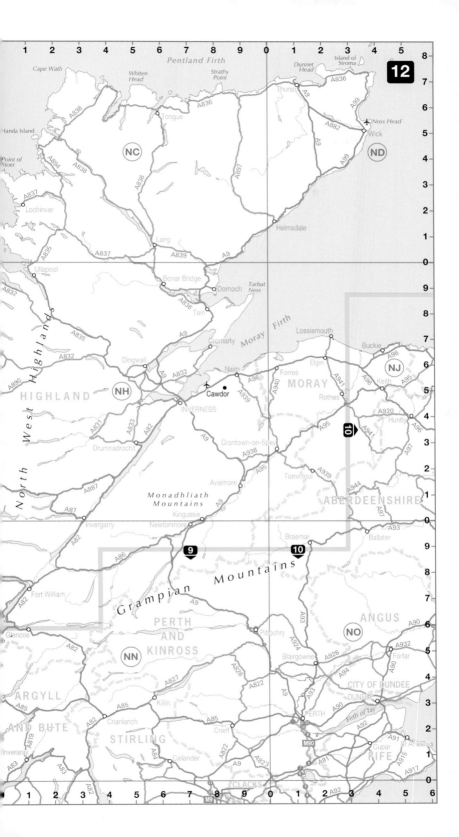

County Map

England

1 Bedfordshire
2 Berkshire
3 Bristol
4 Buckinghamshire
5 Cambridgeshire
6 Greater Manchester
7 Herefordshire
8 Hertfordshire
9 Leicestershire
10 Northamptonshire
11 Nottinghamshire
12 Rutland
13 Staffordshire
14 Warwickshire
15 West Midlands
16 Worcestershire

Scotland

17 City of Glasgow
18 Clackmannanshire
19 East Ayrshire
20 East Dunbartonshire
21 East Renfrewshire
22 Perth & Kinross
23 Renfrewshire
24 South Lanarkshire
25 West Dunbartonshire

Wales

26 Blaenau Gwent
27 Bridgend
28 Caerphilly
29 Denbighshire
30 Flintshire
31 Merthyr Tydfil
32 Monmouthshire
33 Neath Port Talbot
34 Newport
35 Rhondda Cynon Taff
36 Torfaen
37 Vale of Glamorgan
38 Wrexham

Location Index

A

ABERDYFI, Gwynedd
Penhelig Arms Hotel & Restaurant   288

ABERGAVENNY, Monmouthshire
Clytha Arms   289

ALDERMINSTER, Warwickshire
Bell, The   229

ALTON, Hampshire
Anchor Inn, The   111

ALTRINCHAM, Greater Manchester
Victoria, The   109

AMBLESIDE, Cumbria
Drunken Duck Inn   51

ARINAGOUR, Scottish Islands
Coll Hotel   279

ARKESDEN, Essex
Axe & Compasses   89

ARLINGHAM, Gloucestershire
Old Passage Inn, The   94

ASHLEWORTH, Gloucestershire
Queens Arms, The   95

ASTON CREWS, Herefordshire
Penny Farthing Inn, The   125

ASTON, Cheshire
Bhurtpore Inn, The   36

AXFORD, Wiltshire
Red Lion Inn   239

B

BARFORD, Warwickshire
Granville @ Barford, The   229

BARSTON, West Midlands
Malt Shovel at Barston, The   233

BATH, Somerset
Marlborough Tavern, The   187

BAUGHURST, Hampshire
Wellington Arms, The   112

BAWBURGH, Norfolk
Kings Head   154

BELTON, Leicestershire
Queen's Head, The   148

BENTWORTH, Hampshire
Sun Inn, The   113

BETWYS-Y-COED, Conwy
Ty Gwyn Inn   284

BLACK BOURTON, Oxfordshire
Vines, The   171

BLACKBURN, Lancashire
Clog and Billycock   140

BLAKENEY, Norfolk
Blakeney White Horse, The   155

BLETCHLEY, Buckinghamshire
Crooked Billet, The   22

BOLDRE, Hampshire
Red Lion, The   114

BOOT, Cumbria
Boot Inn, The   52

BOROUGHBRIDGE, North Yorkshire
Black Bull Inn, The   253

BOVINGDON GREEN, Buckinghamshire
Royal Oak, The   23

BREARTON, North Yorkshire
Malt Shovel Inn   254

BRECON, Powys
White Swan Inn, The   295

BRETFORTON, Worcestershire
Fleece Inn, The   251

Location Index

BRINKWORTH, Wiltshire
Three Crowns, The   240

BROUGHTON, North Yorkshire
Bull, The   255

BROUGHTON, Cambridgeshire
Crown, The   31

BURFORD, Oxfordshire
Lamb Inn, The   172

BURGHCLERE, Hampshire
Carnarvon Arms   115

BURNHAM MARKET, Norfolk
Hoste Arms, The   156

BURNHAM THORPE, Norfolk
Lord Nelson, The   156

BURPHAM, West Sussex
George & Dragon   218

BURROW, Lancashire
Highwayman, The   141

BURTON BRADSTOCK, Dorset
Anchor Inn, The   82

BURWARDSLEY, Cheshire
Pheasant Inn, The   37

C

CARTHORPE, North Yorkshire
Fox & Hounds, The   256

CASTLE HEDINGHAM, Essex
Bell Inn, The   90

CAWDOR, Highland
Cawdor Tavern   273

CHACOMBE, Northamptonshire
George and Dragon   160

CHALGROVE, Oxfordshire
Red Lion Inn, The   173

CHARLTON, West Sussex
Fox Goes Free, The   219

CHENIES, Buckinghamshire
Red Lion, The   24

CHERITON BISHOP, Devon
Old Thatch Inn, The   61

CHESTER, Cheshire
Albion Inn   37

CHICHESTER, West Sussex
Royal Oak Inn   220

CHIDDINGSTONE, Kent
Castle Inn   133

CHILGROVE, West Sussex
Fish House, The   221

CHILLENDEN, Kent
Griffins Head   134

CHINNOR, Oxfordshire
Sir Charles Napier, The   173

CHIPPING CAMPDEN, Gloucestershire
Eight Bells   95

CHISELHAMPTON, Oxfordshire
Coach & Horses Inn   174

CHOLMONDELEY, Cheshire
Cholmondeley Arms, The   38

CLAVERING, Essex
Cricketers, The   90

CLEOBURY MORTIMER, Shropshire
Crown Inn, The   185

CLITHEROE, Lancashire
Asseton Arms, The   142

CLUTTON, Somerset
Hunters Rest, The   188

CLYST HYDON, Devon
Five Bells Inn, The   62

COATES, Gloucestershire
Tunnel House Inn, The   96

COLEFORD, Devon
New Inn, The   63

Location Index

COLSTON BASSETT, Nottinghamshire
Martin's Arms, The 169

COLTON, Staffordshire
Yorkshireman, The 196

CONISTON, Cumbria
Sun Coniston, The 53

CONWY, Conwy
Groes Inn, The 285

COOKHAM DEAN, Berkshire
Chequers Brasserie, The 17

CORTON DENHAM, Somerset
Queens Arms, The 189

CORTON, Wiltshire
Dove Inn, The 241

COWLEY, Gloucestershire
Green Dragon Inn, The 97

CRAYKE, North Yorkshire
Durham Ox, The 257

CREIGIAU, Cardiff
Caesars Arms 282

CRICKHOWELL, Powys
Nantyffin Cider Mill Inn 296

CROSTHWAITE, Cumbria
Punch Bowl Inn, The 54

D

DANEHILL, East Sussex
Coach and Horses, The 210

DENHAM, Buckinghamshire
Swan Inn, The 25

DITCHLING, East Sussex
Bull, The 211

DODDISCOMBSLEIGH, Devon
Nobody Inn, The 64

DUNSTER, Somerset
Luttrell Arms, The 190

E

EAST COKER, Somerset
Helyar Arms, The 191

EAST END, Hampshire
East End Arms, The 116

EAST GARSTON, Berkshire
Queen's Arms Country Inn, The 18

EAST KNOYLE, Wiltshire
Fox and Hounds, The 242

EAST MORDEN, Dorset
Cock & Bottle, The 82

EAST WITTON, North Yorkshire
Blue Lion, The 258

EASTON, Hampshire
Chestnut Horse, The 116

ELY, Cambridgeshire
Anchor Inn, The 32

EVERSHOT, Dorset
Acorn Inn, The 83

F

FADMOOR, North Yorkshire
Plough Inn, The 259

FALSTONE, Northumberland
Pheasant Inn, The 165

FARINGDON, Oxfordshire
Trout at Tadpole Bridge, The 174

FARNHAM, Surrey
Bat & Ball Freehouse, The 207

FELSTED, Essex
Swan at Felsted, The 91

FLAUNDEN, Hertfordshire
Bricklayers Arms, The 129

FOSSEBRIDGE, Gloucestershire
Inn at Fossebridge, The 98

Location Index

FOTHERINGHAY, Northamptonshire
Falcon Inn, The 160

G

GORING, Oxfordshire
Miller of Mansfield 176

GRAFFHAM, West Sussex
Foresters Arms, The 222

GREAT MISSENDEN, Buckinghamshire
Nags Head, The 26

GREAT SALKELD, Cumbria
Highland Drove Inn
  and Kyloes Restaurant, The 55

GRINTON, North Yorkshire
Bridge Inn, The 260

GUILDTOWN, Perth & Kinross
Anglers Inn 277

GUNWALLOE, Cornwall
Halzephron Inn, The 42

H

HALESWORTH, Suffolk
Queen's Head, The 200

HALIFAX, West Yorkshire
Shibden Mill Inn 269

HALNAKER, West Sussex
Anglesey Arms at Halnaker, The 222

HAMBLE-LE-RICE, Hampshire
Bugle, The 117

HANNINGTON, Hampshire
Vine at Hannington, The 118

HARTFIELD, East Sussex
Hatch Inn, The 212

HAWKSHEAD, Cumbria
Queen's Head, The 56

HEMEL HEMPSTEAD, Hertfordshire
Alford Arms 130

HEMINGFORD GREY, Cambridgeshire
Cock Pub and Restaurant, The 33

HENLEY-ON-THAMES, Oxfordshire
Five Horseshoes, The 176

HEXHAM, Northumberland
Battlesteads Hotel & Restaurant 166

HEYTESBURY, Wiltshire
Angel Coaching Inn, The 243

HINDON, Wiltshire
Lamb at Hindon, The 244

HUNGERFORD, Berkshire
Crown & Garter, The 18

HUNGERFORD, Berkshire
Swan Inn, The 19

HUNSDON, Hertfordshire
Fox and Hounds, The 131

I

ILMINGTON, Warwickshire
Howard Arms, The 230

IVY HATCH, Kent
Plough at Ivy Hatch, The 135

**IWERNE COURTNEY
  OR SHROTON, Dorset**
Cricketers, The 84

K

KESWICK, Cumbria
Horse & Farrier Inn, The 57

KESWICK, Cumbria
Kings Head, The 58

KIMBOLTON, Herefordshire
Stockton Cross Inn 125

KINGS NYMPTON, Devon
Grove Inn, The 65

Location Index

KINGSKERSWELL, Devon
Bickley Mill Inn   66

KNARESBOROUGH, North Yorkshire
General Tarleton Inn, The   261

KNOWL HILL, Berkshire
Bird In Hand Country Inn   20

KNUTSFORD, Cheshire
Dog Inn, The   38

LONGFRAMLINGTON, Northumberland
Anglers Arms, The   167

LONGPARISH, Hampshire
Plough Inn, The   118

LOWER CHICKSGROVE, Wiltshire
Compasses Inn   245

LOWER SHIPLAKE, Oxfordshire
Baskerville, The   177

L

LANLIVERY, Cornwall
Crown Inn, The   43

LAUDER, Scottish Borders
Black Bull, The   278

LEYBURN, North Yorkshire
Sandpiper Inn   262

LIDGATE, Suffolk
Star Inn, The   200

LINGFIELD, Surrey
Hare and Hounds   208

LITTLE HAVEN, Pembrokeshire
Swan Inn, The   293

LLANDDAROG, Carmarthenshire
White Hart Thatched Inn & Brewery   283

LLANDUDNO JUNCTION, Conwy
Queens Head, The   286

LLANTRISANT, Monmouthshire
Greyhound Inn-Hotel, The   290

LODSWORTH, West Sussex
Hollist Arms, The   224

LONDON, SE10, London
North Pole Bar & Restaurant   150

LONDON, WC1, London
Bountiful Cow, The   151

LONDON, WC2, London
Seven Stars, The   152

M

MARLOW, Buckinghamshire
Hand and Flowers, The   27

MARSHWOOD, Dorset
Bottle Inn, The   85

MARTON, Cheshire
Davenport Arms, The   39

MAYFIELD, East Sussex
Middle House, The   213

MILTON, Oxfordshire
Black Boy Inn, The   178

MILVERTON, Somerset
Globe, The   192

MINCHINHAMPTON, Gloucestershire
Weighbridge Inn, The   99

MODBURY, Devon
California Country Inn   67

MONKS ELEIGH, Suffolk
Swan Inn, The   201

MORWENSTOW, Cornwall
Bush Inn, The   44

MOULDSWORTH, Cheshire
Goshawk, The   39

MYLOR BRIDGE, Cornwall
Pandora Inn, The   45

Location Index

N

NEWLAND, Gloucestershire
Ostrich Inn, The 100

NORTH WALTHAM, Hampshire
Fox, The 120

NORTON ST PHILIP, Somerset
George Inn 193

NOSS MAYO, Devon
Ship Inn, The 68

O

OCKLEY, Surrey
Bryce's at The Old School House 208

OVINGTON, Hampshire
Bush, The 121

OXFORD, Oxfordshire
Anchor, The 179

P

PATELEY BRIDGE, North Yorkshire
Sportsmans Arms Hotel, The 262

PATTISWICK, Essex
Compasses at Pattiswick, The 92

PENN, Buckinghamshire
Old Queens Head, The 28

PENSHURST, Kent
Bottle House Inn, The 136

PETWORTH, West Sussex
Grove Inn, The 225

PICKERING, North Yorkshire
Fox & Hounds Country Inn 263

PISHILL, Oxfordshire
Crown Inn, The 180

PITLOCHRY, Perth & Kinross
Moulin Hotel 277

PLOCKTON, Highland
Plockton Hotel, The 274

PLOCKTON, Highland
Plockton Inn & Seafood Restaurant 275

PORTGATE, Devon
Harris Arms, The 70

POYNINGS, West Sussex
Royal Oak Inn 226

PRESTON, Lancashire
Cartford Country Inn & Hotel 143

R

RAMSDEN, Oxfordshire
Royal Oak, The 181

ROCKBEARE, Devon
Jack in the Green Inn 71

ROCKBOURNE, Hampshire
Rose & Thistle, The 122

ROMALDKIRK, County Durham
Rose & Crown 87

ROWDE, Wiltshire
George & Dragon, The 246

ROYAL TUNBRIDGE WELLS, Kent
Beacon, The 137

RUTHIN, Denbighshire
Wynnstay Arms, The 287

RYE, East Sussex
Ypres Castle Inn, The 214

S

SAPPERTON, Gloucestershire
Bell at Sapperton, The 102

SEAVIEW, Isle of Wight
Seaview Hotel & Restaurant, The 235

SEMINGTON, Wiltshire
Somerset Arms, The 247

Location Index

SHALFLEET, Isle of Wight
New Inn, The   236

SHEFFIELD, South Yorkshire
Fat Cat, The   267

SHIELDAIG, Highland
Shieldaig Bar & Coastal Kitchen   275

SHIPLEY, West Sussex
Countryman Inn, The   227

SHIPSTON ON STOUR, Warwickshire
Red Lion, The   230

SHORWELL, Isle of Wight
Crown Inn, The   237

SHROTON OR
  IWERNE COURTNEY, Dorset
Cricketers, The   84

SIBBERTOFT, Northamptonshire
Red Lion, The   161

SIDMOUTH, Devon
Blue Ball, The   72

SIDMOUTH, Devon
Dukes   73

SLAPTON, Devon
Tower Inn, The   74

SNAPE, Suffolk
Crown Inn, The   201

SOUTHROP, Gloucestershire
Swan at Southrop, The   103

SOUTHWOLD, Suffolk
Crown Hotel, The   202

SOUTHWOLD, Suffolk
Randolph, The   203

SPARSHOLT, Hampshire
Plough Inn, The   123

ST AGNES, Cornwall
Driftwood Spars   46

ST ANDREWS, Fife
Jigger Inn, The   272

ST MARGARET'S AT CLIFFE, Kent
Coastguard, The   138

ST MAWES, Cornwall
Victory Inn, The   46

ST MERRYN, Cornwall
Cornish Arms, The   47

STACKPOLE, Pembrokeshire
Stackpole Inn, The   294

STAFFORD, Staffordshire
Holly Bush Inn, The   197

STANTON WICK, Somerset
Carpenters Arms, The   194

STILTON, Cambridgeshire
Bell Inn Hotel, The   34

STROUD, Gloucestershire
Bear of Rodborough Hotel   104

SWERFORD, Oxfordshire
Mason's Arms, The   182

SWETTENHAM, Cheshire
Swettenham Arms, The   40

SYDENHAM, Oxfordshire
Crown Inn, The   182

SYMONDS YAT [EAST], Herefordshire
Saracens Head Inn, The   126

T

TETBURY, Gloucestershire
Gumstool Inn   105

TETBURY, Gloucestershire
Trouble House, The   105

THOMPSON, Norfolk
Chequers Inn   157

THORNTON WATLASS, North Yorkshire
Buck Inn, The   263

TIPTON ST JOHN, Devon
Golden Lion Inn, The   75

321

Location Index

TODENHAM, Gloucestershire
Farriers Arms, The … 107

TOTNES, Devon
Durant Arms, The … 76

TOTNES, Devon
White Hart, The … 77

TREBARWITH, Cornwall
Mill House Inn, The … 48

TREBURLEY, Cornwall
Springer Spaniel, The … 49

TRECASTLE, Powys
Castle Coaching Inn, The … 297

TRELLECH, Monmouthshire
Lion Inn, The … 291

TRENT, Dorset
Rose & Crown Trent … 85

TROUTBECK, Cumbria
Queen's Head … 59

TRUSHAM, Devon
Cridford Inn … 78

WESTLETON, Suffolk
Westleton Crown, The … 205

WESTON, Northamptonshire
Crown, The … 162

WHALLEY, Lancashire
Three Fishes, The … 145

WHITEWELL, Lancashire
Inn at Whitewell, The … 146

WHITLEY, Wiltshire
Pear Tree Inn, The … 249

WIVETON, Norfolk
Wiveton Bell … 158

WOLLASTON, Northamptonshire
Wollaston Inn, The … 163

WOOBURN COMMON, Buckinghamshire
Chequers Inn … 29

WOODBURY SALTERTON, Devon
Digger's Rest, The … 79

WRINEHILL, Staffordshire
Crown Inn, The … 198

W

WADHURST, East Sussex
Best Beech Inn, The … 215

WALBERSWICK, Suffolk
Anchor, The … 204

WALFORD, Herefordshire
Mill Race, The … 127

WARMINGHAM, Cheshire
Bear's Paw, The … 40

WARTLING, East Sussex
Lamb Inn, The … 216

WASS, North Yorkshire
Wombwell Arms … 265

WEST LAVINGTON, Wiltshire
Bridge Inn, The … 248

Y

YANWATH, Cumbria
Yanwath Gate Inn, The … 59

YEALMPTON, Devon
Rose & Crown … 80

Pub Index

A

Acorn Inn, The
EVERSHOT, Dorset — 83

Albion Inn
CHESTER, Cheshire — 37

Alford Arms
HEMEL HEMPSTEAD, Hertfordshire — 130

Anchor Inn, The
ALTON, Hampshire — 111

Anchor Inn, The
BURTON BRADSTOCK, Dorset — 82

Anchor Inn, The
ELY, Cambridgeshire — 32

Anchor, The
OXFORD, Oxfordshire — 179

Anchor, The
WALBERSWICK, Suffolk — 204

Angel Coaching Inn, The
HEYTESBURY, Wiltshire — 243

Anglers Arms, The
LONGFRAMLINGTON, Northumberland — 167

Anglers Inn
GUILDTOWN, Perth & Kinross — 277

Anglesey Arms at Halnaker, The
HALNAKER, West Sussex — 222

Assheton Arms, The
CLITHEROE, Lancashire — 142

Axe & Compasses
ARKESDEN, Essex — 89

B

Baskerville, The
LOWER SHIPLAKE, Oxfordshire — 177

Bat & Ball Freehouse, The
FARNHAM, Surrey — 207

Battlesteads Hotel & Restaurant
HEXHAM, Northumberland — 166

Beacon, The
ROYAL TUNBRIDGE WELLS, Kent — 137

Bear of Rodborough Hotel
STROUD, Gloucestershire — 104

Bear's Paw, The
WARMINGHAM, Cheshire — 40

Bell at Sapperton, The
SAPPERTON, Gloucestershire — 102

Bell Inn Hotel, The
STILTON, Cambridgeshire — 34

Bell Inn, The
CASTLE HEDINGHAM, Essex — 90

Bell, The
ALDERMINSTER, Warwickshire — 229

Best Beech Inn, The
WADHURST, East Sussex — 215

Bhurtpore Inn, The
ASTON, Cheshire — 36

Bickley Mill Inn
KINGSKERSWELL, Devon — 66

Bird In Hand Country Inn
KNOWL HILL, Berkshire — 20

Black Boy Inn, The
MILTON, Oxfordshire — 178

Black Bull Inn, The
BOROUGHBRIDGE, North Yorkshire — 253

Black Bull, The
LAUDER, Scottish Borders — 278

Blakeney White Horse, The
BLAKENEY, Norfolk — 155

Pub Index

Blue Ball, The
SIDMOUTH, Devon · 72

Blue Lion, The
EAST WITTON, North Yorkshire · 258

Boot Inn, The
BOOT, Cumbria · 52

Bottle House Inn, The
PENSHURST, Kent · 136

Bottle Inn, The
MARSHWOOD, Dorset · 85

Bountiful Cow, The
LONDON, WC1 · 151

Bricklayers Arms, The
FLAUNDEN, Hertfordshire · 129

Bridge Inn, The
GRINTON, North Yorkshire · 260

Bridge Inn, The
WEST LAVINGTON, Wiltshire · 248

Bryce's at The Old School House
OCKLEY, Surrey · 208

Buck Inn, The
THORNTON WATLASS, North Yorkshire · 263

Bugle, The
HAMBLE-LE-RICE, Hampshire · 117

Bull, The
BROUGHTON, North Yorkshire · 255

Bull, The
DITCHLING, East Sussex · 211

Bush Inn, The
MORWENSTOW, Cornwall · 44

Bush, The
OVINGTON, Hampshire · 121

C

Caesars Arms
CREIGIAU, Cardiff · 282

California Country Inn
MODBURY, Devon · 67

Carnarvon Arms
BURGHCLERE, Hampshire · 115

Carpenters Arms, The
STANTON WICK, Somerset · 194

Cartford Country Inn & Hotel
PRESTON, Lancashire · 143

Castle Coaching Inn, The
TRECASTLE, Powys · 297

Castle Inn
CHIDDINGSTONE, Kent · 133

Cawdor Tavern
CAWDOR, Highland · 273

Chequers Brasserie, The
COOKHAM DEAN, Berkshire · 17

Chequers Inn
THOMPSON, Norfolk · 157

Chequers Inn
WOOBURN COMMON, Buckinghamshire · 29

Chestnut Horse, The
EASTON, Hampshire · 116

Cholmondeley Arms, The
CHOLMONDELEY, Cheshire · 38

Clog and Billycock
BLACKBURN, Lancashire · 140

Clytha Arms
ABERGAVENNY, Monmouthshire · 289

Coach & Horses Inn
CHISELHAMPTON, Oxfordshire · 174

Coach and Horses, The
DANEHILL, East Sussex · 210

Coastguard, The
ST MARGARET'S AT CLIFFE, Kent · 138

Cock & Bottle, The
EAST MORDEN, Dorset · 82

327

Pub Index

Cock Pub and Restaurant, The
HEMINGFORD GREY, Cambridgeshire   33

Coll Hotel
ARINAGOUR, Scottish Islands   279

Compasses at Pattiswick, The
PATTISWICK, Essex   92

Compasses Inn
LOWER CHICKSGROVE, Wiltshire   245

Cornish Arms, The
ST MERRYN, Cornwall   47

Countryman Inn, The
SHIPLEY, West Sussex   227

Cricketers, The
CLAVERING, Essex   90

Cricketers, The
IWERNE COURTNEY
  OR SHROTON, Dorset   84

Cridford Inn
TRUSHAM, Devon   78

Crooked Billet, The
BLETCHLEY, Buckinghamshire   22

Crown & Garter, The
HUNGERFORD, Berkshire   18

Crown Hotel, The
SOUTHWOLD, Suffolk   202

Crown Inn, The
CLEOBURY MORTIMER, Shropshire   185

Crown Inn, The
LANLIVERY, Cornwall   43

Crown Inn, The
PISHILL, Oxfordshire   180

Crown Inn, The
SHORWELL, Isle of Wight   237

Crown Inn, The
SNAPE, Suffolk   201

Crown Inn, The
SYDENHAM, Oxfordshire   182

Crown Inn, The
WRINEHILL, Staffordshire   198

Crown, The
BROUGHTON, Cambridgeshire   31

Crown, The
WESTON, Northamptonshire   162

D

Davenport Arms, The
MARTON, Cheshire   39

Digger's Rest, The
WOODBURY SALTERTON, Devon   79

Dog Inn, The
KNUTSFORD, Cheshire   38

Dove Inn, The
CORTON, Wiltshire   241

Driftwood Spars
ST AGNES, Cornwall   46

Drunken Duck Inn
AMBLESIDE, Cumbria   51

Dukes
SIDMOUTH, Devon   73

Durant Arms, The
TOTNES, Devon   76

Durham Ox, The
CRAYKE, North Yorkshire   257

E

East End Arms, The
EAST END, Hampshire   116

Eight Bells
CHIPPING CAMPDEN, Gloucestershire   95

F

Falcon Inn, The
FOTHERINGHAY, Northamptonshire   160

Pub Index

Farriers Arms, The
TODENHAM, Gloucestershire   107

Fat Cat, The
SHEFFIELD, South Yorkshire   267

Fish House, The
CHILGROVE, West Sussex   221

Five Bells Inn, The
CLYST HYDON, Devon   62

Five Horseshoes, The
HENLEY-ON-THAMES, Oxfordshire   176

Fleece Inn, The
BRETFORTON, Worcestershire   251

Foresters Arms, The
GRAFFHAM, West Sussex   222

Fox & Hounds Country Inn
PICKERING, North Yorkshire   263

Fox & Hounds, The
CARTHORPE, North Yorkshire   256

Fox and Hounds, The
EAST KNOYLE, Wiltshire   242

Fox and Hounds, The
HUNSDON, Hertfordshire   131

Fox Goes Free, The
CHARLTON, West Sussex   219

Fox, The
NORTH WALTHAM, Hampshire   120

G

General Tarleton Inn, The
KNARESBOROUGH, North Yorkshire   261

George & Dragon
BURPHAM, West Sussex   218

George and Dragon
CHACOMBE, Northamptonshire   160

George & Dragon, The
ROWDE, Wiltshire   246

George Inn
NORTON ST PHILIP, Somerset   193

Globe, The
MILVERTON, Somerset   192

Golden Lion Inn, The
TIPTON ST JOHN, Devon   75

Goshawk, The
MOULDSWORTH, Cheshire   39

Granville @ Barford, The
BARFORD, Warwickshire   229

Green Dragon Inn, The
COWLEY, Gloucestershire   97

Greyhound Inn-Hotel, The
LLANTRISANT, Monmouthshire   290

Griffins Head
CHILLENDEN, Kent   134

Groes Inn, The
CONWY, Conwy   285

Grove Inn, The
KINGS NYMPTON, Devon   65

Grove Inn, The
PETWORTH, West Sussex   225

Gumstool Inn
TETBURY, Gloucestershire   105

H

Halzephron Inn, The
GUNWALLOE, Cornwall   42

Hand and Flowers, The
MARLOW, Buckinghamshire   27

Hare and Hounds
LINGFIELD, Surrey   208

Harris Arms, The
PORTGATE, Devon   70

Hatch Inn, The
HARTFIELD, East Sussex   212

Pub Index

Helyar Arms, The
EAST COKER, Somerset — 191

Highland Drove Inn and Kyloes Restaurant, The
GREAT SALKELD, Cumbria — 55

Highwayman, The
BURROW, Lancashire — 141

Hollist Arms, The
LODSWORTH, West Sussex — 224

Holly Bush Inn, The
STAFFORD, Staffordshire — 197

Horse & Farrier Inn, The
KESWICK, Cumbria — 57

Hoste Arms, The
BURNHAM MARKET, Norfolk — 156

Howard Arms, The
ILMINGTON, Warwickshire — 230

Hunters Rest, The
CLUTTON, Somerset — 188

I

Inn at Fossebridge, The
FOSSEBRIDGE, Gloucestershire — 98

Inn at Whitewell, The
WHITEWELL, Lancashire — 146

J

Jack in the Green Inn
ROCKBEARE, Devon — 71

Jigger Inn, The
ST ANDREWS, Fife — 272

K

Kings Head
BAWBURGH, Norfolk — 154

Kings Head, The
KESWICK, Cumbria — 58

L

Lamb at Hindon, The
HINDON, Wiltshire — 244

Lamb Inn, The
BURFORD, Oxfordshire — 172

Lamb Inn, The
WARTLING, East Sussex — 216

Lion Inn, The
TRELLECH, Monmouthshire — 291

Lord Nelson, The
BURNHAM THORPE, Norfolk — 156

Luttrell Arms, The
DUNSTER, Somerset — 190

M

Malt Shovel at Barston, The
BARSTON, West Midlands — 233

Malt Shovel Inn
BREARTON, North Yorkshire — 254

Marlborough Tavern, The
BATH, Somerset — 187

Martin's Arms, The
COLSTON BASSETT, Nottinghamshire — 169

Mason's Arms, The
SWERFORD, Oxfordshire — 182

Middle House, The
MAYFIELD, East Sussex — 213

Mill House Inn, The
TREBARWITH, Cornwall — 48

Mill Race, The
WALFORD, Herefordshire — 127

Miller of Mansfield
GORING, Oxfordshire — 176

Pub Index

Moulin Hotel
PITLOCHRY, Perth & Kinross 277

N

Nags Head, The
GREAT MISSENDEN, Buckinghamshire 26

Nantyffin Cider Mill Inn
CRICKHOWELL, Powys 296

New Inn, The
COLEFORD, Devon 63

New Inn, The
SHALFLEET, Isle of Wight 236

Nobody Inn, The
DODDISCOMBSLEIGH, Devon 64

North Pole Bar & Restaurant
LONDON, SE10 150

O

Old Passage Inn, The
ARLINGHAM, Gloucestershire 94

Old Queens Head, The
PENN, Buckinghamshire 28

Old Thatch Inn, The
CHERITON BISHOP, Devon 61

Ostrich Inn, The
NEWLAND, Gloucestershire 100

P

Pandora Inn, The
MYLOR BRIDGE, Cornwall 45

Pear Tree Inn, The
WHITLEY, Wiltshire 249

Penhelig Arms Hotel & Restaurant
ABERDYFI, Gwynedd 288

Penny Farthing Inn, The
ASTON CREWS, Herefordshire 125

Pheasant Inn, The
BURWARDSLEY, Cheshire 37

Pheasant Inn, The
FALSTONE, Northumberland 165

Plockton Hotel, The
PLOCKTON, Highland 274

Plockton Inn & Seafood Restaurant
PLOCKTON, Highland 275

Plough at Ivy Hatch, The
IVY HATCH, Kent 135

Plough Inn, The
FADMOOR, North Yorkshire 259

Plough Inn, The
LONGPARISH, Hampshire 118

Plough Inn, The
SPARSHOLT, Hampshire 123

Punch Bowl Inn, The
CROSTHWAITE, Cumbria 54

Q

Queens Arms, The
ASHLEWORTH, Gloucestershire 95

Queens Arms, The
CORTON DENHAM, Somerset 189

Queen's Arms Country Inn, The
EAST GARSTON, Berkshire 18

Queen's Head
TROUTBECK, Cumbria 59

Queen's Head, The
BELTON, Leicestershire 148

Queen's Head, The
HALESWORTH, Suffolk 200

Queen's Head, The
HAWKSHEAD, Cumbria 56

Queens Head, The
LLANDUDNO JUNCTION, Conwy 286

Pub Index

R

Randolph, The
SOUTHWOLD, Suffolk 203

Red Lion Inn
AXFORD, Wiltshire 239

Red Lion Inn, The
CHALGROVE, Oxfordshire 173

Red Lion, The
BOLDRE, Hampshire 114

Red Lion, The
CHENIES, Buckinghamshire 24

Red Lion, The
SHIPSTON ON STOUR, Warwickshire 230

Red Lion, The
SIBBERTOFT, Northamptonshire 161

Rose & Crown
ROMALDKIRK, County Durham 87

Rose & Crown
YEALMPTON, Devon 80

Rose & Crown Trent
TRENT, Dorset 85

Rose & Thistle, The
ROCKBOURNE, Hampshire 122

Royal Oak Inn
CHICHESTER, West Sussex 220

Royal Oak Inn
POYNINGS, West Sussex 226

Royal Oak, The
BOVINGDON GREEN, Buckinghamshire 23

Royal Oak, The
RAMSDEN, Oxfordshire 181

S

Sandpiper Inn
LEYBURN, North Yorkshire 262

Saracens Head Inn, The
SYMONDS YAT [EAST], Herefordshire 126

Seaview Hotel & Restaurant, The
SEAVIEW, Isle of Wight 235

Seven Stars, The
LONDON, WC2 152

Shibden Mill Inn
HALIFAX, West Yorkshire 269

Shieldaig Bar & Coastal Kitchen
SHIELDAIG, Highland 275

Ship Inn, The
NOSS MAYO, Devon 68

Sir Charles Napier, The
CHINNOR, Oxfordshire 173

Somerset Arms, The
SEMINGTON, Wiltshire 247

Sportsmans Arms Hotel, The
PATELEY BRIDGE, North Yorkshire 262

Springer Spaniel, The
TREBURLEY, Cornwall 49

Stackpole Inn, The
STACKPOLE, Pembrokeshire 294

Star Inn, The
LIDGATE, Suffolk 200

Stockton Cross Inn
KIMBOLTON, Herefordshire 125

Sun Coniston, The
CONISTON, Cumbria 53

Sun Inn, The
BENTWORTH, Hampshire 113

Swan at Felsted, The
FELSTED, Essex 91

Swan at Southrop, The
SOUTHROP, Gloucestershire 103

Swan Inn, The
DENHAM, Buckinghamshire 25

Pub Index

Swan Inn, The
HUNGERFORD, Berkshire   19

Swan Inn, The
LITTLE HAVEN, Pembrokeshire   293

Swan Inn, The
MONKS ELEIGH, Suffolk   201

Swettenham Arms, The
SWETTENHAM, Cheshire   40

T

Three Crowns, The
BRINKWORTH, Wiltshire   240

Three Fishes, The
WHALLEY, Lancashire   145

Tower Inn, The
SLAPTON, Devon   74

Trouble House, The
TETBURY, Gloucestershire   105

Trout at Tadpole Bridge, The
FARINGDON, Oxfordshire   174

Tunnel House Inn, The
COATES, Gloucestershire   96

Ty Gwyn Inn
BETWYS-Y-COED, Conwy   284

V

Victoria, The
ALTRINCHAM, Greater Manchester   109

Victory Inn, The
ST MAWES, Cornwall   46

Vine at Hannington, The
HANNINGTON, Hampshire   118

Vines, The
BLACK BOURTON, Oxfordshire   171

W

Weighbridge Inn, The
MINCHINHAMPTON, Gloucestershire   99

Wellington Arms, The
BAUGHURST, Hampshire   112

Westleton Crown, The
WESTLETON, Suffolk   205

White Hart Thatched Inn & Brewery
LLANDDAROG, Carmarthenshire   283

White Hart, The
TOTNES, Devon   77

White Swan Inn, The
BRECON, Powys   295

Wiveton Bell
WIVETON, Norfolk   158

Wollaston Inn, The
WOLLASTON, Northamptonshire   163

Wombwell Arms
WASS, North Yorkshire   265

Wynnstay Arms, The
RUTHIN, Denbighshire   287

Y

Yanwath Gate Inn, The
YANWATH, Cumbria   59

Yorkshireman, The
COLTON, Staffordshire   196

Ypres Castle Inn, The
RYE, East Sussex   214

Credits

The Automobile Association would like to thank the following photographers, companies and picture libraries for their assistance in the preparation of this book.

Abbreviations for the picture credits are as follows: (t) top; (b) bottom; (l) left; (r) right; (c) centre; (AA) AA World Travel Library.

4 AA/C Sawyer; 5 AA/S Montgomery; 6 Huw Evans; 8 ; 10 AA/C Sawyer; 14/15 AA/T Mackie; 16 AA/V Bates; 19b AA/W Voysey; 21 AA/J Tims; 29b AA/M Birkitt; 30 AA/M Moody; 32b AA/M Birkitt; 35 AA/C Jones; 41 AA/J Wood; 47b AA/J Wood; 49b AA/N Ray; 50 AA/R Coulam; 52b AA/T Mackie; 54b AA/R Coulam; 60 AA; 62b AA/R Moss; 65b AA/N Hicks; 69 AA/H Williams; 72b AA/N Hicks; 74b AA/N Hicks; 76b AA/N Hicks; 78b AA/C Jones; 81 AA/S&O Mathews; 86 AA/C Lees; 87b AA/R Coulam; 88 AA/M Birkitt; 93 AA/M Moody; 101 AA/D Hall; 106 AA/D Hall; 108 AA/C Molyneux; 110 AA/A Burton; 119 AA/M Moody; 124 AA/H Palmer; 128 AA/M Moody; 131b AA/M Moody; 132 AA/N Setchfield; 134b AA/M Busselle; 138b AA/D Forss; 139 A/J Beazley; 144 AA/J Blandford; 146b AA/T Griffiths; 147 AA/A Tryner; 148b AA/R Newton; 149 AA/N Setchfield; 153 AA/T Mackie; 154b AA/L Whitwam; 159 AA/M Birkitt; 164 AA/R Coulam; 168 AA/M Birkitt; 170 AA/M Birkitt; 171b AA/S Day; 175 AA/C Jones; 179b AA/V Greaves; 183 AA/S Day; 184 AA/M Hayward; 186 AA/S Day; 187b AA/S Day; 191b AA/C Jones; 193b AA/R Moss; 195 AA/T Mackie; 196b AA/V Greaves; 199 AA/T Mackie; 202b AA/P Davies; 206 AA/J Tims; 209 AA/J Miller; 210b AA/P Baker; 217 AA/J Miller; 223 AA/J Miller; 224b AA/P Brown; 228 AA/M Moody; 231 AA/V Greaves; 232 AA/J Welsh; 233b AA/J Welsh; 234 AA/A Burton; 236b AA/S McBride; 238 AA/M Moody; 239b AA/S Day; 245b AA/J Tims; 248b AA/M Moody; 250 AA/M Moody; 251b AA/M Moody; 252 AA/M Kipling; 256b AA/M Kipling; 258 AA/S&O Mathews; 264 AA/M Kipling; 266 AA; 267b AA/J Morrison; 268 AA/L Whitwam; 270/271 AA/J Smith; 273b AA/J Carnie; 276 AA/J Smith; 278/279 AA/S Anderson; 280/281 AA/N Jenkins; 283b AA; 285b AA/S Lewis; 287b AA/N Jenkins; 288/289 AA/S Lewis; 292 AA/R Ireland; 295b AA/D Santillo; 298 AA/C&A Molyneux; 323 AA/R Ireland; 324/325 AA/C Sawyer; 334/335 AA/C Sawyer;

Every effort has been made to trace the copyright holders, and we apologise in advance for any accidental errors. We would be happy to apply any corrections in the following edition of this publication.